Religion, Disease, and Immunology

Also Available from Bloomsbury

Scientific Studies of Religion: Inquiry and Explanation

Series editors: Luther H. Martin, Donald Wiebe, Radek Kundt
and Dimitris Xygalatas

Scientific Studies of Religion: Inquiry and Explanation publishes cutting-edge research in the new and growing field of scientific studies in religion. Its aim is to publish empirical, experimental, historical, and ethnographic research on religious thought, behaviour, and institutional structures. The series works with a broad notion of scientific that includes innovative work on understanding religion(s), both past and present. With an emphasis on the cognitive science of religion, the series includes complementary approaches to the study of religion, such as psychology and computer modelling of religious data. Titles seek to provide explanatory accounts for the religious behaviors under review, both past and present.

The Attraction of Religion, edited by D. Jason Slone and James A. Van Slyke
The Cognitive Science of Religion, edited by D. Jason Slone and William W. McCorkle Jr.
The Construction of the Supernatural in Euro-American Cultures, Benson Saler
Contemporary Evolutionary Theories of Culture and the Study of Religion, Radek Kundt
Death Anxiety and Religious Belief, Jonathan Jong and Jamin Halberstadt
Gnosticism and the History of Religions, David G. Robertson
The Impact of Ritual on Child Cognition, Veronika Rybanska
Language, Cognition, and Biblical Exegesis, edited by Ronit Nikolsky, Istvan Czachesz, Frederick S. Tappenden and Tamas Biro
The Learned Practice of Religion in the Modern University, Donald Wiebe
The Mind of Mithraists, Luther H. Martin
Naturalism and Protectionism in the Study of Religion, Juraj Franek
New Patterns for Comparative Religion, William E. Paden
Philosophical Foundations of the Cognitive Science of Religion, Robert N. McCauley with E. Thomas Lawson
Religion Explained?, edited by Luther H. Martin and Donald Wiebe
Religion in Science Fiction, Steven Hrotic
Religious Evolution and the Axial Age, Stephen K. Sanderson
The Roman Mithras Cult, Olympia Panagiotidou with Roger Beck
Solving the Evolutionary Puzzle of Human Cooperation, Glenn Barenthin
Understanding Religion Through Artificial Intelligence, Justin E. Lane

Religion, Disease, and Immunology

Thomas B. Ellis

BLOOMSBURY ACADEMIC
LONDON • NEW YORK • OXFORD • NEW DELHI • SYDNEY

BLOOMSBURY ACADEMIC
Bloomsbury Publishing Plc
50 Bedford Square, London, WC1B 3DP, UK
1385 Broadway, New York, NY 10018, USA
29 Earlsfort Terrace, Dublin 2, Ireland

BLOOMSBURY, BLOOMSBURY ACADEMIC and the Diana logo are trademarks of Bloomsbury Publishing Plc

First published in Great Britain 2022
This paperback edition published 2024

Copyright © Thomas B. Ellis, 2022, 2024

Thomas B. Ellis has asserted his right under the Copyright, Designs and Patents Act, 1988, to be identified as Author of this work.

For legal purposes the Acknowledgments on p. viii constitute an extension of this copyright page.

Cover image © Shutterstock

All rights reserved. No part of this publication may be reproduced or transmitted in any form or by any means, electronic or mechanical, including photocopying, recording, or any information storage or retrieval system, without prior permission in writing from the publishers.

Bloomsbury Publishing Plc does not have any control over, or responsibility for, any third-party websites referred to or in this book. All internet addresses given in this book were correct at the time of going to press. The author and publisher regret any inconvenience caused if addresses have changed or sites have ceased to exist, but can accept no responsibility for any such changes.

A catalogue record for this book is available from the British Library.

Library of Congress Control Number: 2021952921

ISBN: HB: 978-1-3501-8824-2
PB: 978-1-5266-2924-1
ePDF: 978-1-3501-8825-9
eBook: 978-1-3501-8826-6

Series: Scientific Studies of Religion: Inquiry and Explanation

Typeset by Deanta Global Publishing Services, Chennai, India

To find out more about our authors and books visit www.bloomsbury.com and sign up for our newsletters

For Megan and Maddie

Contents

Acknowledgments — viii

1. Introduction — 1
2. The Biology of Religion: There Will Never Be a Darwin for the Crown of Thorns? — 15
3. Religion's Tribalism: The Behavioral Immune System — 49
4. Religion's Vital Lies and Illusions of Control: The Psychological Immune System — 81
5. Religion's Curative Violence: The Physiological Immune System — 111
6. At War with the Body: When Religion Becomes the Infection — 143
7. Conclusion — 175

Notes — 181
References — 194
Index — 227

Acknowledgments

I began this project in earnest in 2019. Clearly, I had no idea that the topic would become, fortunately, but certainly also tragically, timely. My sabbatical semester from Appalachian State University in the spring semester of 2020 saw not only progress on the manuscript but also the irruption of a pandemic. The death toll from Covid-19 is both breathtaking and heartbreaking. As I write, the Delta and Omicron variants are on the march, especially among the unvaccinated. Regrettably, a public health issue has been politicized. This only promises a higher death toll. Perhaps this volume can shed some light on the issues at hand. I can only hope so.

I would first like to thank Luther Martin and Don Wiebe for their encouragement upon reading the proposal. I would also like to thank the reviewers for their comments and their endorsement. I especially thank Bob Fuller for his extensive comments and suggestions on how to improve the manuscript. I, of course, take the credit for all remaining flaws in the arguments and presentation. I also thank Lalle Pursglove and Lily McMahon at Bloomsbury for their assistance in preparing the manuscript.

I want to thank Oxford University Press and *The Journal of the American Academy of Religion* for granting me permission to reuse some material I published with them. Chapter 6 contains passages from "Disgusting Bodies, Disgusting Religion: The Biology of Tantra." Chapter 3 contains passages from "Evoked Puja: The Behavioral Ecology of an Equatorial Ritual." I would also like to thank Brill and *Method and Theory in the Study of Religion* for granting me permission to reuse some material I published with them. Chapters 2 and 4 contain passages from "Of Gods and Devils: Differential Cognition and the Adaptive Illusions of Control."

Lastly, I thank my family for their patience and support over the past couple of years. I couldn't have done it without them.

1

Introduction

Religious commitments are often attributed to an experience (Proudfoot 1985; Boyer and Bergstrom 2008; Taves 2009). The experience purportedly involves an immediate apprehension of the sacred (James 1961 [1902]). However else one may wish to characterize it, the sacred is perceived to be transcendent to the natural world (Segal 1983; Bulbulia and Slingerland 2012). Should such transcendence turn out to be more than mere perception, religion would presumably be immune to natural assessment and explanation (Haught 2008). Causal accounts of the origin and functions of religion would thus, necessarily, include the religious perspective, rendering thereby any exclusively natural explanation of religion interminably incomplete. To suggest otherwise risks courting accusations of reductionism (Eliade 1958; Cho and Squier 2008). Some are willing to run the risk (Preus 1987; McCutcheon 2001; Smith 2004; Dennett 2006). I'm willing to run the risk.

One of the more influential books in the study of religion in the twentieth century to promote the insider's perspective, so-called, was Rudolf Otto's *The Idea of the Holy*. Otto (in)famously proposed that the reader who could not recollect "a moment of deeply-felt religious experience . . . is requested to read no farther" (Otto 1923 [1917], 8). His was a "privileged" audience (Eliade 1964, 7).[1] The German theologian was both right and wrong. Otto was right to suggest that there is an experience at the core of religion. He was wrong to imply that this experience was limited to a select few. The experience upon which religion rests has been had by all. No one will need to put this volume down.

We've all had the experience. We all know the feeling. No one has ever been spared. The body starts aching. The lungs start convulsing. The nose starts running. The head starts throbbing. The body's temperature starts rising. No Tamiflu in the medicine cabinet? Not to worry. There's always religion.

All living organisms have experienced the pain and suffering that accompanies infectious disease.[2] It is "the most familiar and universal aspect of all human experiences," notes A. Glucklich, "and it binds us with many animals as well" (2001, 11). The threat of morbidity and mortality due to an infectious disease is persistent and ubiquitous. It is a "universal aspect of the human experience" (Inhorn and Brown 1997, 54). That I am here writing this book, and that you are now reading it, attests to the fact that our evolutionary forebears figured out how to manage the transmission, contraction, and eradication of infectious disease (Hart 2011). How they did so is the subject matter of this book. This book is about religion.

Religion is "our most defining cultural invention" (Sapolsky 2017, 621). It is "what is most distinctive about man" (Becker 1975, 4). Religion's "stunning universality" (Dubuisson 2003, 168), as well as its own "persistence and ubiquity" (Sterelny 2018, 408; Schmitt and Fuller 2015; McGuire and Tiger 2009), is well attested in both the historical and ethnographic records (Burkert 1996; Rappaport 1999; Boyer 2001; Hayden 2003; Dennett 2006). For the practitioner, such persistence and ubiquity presumably attest to the reality of the sacred. For those not so persuaded, it is a bit of a mystery. It is a mystery because religion appears to be singularly irrational, both philosophically (Mackie 1982; Flanagan 2002; Philipse 2014) and economically (Atran 2002; Sosis and Alcorta 2003; Kirkpatrick 2005). "Religions are strange," notes J. Slone, "because they require people to engage in activities that seem, from a biological point of view, to be *costly* and apparently *useless*" (2008, 181). The perceived irrationality and profligacy of religion makes some question how it could survive natural selection's systematic pruning of gratuitous expenditures (Bulbulia 2006). Behaviors that do not improve an organism's inclusive fitness are usually targets for elimination. Is religion a curious exception to this rather general rule in biology? Perhaps not. B. Hayden points out that "(a) when people spend large amounts of time, effort, and resources on a specific type of behavior, (b) when that behavior persists over long periods of time, and (c) when the behavior is widespread, then there is likely to be some adaptive benefits to such behaviors" (2003, 12). All three of Hayden's qualifications surely apply to religion. Accordingly, "the spatiotemporal ubiquity, recurrent morphology, and *apparently* maladaptive nature of religion cry out for evolutionary explanation" (Powell and Clarke 2012, 459, emphasis added). Agreed. In the chapters that follow, we will consider the possibility that there is a significant, and quite possibly adaptive, correlation between the persistence and ubiquity of religion and the persistence and ubiquity of infectious disease.

This volume contributes to a fertile, though often contested, approach to the study of religion. The approach effectively began with E. O Wilson's 1975 publication, *Sociobiology: The New Synthesis*. Wilson proposed that the time had finally arrived for biology to have its turn at interpreting and explaining religious phenomena. He sensed, for instance, that religion was a biological adaptation for collective living. For this reason, it ought to be considered a part of the human animal's extended phenotype (Dawkins 1982). Wilson's book received mixed reviews. Some cheered it. Others jeered it.

The next fifteen years or so were rather fallow for the biology of religion. Perhaps the most significant contribution during this time came in 1983 with the publication of V. Reynolds's and R. Tanner's *The Biology of Religion*. Reynolds and Tanner identified religion's role in promoting a host of adaptive behaviors pertaining to reproduction, childhood, adolescence, adulthood, and senescence. The book was emended and re-released in the 1990s as *The Social Ecology of Religion* (1995), the decade when the biology of religion really began to take off.

Perhaps of singular importance to the biology of religion during the 1990s was S. Guthrie's *Faces in the Clouds: A New Theory of Religion* (1993). Guthrie documented the human animal's irrepressible tendency to anthropomorphize. From faces in the clouds to saintly visages in croissants, we tend to see human agents, and traces thereof, practically everywhere. Guthrie claimed that such anthropomorphizing rests at the base of religion. The first of many to come, Guthrie's book proposed a cognitive explanation of religion. The human brain was naturally selected to be hypersensitive to the presence of conspecific agents. As we will see in the next chapter, God is often perceived to be a disembodied, anthropomorphic agent. It would appear that the book of Genesis has it backwards. We are not made in God's image. God is made in ours. The other significant contribution to the biological study of religion in the 1990s was W. Burkert's *Creation of the Sacred: Tracks of Biology in Early Religions* (1996). Burkert argued that biological anthropology was essential for understanding religion. He suggested, for instance, that some religious rituals appear calibrated for engagements with predators of a distant past. These authors kept afloat an underappreciated yet burgeoning approach to religion in the last quarter of the previous century. The past two decades of the present one tell a different story.

The twenty-first century has seen the biology of religion flourish. We now have impressive contributions from cognitive science (Boyer 2001), evolutionary psychology (Kirkpatrick 2005), ethology (Feierman 2009a), neuroscience (McNamara 2009; McGuire and Tiger 2009), and human behavioral ecology (Sosis and Bulbulia 2011). We now know, for instance, why religious practitioners in prayer often assume postures that make them appear lower, smaller, and more vulnerable (Feierman 2009b). These are the same behaviors many species of animals perform when confronted with a dominant other. They deescalate any possible conflict. We will have ample opportunity to discuss many of the adaptations the human animal came to possess that contribute to religion's origins and functions in the next chapter. For now, we can note that the success these approaches have enjoyed has led some to propose that the biology of religion is the only real game in town today (Slingerland and Bulbulia 2011). Though traditionally associated with the humanities, the academic study of religion must find a way to integrate itself with the life sciences (Wilson 1999; Slingerland 2008; Fuller 2008). This volume works toward that integration. It presents for the first time a systematic consideration of the relationship between religious phenomena and the human animal's immunological needs.

Most animals possess two systems for managing the transmission, contraction, and eradication of infectious disease (McCabe et al. 2015). The first is the physiological immune system. This system eradicates parasites and pathogens that have breached the body's first lines of defense, the skin and mucosal membranes. The physiological immune system is, however, both calorically expensive and occasionally flawed. Some infections are lethal. Clearly, it is always better not to get sick in the first place. For this reason, natural selection sculpted a second system. This second system is composed of a suite of psychological dispositions and behavioral tendencies to avoid prophylactically the transmission and contraction of infectious disease. This is the behavioral immune system. There is yet a third system unique to the human animal, the psychological immune system. This system protects mental health. It solves the problems issuing from chronic stress and major depression, both of which directly contribute to immunosuppression and subfecundity.[3] The eradicative nature of the physiological immune system combined with the prophylactic natures of the behavioral and psychological immune systems constitutes what some have called "the integrated immune system" (Gangestad and Grebe 2014, 227). Facilitating the success of the integrated immune system is one of religion's primary functions. The persistence and ubiquity of religion thus correlate not with the persistence and ubiquity of the theologian's god or the phenomenologist's sacred. Rather, the persistence and ubiquity of religion correlate with the persistence and ubiquity of infectious disease, that is, the Fourth Horseman of the Apocalypse, Pestilence.[4]

The discussion unfolds over five chapters. The next chapter, "The Biology of Religion: There Will Never Be a Darwin for the Crown of Thorns?" provides an overview of biological studies of religion to date. It thereby sets the stage for the larger discussion of the integrated immunology of religion throughout the rest of the volume. The chapter begins with a consideration of the physical aspects of life. It pays particular attention to the second law of thermodynamics, what A. Rosenberg calls "the ruling principle of this universe" (2011, 30). The second law states that all things are headed toward entropy, that is, heat death. There is only one process capable of forestalling temporarily this inevitable fate, evolution by natural selection. Evolution by natural selection accounts for the design of all organisms, the human brain and the mind it produces included (Barrett 2015). The constitution of the human mind/brain reflects the various pressures the human animal had to negotiate to ensure its inclusive fitness in an ancestral past. Among such pressures were those issuing from other agents. The human animal thus came to possess what evolutionary psychology and cognitive science have come to call a theory of mind (ToM) and a hyperactive agency detection device (HADD). Both contribute directly to the production of religion.

Evolutionary psychology and cognitive science demonstrate how the human mind typically processes specific types of information from both the external and internal worlds. Such information informs behavior. In addition to addressing the evolution of the human brain and mind, chapter two reviews the human animal's capacity to adjust its behavioral strategies according to the prevailing conditions of the time and place. It addresses what has come to be called, human behavioral ecology (HBE). HBE assesses the extent to which behavior is plastic, that is, responsive to environmental contingencies rather than wholly determined by genes.

Chapter 2 then addresses what many believe to be the primary selection pressure that led to the emergence of religion, the need to cooperate. Many have thus corroborated E. O. Wilson's initial proposal (Irons 2001; Sosis and Alcorta 2003; Haidt 2012; Greene 2013; Norenzayan 2013). As we will see, cooperation was the common solution to a host of problems pertaining to subsistence and reproduction. Though common, the solution is hard to achieve. Cooperative tasks always run the risk of being exploited by either the free rider or the promiscuous rider. The free rider is one who enjoys collective benefits but pays none of the costs. The promiscuous rider is one who enjoys many children with different partners but invests resources only in a limited few, if any at all. Some suggest that religion affords opportunities for individuals to demonstrate their trustworthiness when it comes to such collective action problems. These opportunities often involve costly and hard-to-fake signs of commitment. A circumcised penis is one such sign. There is yet a third cooperation problem that has heretofore remained unaddressed. Economic and reproductive success depend upon healthy bodies and minds. The human community is equally concerned with the infected rider. Infections and infected riders are the subject matter for the remaining chapters of this volume.

Chapter 3, "Religion's Tribalism: The Behavioral Immune System," addresses the selection pressure for individual and collective hygiene. Contracting an infection is both calorically expensive and debilitating. It is also often deadly. From a life-history perspective (Hill 1993; Kaplan et al. 2000; McDade 2003), calories spent fighting off an infection are calories not spent procuring resources, both economic and sexual, or tending to progeny. Many species have thus developed strategies for maintaining health. These strategies have come to be called, the behavioral immune system. This arm of the integrated immune system is calibrated to respond adaptively to the local disease ecology. Because disease ecologies vary, the behavioral immune system enjoys a degree of plasticity (West-Eberhard 2003). Behavioral plasticity contributes to cultural variability. It turns out that culture is, indeed, part of the human animal's extended phenotype (Dawkins 1982). Religion's tribalism, with its oft-accompanying xenophobia and ethnocentrism, appears particularly calibrated to forestalling the transmission and contraction of infectious diseases. It is an iteration of collectivism. As we will see, collectivism is strategically prophylactic. This is the case because local groups, or tribes, become adapted to their local disease pools. Different tribes have different immunological profiles. Religion's tribalism reflects in this way the geography of immunocompetence.

Extra-tribal others may be harbingers of infectious agents concerning which the local group's immunity may be naïve. Introduction of a novel infectious disease often results in outbreaks. Outbreaks have the potential to decimate the local group (Diamond 1997). It is thus adaptive to be wary of such extra-tribal others. One's tribal identity is often established through irrational religious claims and locally contingent purity and pollution codes. Both are pronounced features of all religious tribes. Those who do not recognize and abide the local religion's propositional commitments and purity and pollution codes evoke disgust, an emotional response equally evoked in the presence of the free and promiscuous riders. Disgust is essential for religion (Ellis 2011). Religion's purity and pollution codes not only establish tribal boundaries. They equally inform hygiene practices. Purity and pollution codes amount to a public health policy. It would appear that religion was "the original health promoting system" (Fabrega, Jr. 2004, 737).

Successful tribes depend upon individuals maintaining a commitment to the welfare of the group. Collectivism depends in this way upon a certain personality profile. Most determinative of a personality profile is environmental input. There is no environmental input of greater significance for the developing child than parental behavior. A parent's childrearing strategy greatly affects the child's personality profile, the one that will accompany her throughout life. Infectious disease ecologies have a direct impact on the types of childrearing practices a culture adopts. The childrearing practice most adopted amid robust disease ecologies has been called, the pediatric style. This style tends to nurture what are called insecure-anxious attachments. Insecure-anxious attachments are particularly correlated with the personality profile most conducive to collectivism. The prominence of childrearing strategies for prophylactic personalities is glaringly absent from the behavioral immune system literature. This is an omission in need of rectification. "The arena of mother-infant behavior and nurturing behavior more generally" are, according to B. King, "too-often-neglected aspects of evolutionary theorizing" (quoted in Weingarten and Chisholm 2009, 774). Chapter 3 so rectifies. From the disease-evoked, pediatric childrearing practices to insecure-anxious attachments to the purity and pollution codes promoting collectivist ethnocentrism and xenophobia, infectious disease proves to be a significant driver of religion's tribalism. Religion's tribalism is a direct expression of the behavioral immune system.

Chapter 4, "Religion's Vital Lies and Illusions of Control: The Psychological Immune System," introduces the second arm of the integrated immune system. The psychological immune system is in the business of maintaining psychological health. One of religion's primary functions is to manage stress, both acute and chronic. Detractors of the "comfort hypothesis," so-called, are correct to note that evolution would not have selected for happiness as such (Kirkpatrick 2006). Evolution by natural selection is blind to the human animal's preference for happiness. What selection is not blind to, however, are states of mind leading to immunosuppression and subfecundity. Immunosuppression renders an organism most susceptible to infectious disease. Subfecundity, on the other hand, is the failure to achieve optimal reproductive success. If chronic stress and massive depression led to immunoenhancement and reproductive success, most of us would be chronically stressed and massively depressed most of the time. That, however, is not the case. Chronic stress is a direct contributor to immunosuppression and major depression. The latter is a major cause of subfecundity. The environment in which the human animal evolved was replete with stressors. Our evolutionary forebears were no strangers to chronic stress and depression. Religion mitigates stress and depression by telling stories about reality that are less than truthful. Religion promotes vital lies.

Foremost among religion's vital lies is the one pertaining to immortality. Most of the popular religions to this day articulate visions of life everlasting. Abiding such a lie, one can fend off the stress and depression associated with immunosuppression and subfecundity. Perhaps it is better to live in a fantasy world of health and reproductive success than to curl up in a corner and sob one's life away due to an accurate assessment of reality. Religion's vital lies are not the only remedy for stress and depression. Religion equally fosters adaptive illusions of control. One of the major conundrums contributing to chronic stress and depression is the perception that one has lost control over one's situation. Of all the things over which one clearly lacks exhaustive control are precisely disease and death. Illusions of control, especially as manifested in religious rituals, mitigate such stress. Religion promotes stories about the human animal's ability to appeal to gods and spirits for aid in times of trouble. If one gets sick, for instance, a prayer to the gods may help. This is one of the key claims of psychoneuroimmunology (Segerstrom and Miller 2004). One's frame of mind can directly affect one's health (Clark and Fessler 2014). The religious animal thus entertains the illusion that it enjoys a modicum of control even when that is not in fact the case. Natural selection did not select for happiness, nor did it select cognitive predilections to discover what is in fact true. Natural selection only selects for predilections that enable reproductive success. If a religious lie and illusion can do the trick, then a religious lie and illusion will do.

Humans appeal to gods when they cannot procure the necessary means for survival (Stark and Finke 2000). Resource-starved individuals are most prone to religion (Gray and Wegner 2010). Of the many resources that may show up in short supply, there is one resource that is truly in short supply and most motivating for the adoption of a religious worldview. Life is *the* limited resource (Pinker 2018). We can be relatively certain that we will all get sick again (assuming one is not sick now). We can be equally certain that we will all die. It is against this reality that many a religious practitioner will protest. This reality constitutes the basis of terror management theory, or TMT (Pyszczynski et al. 2003). TMT suggests that humans construct cultures and pursue self-esteem because such things mitigate existential anxiety. Chapter 4 thus reviews terror management theory. TMT recognizes that the vital lie is precarious. Precarity necessarily correlates with the lack of empirical and philosophical warrant for religious claims (Flanagan 2002). It also attends symbolic solutions to material problems. Symbols simply cannot overcome material realities. No lie is foolproof. Confidence in a lie is only purchased through consensus. Accordingly, the religious other has both dirty practices and dirty ideas. Like the behavioral immune system, the psychological immune system employs disgust in its dealings with the ideationally strange other. Religious commitments can serve in this way as a cognitive immunity against ideas that would trouble one's confidence in one's own religion. To find the other's behaviors and ideas dirty serves to maintain psychological health, and thus physical and reproductive health. Occasionally, the psychological immune system's disgust with the other can lead to the violent eradication of the threat. The psychological and physiological immune systems are calibrated to destroy that which would threaten the well-being of the host.

Chapter 5, "Religion's Curative Violence: The Physiological Immune System," introduces the physiological immune system. It is the third and final arm of the integrated immune system. As Chapters 3 and 4 demonstrate, the behavioral and psychological immune systems are prophylactic in nature. They attempt to forestall the transmission and contraction of disease. The physiological immune system is calibrated to heal the infected body. Its task is to eradicate disease. The physiological immune system does so through two components, the innate and the adaptive. The innate component is the first to attack the infection. It is associated with inflammation. The adapted component is what remembers the identity of the particular infection. Immunological memory provides a more robust immunological response upon re-exposure to the antigen. Following the introduction of the physiological immune system, the chapter turns to what some have considered to be not only the first religion but also the one that informs all future religions. The chapter turns to shamanism. The shaman was the first religious authority as well as the first physician and therapist.

The shaman's medical practice is multifaceted. This is the case because there is a range of illnesses that require the shaman's ministrations. Illness can befall both the individual and the group. Regarding the latter, a group can be infected with a free rider. As Chapter 2 demonstrates, the free rider is a constant threat to the cooperative, economic unit. One function of shamanic ritual is to facilitate confession and contrition, thereby reintegrating the free rider into the group. The shaman also ministers to the sick individual. An individual can suffer from both psychological and physical malaise. Regarding the former, and as Chapter 3 demonstrates, an individual can suffer from attachment anxieties. Similarly, and as Chapter 4 demonstrates, an individual can suffer from existential anxieties. These two anxieties are not wholly unrelated. Those with insecure-anxious attachments styles are especially prone to existential anxieties (Mikulincer et al. 1990). The relevant literature on shamanism is explicit on this score: shamans minister to the insecure-anxiously attached. Through a variety of techniques, especially the induction of altered states of consciousness, shamans facilitate mental healing for the psychologically ill individual and group.

Social and psychological illnesses are problems that require the shaman's therapeutic intervention. The physically ill equally requires the shaman's intervention. Such intervention occurs on three separate registers. The first register pertains to folk pharmacology. Folk pharmacology describes those indigenous practices wherein the shaman identifies material resources believed to have medicinal effects. Such resources are often placebos, although an occasional identification of a bioactive substance is not out of the question. In addition to pharmacological interventions, whether placebo or truly bioactive, a shaman also resorts to a range of psychological manipulations. These manipulations routinely involve inducing an altered state of consciousness. Altered states of consciousness include hypnosis and dissociation. Hypnosis and dissociation can cure both psychological and psychosomatic disorders. The third and final technique the shaman engages in is acute-stress induction. Here is where things can get violent.

The literature on stress is robust. Chronic stress is incontestably debilitating. It leads to immunosuppression as well as major depression and thus subfecundity. Religion promotes vital lies and adaptive illusions of control to manage the threats associated with chronic stress. Religion occasionally induces an acute-stress response. Managing stress is not exclusively tied to eradication. This is important because many authors have suggested that such inductions belie the comfort hypothesis. Some argue that acute-stress-inducing rituals are incompatible with healing. This is not the case. Chapter 5 presents for the first time the acute-stress induction theory of ritual healing.

Chronic stress is immunosuppressing. Acute stress is immunoenhancing. Subjecting an individual to a gory, disgusting scene induces an acute-stress response which in turn potentiates the physiological immune system. This is the case because throughout evolutionary history gory scenes would have been potential sources of infection. An acute-stress-induced, prophylactic upregulation of the physiological immune system in advance of the infectious threat would have been adaptive. An acute-stress response similarly upregulates immune function in the infected individual. An acute-stress-inducing ritual, such as blood sacrifice, is not a confound for ritual healing theory (McClenon 2006). Rather, it supports it. Religious violence cures.

Chapter 6, "At War with the Body: When Religion Becomes the Infection," addresses those moments when religion motivates maladaptive behavior. Religion occasionally becomes an autoimmune disorder. Autoimmunity arises when religion encourages behaviors and beliefs that appear to be beneficial only to the religion, that is, beneficial to the spread of the religion, and this at the expense of the biological body. Religion can become a set of parasitic ideas. Parasitic ideas are deleterious memes.

The status of memes is highly contested. Intended to account for cultural evolution, memes are supposed to be units of cultural information capable of replication with a modicum of fidelity and fecundity. The original niche for the meme was the human brain. By way of demonstration and articulation, a human can pass its memes on to another. Some memes enjoy greater reproductive success than others. Some memes go extinct. No one today is interested in the combustible substance of phlogiston. Memetics attempt to account for why some ideas replicate and spread while others do not. Memetics addresses in this way the epidemiology of culture (Sperber 1996).

Most successful memes are so because the meme's "interest" dovetails with those of the host. For much of its history, religion has provided an adaptive advantage for those animals capable of adopting and abiding purity and pollution codes, vital lies, adaptive illusions of control, and immunoenhancing, acute stress. Religious memes and human genes have enjoyed a long-standing mutualism. There are moments, however, when the meme's interests and the host's genetic interests diverge. Some memeticists suggest that in some instances memes replicate simply for their own replication's sake, that is, without regard for the well-being of their host. This may be the case for religion in the post-industrial world. Certain religious beliefs and behaviors may have become memetic infections.

The memetic infection is often a pathological development of the vital lie. Chapter 4 addresses religion's management of chronic stress. This management is largely accomplished through the promotion of vital lies, the most vital one of which being the promise of immortality. The human animal's natural drive to survive runs directly into the countervailing fact that survival in perpetuity is impossible. Despite the intuitive appeal of dualism, itself the metaphysical commitment underwriting most religious traditions, when the body dies so too does the "soul." This fact often evokes both terror and disgust. Disgust research demonstrates that the human animal finds free, promiscuous, and infected riders disgusting. It also demonstrates that the human animal finds its embodiment disgusting. Humans are prone to experiencing animal-nature disgust.

Animal-nature disgust is the affective component of dualism. Dualism allows us to believe that we have a soul. Souls are capable of escaping the body upon death, and quite possibly many times prior thereto. Dualism allows us to deny that we are 100 percent animals. If persuasive, this denial enables religion's détente dualism. Most religious practitioners can get on with the business of the biological body, for instance, sexual intercourse, without great anxiety because of this overarching belief system. In fact, religions often counsel behaviors that are positively healthy for the body. The body is, after all, a temple and should be shown the respect such a sacred space deserves. For a select few, however, this isn't good enough. They eventually become religion's charismatics, or virtuosi. Détente dualism often incentivizes the laity. Militant dualism incentivizes the charismatics.

Militant dualists masochistically attack the body. They do this in order to assert the dominion of mind over matter, the true antidote to animal-nature disgust. The dominion involves behaviors that are wholly maladaptive. This is the memetic infection. We will address several moments when religion appears to counsel behaviors that can only be seen as beneficial to the memes themselves. One particular example of such memetically driven behavior, and certainly one that is no stranger to the contemporary world, is anti-vaccination behavior often associated with religion. Religiously motivated, anti-vaccination ideologies ultimately serve the interests of religious memes, and quite possibly the infectious diseases as well. When there is a robust social safety net, a net including not only economic and educational safety but health as well, religion declines. Religious memes promoting anti-vaccination behaviors are ultimately self-serving. A sick population is a population that needs religion. Admittedly, I am a South Asianist by training. I do not believe, however, that I am expressing bias when I claim that there is perhaps no better presentation of the memetic infection than what is called classical Hindu Yoga and Tantra.

Popular characterizations of Hindu Yoga and Tantra today portray these traditions as salubrious for both mind and body. These would be mischaracterizations were they to apply to the classical traditions. Classical Hindu Yoga and Tantra often involved behaviors particularly suited to insulting the naturally selected human body. Yoga often involved assuming postures and behaviors that beleaguer the human body. Tantra counseled the consumption of pathogen-rich excreta and the practice of maximally suboptimal sexual intercourse. Both are disgusting. The tantric practitioner is often referred to as a *vira*, that is, a hero, an appellation most appropriate in the context of militant dualism. The tantric hero does not deny the material, as an idealist would. Rather, the tantric hero attacks the material, behaving in the most maladaptive ways possible, with but one exception. Tantric heroes seldom take their militant dualism to the next level. The next level is suicidal dualism. Some religious traditions counsel suicide. The suicidal dualist is so bothered by the uncontrollability and unpredictability of death that he takes it upon himself to expedite mortality. For good or ill, religious memes can become parasitic. They can become an autoimmune disorder.

Chapter 7, "Conclusion," recaps the arguments made throughout the previous five chapters. It maintains that religion, on the whole, has been an adaptive suite of perceptions, beliefs, behaviors, and experiences calibrated to manage the transmission, contraction, and eradication of infectious disease. Our evolutionary ancestors may not have survived the Paleolithic past without it. The extent to which religion remains adaptive in a post-industrial world is a topic worth considering. As Chapter 6 will show, some religious communities today are intentionally keeping themselves, and some of us, sick and thus in need of religion. Whether religion is, on the whole, good or bad for us today is something about which we will remain agnostic for the present discussion. That said, and as previously noted, all bodies and minds, both infected and healthy, eventually succumb to the passage of time. To borrow from the late poet and lead singer of *The Doors*, Jim Morrison, no one here gets out alive. Such is the reality of the second law of thermodynamics, to which we now turn.

2

The Biology of Religion

There Will Never Be a Darwin for the Crown of Thorns?

The German philosopher Immanuel Kant once proclaimed that there would never be a Newton for the blade of grass. While Newton may have banished purpose and design from the inanimate world, a similar fate was certainly not forthcoming for the animate one. The seemingly incomparable difference between the simple trajectories of planets and the complex intricacy of a blade of grass had to admit of different explanations. The living world required a teleological explanation, not a mechanistic, historical one, or so Kant thought. The lesson to be learned here? Even a philosophical genius can occasionally suffer an impoverished imagination.

In 1859, Charles Darwin published, *On the Origin of Species by Means of Natural Selection, or the Preservation of Favoured Races in the Struggle for Life*. There the argument was made that all of life descended from a common ancestor. What is more, such descent appeared mechanistic and unguided. Speciation via evolution by natural selection was based solely on chance and necessity (Monod 1971). Darwin completed Newton's project (Rosenberg 2011, 2018). Banishing purpose and intentional design from the living world is, to be sure, "the *defining feature* of Darwin's theory" (Stewart-Williams 2010, 64). What Kant insisted must be designed turned out to be "nothing but slow accretion of fortuitous change" (Wright 1994, 232). Although certain of the reality of evolution, Darwin could not provide at that time the precise mechanism by which evolution and eventual speciation occurred. The discovery of that mechanism took place a few years later when the Catholic monk and scientist Gregor Mendel demonstrated generational inheritance using pea plants. Mendel discovered how the traits of a pea plant are the result of pairs of, what would eventually be called, genes. The pair of genes were, and are, inherited, one set of the pair from each parent.

Mendel also demonstrated that some genes appeared dominant, while others recessive. Darwin and Mendel provided the two components of what eventually came to be known as the "modern synthesis" (Huxley 2009 [1942]).

The modern synthesis proposes that an organism's appearance and behavior (i.e., its phenotype) is the result of a randomly reshuffled set of genes (i.e., its genotype) interacting with the environment (i.e., its niche). The extent to which a *random* reshuffling of genes led or leads to an organism's flourishing and reproducing in a particular environment is the *necessary* outcome. Insofar as each organism is genetically unique, save perhaps identical twins, there will necessarily be differences in reproductive success among a population of organisms. Some organisms will simply produce more descendants than others. The genes, or better yet, the alleles of such prolific organisms will of necessity be more numerous in the following generation.[1] When the aggregate of genes present in any one population changes over time, that's evolution. That's natural selection. That's the basis of the life sciences. Some suggest it ought to be the basis of the humanities and social sciences, as well (Slingerland 2008; Bulbulia and Slingerland 2012; Rosenberg 2017).[2]

In 1973, Theodor Dobzhansky proclaimed unequivocally, "nothing in biology makes sense except in the light of evolution" (1973, 125). Perhaps the famous biologist was too conservative. It is possible that nothing whatsoever makes sense except in the light of evolution. From cosmogony and cosmology to cosmetics and communion, evolutionary dynamics seem to be in play (Smolin 1999; Richerson and Boyd 2005; Dennett 2006; Ridley 2015; Stewart-Williams 2018). The twenty-first century is "the Age of Universal Darwinism" (Aunger 2001, 1).[3] In the same way Kant was mistaken about there never being a Newton for the blade of grass, one would similarly be mistaken to maintain, as many are often wont to do (Haught 2006, 2008; Oviedo 2016), that there will never be a Darwin for Jesus's Crown of Thorns. In other words, impoverished imaginations cannot imagine an exhaustive, *biological* account of religion. The "biophobia" (Irons and Cronk 2000, 13) of impoverished imaginations cannot withstand the "universal acid" that is Darwinian science (Dennett 1995). It is time for a thorough "behavioral biology of religion" (Sweek 2002, 197). "Biological approaches to religion are not merely optional, one among the many 'theories' or 'methods' on offer in the marketplace of ideas," argue J. Bulbulia and E. Slingerland, "Recent biological studies of religion afford a glimpse of how most scholarship in religious studies will be conducted in the future. The principles of hypothesis testing, of intellectual consistency, and of methodological naturalism will eventually bring a unification of religious studies with the rest of the biological sciences" (2012, 602). The discussion that unfolds over the present and following chapters contributes to such a unification.

The present chapter provides a general introduction to the biology of religion. This will involve a few steps. The first step considers the extent to which the Standard Social Science Model (Tooby and Cosmides 1992) fails to account for religion. The second step considers the success the Standard Model (Carroll 2016) enjoys in the same endeavor. This has to be the case. Nothing in biology makes sense except in the light of evolution because nothing makes sense except in the light of the second law of thermodynamics. The protestations of the intelligent design community notwithstanding, evolution does not falsify the second law (Pennock 1999; Young and Edis 2005). It confirms it.

The chapter then turns to a consideration of some of the biological theories of human behavior on offer today. Attention will be paid particularly to evolutionary psychology—and the closely associated cognitive sciences—and human behavioral ecology, approaches employed throughout this volume. The cognitive adaptations the human animal uniquely enjoys, for instance, theory of mind (ToM) and the hyperactive agency detection device (HADD), appear essential for the production and performance of religion, a precise definition of which is on offer in what's to come. Evolutionary psychology demonstrates how many of our behavioral programs appear calibrated for success in an ancestral past. It is possible that some of these are no longer adaptive today. The chapter concludes with a consideration of some of the biological theories that have been applied successfully to religion, among which include costly-signaling theory (Irons 2001; Sosis and Alcorta 2003; Norenzayan 2013)—the predominant theory in the biology of religion to date—sexual selection theory (Slone and Van Slyke 2015), and the descendant-leaving hypothesis (Palmer and Begley 2015). These theories demonstrate how religion may have evolved to solve what some consider to be biology's foremost problem, the evolution of cooperation among nonkin for economic and reproductive success. The theories are persuasive. They are not exhaustive. One of religion's primary functions—if not in fact the primary one—is to manage the transmission, contraction, and eradication of infectious disease, topics to be addressed in the chapters that follow.

Nothing Makes Sense except in the Light of the Second Law

The goal in this and the following chapters is a biological explanation of *religious* behavior. L. A. Kirkpatrick provides some counsel for such a project.

He proposes that the qualifying coefficient "religious" does not identify what may be called a difference in kind, a point W. James similarly made a century prior (Kirkpatrick 2005; James 1961 [1902]). Kirkpatrick suggests, for instance, that if one wants to understand *religious* motivation, one ought to start with a theory of motivation in general. Likewise, and for those who believe religion is a part of human nature, he suggests that "we need to begin with a good theory of human nature" (2005, 13). Agreed. An explanation of religious behavior must begin with a good theory of behavior in general. What and why is there behavior?

Behavior is simply the movement of things (Feierman 2009a). Things behave for one of two reasons. First, to behave is to move in such a way that one's actions, one's movements are consistent with the expectations of the group to which one belongs. To do otherwise is to misbehave. This is moral behavior (Sapolsky 2017). A discussion of moral behavior follows below. The other type of behavior can be considered amoral. There are two explanations for amoral behavior. The amoral movement of some things can be attributed solely to other things. For instance, when I strike the cue ball, it will move in the proper direction to hit the eight ball—operator errors notwithstanding—sending the latter into the corner pocket for a win. The eight ball cannot do otherwise. Billiard-ball behavior is insentient and non-agential. Insentient, non-agential behavior is not *religious* behavior. Religious behavior is sentient and agential. "Agents are different from things," Slingerland observes, "Agents actively think, choose, and move themselves; things can only be passively moved" (2008, 281). Passively moved things are not of interest here. Sentient, agential behavior is.

Any explanation of sentient, agential behavior must satisfy two requirements. First, the explanation must be consistent with evolutionary theory (Pyszczynski et al. 2003). Second, it must be consistent with the second law of thermodynamics. To be sure, "if your theory is found to be against the second law of thermodynamics," A. Edington warned, "there is nothing for it but to collapse in deepest humiliation" (quoted in Pinker 2018, 17). The theory of evolution by natural selection is in no such danger. It's quite the opposite. "The phenomenon of evolution," notes E. O. Wiley, "can be explained as a consequence of . . . the second law of thermodynamics" (1988, 173–4). J. Tooby et al. similarly remark, "The second law of thermodynamics (in both its classical and informational versions) is a fundamental law of biology and psychology as well as of physics because organisms and their brains are physical systems" (2003, 861). A biological explanation of religious behavior thus ought not to look to the Standard Social Science Model, but rather the Standard Model.

The Standard Social Science Model, or SSSM (Tooby and Cosmides 1992), includes in its intellectual pedigree such influential authors as Emile Durkheim (1962 [1895]), Mary Douglas (2010 [1966]), and Clifford Geertz (1973). It contends that biology merely provides a "blank slate" upon which culture inscribes its biologically independent system of arbitrary symbols and meanings, never pausing to consider what enables the acquisition of culture in the first place (Barkow et al. 1992). Cultural symbols and meanings are, for the SSSM, irreducible or, and what amounts to the same, sui generis (Rue 2005). Only culture can explain culture (Lowie 1966 [1917]). A pioneer of American anthropology, G. P. Murdock was explicit: culture is "independent of the laws of biology and psychology" (1932, 200). Cultural anthropology remains committed to "the myth of culture as causal explanation" (Buss 2001, 968). According to some, it is the discipline's "disastrous mistake" (Boyer 2018, 1; Bloch 2005). "The most scientifically damaging aspect of this value system," Tooby and Cosmides contend, "has been that it leads anthropologists to actively reject conceptual frameworks that identify meaningful dimensions of cross-cultural uniformity in favor of alternative vantage points from which cultures appear maximally differentiated" (1992, 44). Despite the SSSM's widespread appeal in the humanities and postmodern social sciences, such a position is not only unwarranted, it is simply wrong, and quite possibly harmful as well (Pluckrose and Lindsay 2020; Saad 2020). "The fact that this [common psychological] design is a common human possession that we share through biological endowment is a scientific discovery," Bulbulia claims, "not word play" (2005, 73). H. C. Barrett similarly asserts, "the fact that human minds are the products of evolution is something that we can be as sure of as any other fact in biology" (2015, 12). Minds make societies (Boyer 2018). The SSSM collapses in deepest humiliation.

The Standard Model of particle physics accounts for sentient, agential behavior. Essential to the Standard Model are the laws of thermodynamics. Thermodynamics pertain to "the energy transformations that occur in a collection of matter" (Campbell 1987, 95). Though there are officially four such laws, attention needs to be paid here only to the first two. The first law holds that energy is neither created nor destroyed. The *quantity* of energy in the universe remains constant. The universe is a closed system. Closed systems do not receive supplemental energy input from external sources, for example, God. The second law addresses the *quality*. "The quantity of energy in the universe is constant, but its quality is not," writes N. A. Campbell, "Everything that happens converts organized forms of energy to random molecular motion, or heat" (1987, 95). Energy is either organized and thus usable, or disorganized and thus unusable.

Unusable, disorganized energy is entropy. The second law states that a maximally entropic state is the inevitable fate for the universe and everything in it. All usable energy will be rendered useless. It is for this reason that the second law of thermodynamics is "a foundation of our understanding of the universe and our place in it" (Pinker 2018, 16).

The Standard Model holds that there are only two types of things that exist in this universe, fermions and bosons; "there is no third kind" (Rosenberg 2011, 21). Fermions and bosons are the proverbial building blocks of everything that exists and happens in the universe, from the "atomic to bodily to mental" (Rosenberg 2011, 21). But if that is the case, what distinguishes the subject matter of biology and its blades of grass, that is, life, from the subject matter of physics and its inanimate billiard balls?

A precise definition of life is a bit elusive. After all, "there is no real dividing line between these categories [i.e., life and non-life] in evolutionary history" (Stewart-Williams 2010, 158). Some suggest that living systems are physical systems that temporarily, not to mention locally, "cheat" the second law of thermodynamics. Life delays the onset of entropy (Wiley 1988). According to N. Lane, "Life somehow resists the universal tendency to decay, the increase in entropy (disorder) that is stipulated by the second law of thermodynamics" (2015, 22). A. Damasio similarly notes, "Life . . . can be defined by these two traits: the ability to regulate *its* life by maintaining internal structures and operations for as long as possible, and the possibility of reproducing itself and taking a stab at perpetuity" (2018, 40). A living, physical system thus behaves in such a way as to maintain its structural integrity in the face of the second law of thermodynamics, and, if given the opportunity, replicates. "From an Olympian vantage point," observes S. Pinker, "it [i.e., the Second Law] defines the fate of the universe and the ultimate purpose of life, mind, and human striving: to deploy energy and knowledge to fight back the tide of entropy and carve out refuges of beneficial order" (2018, 17). Evolution by natural selection is the only known process capable of such carving (Tooby et al. 2003).

Life temporarily delays the onset of entropy. It can do so because living systems are open systems. Open systems utilize external sources of usable energy. "Basic thermodynamic constraints derived from exact considerations in statistical physics tell us that a self-replicator's maximum potential fitness is set by how effectively it exploits sources of energy in its environment to catalyze its own reproduction," writes J. England, "the empirical, biological fact that reproductive fitness is intimately linked to efficient metabolism now has a clear and simple basis in physics" (2013, 3). Although the metabolism may be efficient, the exploitation of usable energy is prodigal. Local order is bought at the expense of an increase in disorder (Wiley 1988). The amount of usable energy required to drive open systems away from thermodynamic equilibrium inevitably leads to an *increase* in the amount of unusable energy in the universe. Provincial life hastens universal death (Shanks and Karsai 2005).

Procuring usable energy presents its own unique problem. Due to the inevitable increase in unusable energy, sources of usable energy are scarce, and becoming more so by the minute, by the second. What is more, such a source of usable energy is often another open system itself attempting to thwart the second law of thermodynamics. Open systems competing for usable energy for their own maintenance and regeneration is what led Lord Tennyson to quip that nature was red in tooth and claw. Competition for *limited* sources of usable energy provides the passive filter by which the life world is naturally culled. Given the locally contingent circumstances, some systems simply outcompete others at acquiring and allocating the necessary energy to self-sustain and replicate. D. Dennett suggests that the ability of one system to distinguish itself from another is essential to this process. Self-identity and life are co-constitutive. "As soon as something gets into the business of self-preservation, boundaries become important," D. Dennett argues, "You become, in a word, *selfish*.... 'Me against the world'—this distinction between everything on the inside of a closed boundary and everything in the external world—is at the heart of all biological processes... ingestion and excretion, respiration and transpiration... (and) the immune system" (1991, 174).[4] Herein lies the ultimate explanation for sentient, agential behavior. Sentient agents are in the business of thwarting momentarily the second law of thermodynamics in order to take a shot at replication. That's it. There are, of course, degrees of such agency.

The degree of agency reflects the degree to which behavior is under the system's voluntary control. "Gaining control over the production of behavior is the way in which increasingly sophisticated forms of behavior—and the increasing *variety* of behaviors—come about," note R. Aunger and V. Curtis, "Control in this context refers to the psychological ability to develop 'command sequences' for the motor system to execute as a stream of behavior—which may last for a shorter or longer time, and consist of more or fewer actions—and to select among alternative command sequences based on some criteria" (2015, 3–4). Evolution began with organisms that could only reflexively respond to their current environment, for instance, bacteria (Thompson and Derr 2000). Over time, behavior came evermore under the control of the organism in question (Churchland 2005). Enjoying control over behavior has everything to do with the capacity to incur immediate costs for a delayed reward. The degree to which an organism enjoys such control, and thus an advantage in the tasks of surviving and reproducing, is greatly linked to the degree to which it is "minded." "Minded organisms" come "equipped to process information in ways that enable them to flourish," notes Bulbulia, "they gather, store, and access information about the external world and their various internal states, which they exploit to respond and behave to enhance biological success. ['Behave' in the widest sense: on this view, *an immunological response* or dying old (lifespan) is behavior]" (2005, 79, emphasis added). The more an organism is minded, the more it is able to process a greater amount and variety of incoming streams of adaptively relevant information from both the external and internal worlds. This is an adaptive feature because such cognitive complexity facilitates behavioral plasticity.

Minds, Brain, and Behavior

The human animal is unique in two ways. First, it is singularly reliant upon its massive brain for survival and reproduction (Sapolsky 2004). This is the case because the human animal is relatively weak, small, and slow. Humans cannot outrun a big cat or overpower an ungulate. Our ancestors had to rely upon their wits to survive. We have thus been uniquely selected for a life lived in "the cognitive niche" (Boyer 2001, 120). The vital resource within this niche is information. The amount of information any one person can know is greatly enhanced by its exchange with others. This is the second unique aspect. The pressure to acquire information selected for sociality. Sociality requires cooperation. "Humans have two primary evolutionary niches," writes D. Bell, "cognition and social/cooperative behavior" (2015, 181). J. M. Tybur et al. similarly note, "Interdependence was an enduring feature of the human ancestral environment, and it has led to the evolution of multiple psychological adaptations dedicated to navigating social situations" (2018, 7). Identifying these psychological adaptations is within the remit of cognitive science. Explaining how it is that we came to have such adaptations is within the remit of evolutionary psychology (Buss 2005).

Evolutionary psychology, which is "just evolutionary biology applied to the mind" (Barrett 2015, 12), proposes that the mind is a "massively modular" (Barrett 2015, 3; Pinker 1999), "massively parallel processing system" (Flanagan 2002, 99). To be massively modular is to admit of having discreet functions. A discreet function is a neuronally instantiated, specialized algorithm, or, intuitive inference system calibrated to monitor a specific type of information relevant to survival and reproduction in an ancestral past. Capable of sharing information today (Mithen 1996), these modules originally ran in parallel, that is, simultaneously and independently. It has been suggested that these modules actually compete for executive control of attention (McNamara 2009). This "cognitive division of labor" (Barrett 2015, 115) has led some cognitive scientists to employ the metaphor of a Swiss Army Knife (Tooby and Cosmides 1992). In much the same way that a *new* Swiss Army Knife comes equipped ready to handle any problem for which it has the predesigned tools to address, so too a new mind, that is, an infant's mind is similarly so equipped. Evolutionary psychology and cognitive science directly contest in this way the suggestion that human infants come into the world with a mind like a blank slate, that is, without any expectations of how the world works and must therefore learn everything de novo. The blank slate hypothesis is inconsistent with a wealth of empirical results issuing from research on preverbal, infant cognition.

Developmental psychologists have persuasively shown how infants, some no older than a month, experience surprise when objects in the world behave in "inappropriate" ways. Such surprise is assessed using either "violation-of-expectation gazing" (Barrett 2015, 123) or "the habituation/dishabituation paradigm" (Rochat 2001, 11). For instance, if you roll a ball off of a table and it appropriately falls to the floor, an infant's attention is not sustained; the infant looks away. Should you roll a ball off of a table and it hovers in midair (suspended perhaps by some imperceptible, monofilament string), an infant will gaze at the "floating ball" for an extended duration. This is generally interpreted as revealing surprise, a reaction only the unexpected can evoke. Infants innately presume that unsupported objects fall. Kirkpatrick notes, "certain forms of concept acquisition and reasoning abilities seem to emerge very early, spontaneously, and in the *absence of explicit training or experience*" (2005, 271, emphasis added).[5] Infants possess the capacity for "folk physics" (Atran 2002), the "basics" of which "are not only precultural but pan-species" (Slingerland 2008, 124).

Folk physics categorizes the furniture of the world into two fundamentally distinct categories, that is, the animate and the inanimate.[6] Things that are animate are either human, animal, or plant.[7] Natural objects and artifacts/tools are inanimate. These basic ontological categories are rich in "inferential potential," that is, a set of expectations attends each category (Boyer 2001). For instance, if I correctly place "a knife" in the tool category, then I can infer that some agent made it for a purpose, most likely cutting. I can also infer that I don't need to feed the knife and that if it isn't where I thought I left it last, this is not because it got up and went somewhere. Should the latter so happen to be the case, not only would that violate my expectations, it would equally be quite striking and thereby memorable (more on that shortly). Folk physics may do quite well at handling inanimate objects. It is not so suited to handle the animate world. The animate world requires other forms of "folk science." The animate world requires "folk biology" and "folk psychology."

Folk biology pertains to the evolved capacity to categorize living animals into taxa depending on their, presumably, essential traits. All rabbits are rabbits because they possess rabbit-ness. The tendency to attribute essences to things is something the human animal naturally does, from infancy to adulthood.[8] It is incorrect. The "biological species concept" (Mayr 2001) recognizes that species are populations of genetically unique organisms with the capacity to reproduce successfully. There are no deep essences. Our folk sciences get it wrong (Slingerland 2008; Rosenberg 2011, 2018; Boyer 2018). This is not necessarily a surprise. Once again, natural selection did not select for cognitive skills calibrated to know what is true. It selected skills needed for reproduction. "The mind, like any other complex aspect of the organism," Stewart-Williams writes, "is the product of a slow and gradual accumulation of variants that, at each stage in the process, enhanced the fitness of the individuals possessing them" (Stewart-Williams 2010, 147). Flawed cognition often outcompetes truthful cognition in the game of life. This appears to pertain equally to our "folk psychology."

Foremost among the human animal's folk sciences is "folk psychology." Folk psychology reflects the ability to endow objects with minds. Minds produce beliefs, desires, and intentions. Herein rests the momentous distinction between billiard balls and pool sharks. Because "the function of all cognition is prediction in the service of action" (Barrett 2015, 254), different strategies are required when predicting the behavior of these different types of objects. Folk physics tells us that objects have to behave according to physical laws. All unsupported objects fall. Folk physics enjoys great predictive power. Folk biology similarly enables accurate predictions. A hungry frog simply cannot help but shoot out its tongue when the appropriate stimulus, a fly for instance, crosses its visual field (Rosenberg 2011). Such determinism and the accompanying ability to predict with great precision is not on the cards for folk psychology. When we attribute a mind to something, including ourselves of course, behavior suddenly becomes of a different order altogether, or so commonsense intuition would have us believe (Rosenberg 2018). It is for this reason that there would seem to be a need for two different types of explanation for the behavior of objects in the world, one based on sheer mechanism and the other on interpretation (Slingerland and

Bulbulia 2011). We mechanistically explain why billiard balls move as they do. We interpret why someone would want to play pool as opposed to darts (Cohen 2007).[9]

The cognitive core of folk psychology is the "theory of mind," or ToM (Bloom 2004; Barrett 2015). The theory of mind allows us to infer the presence of intentions, beliefs, and desires behind the other's behaviors. For instance, while a tree limb may move because the wind is blowing it, a person goes inside because they don't want the wind to mess up their hair. The limb cannot help but move. The person could do otherwise. This capacity to interpret behaviors based on opaque intentions, that is, mindreading, appears innate. "Prior to the well-documented emergence of theories of mind in the verbal child," P. Rochat argues, "infants develop a sophisticated, although implicit (not yet verbalized) understanding of others as intentional—as having desires, feelings, and fluctuating affects" (2001, 164). If cognition is in the service of prediction, the intractable problem regarding agents is that one can never truly know what the other agent will do next. The best one can do is guess. Fortunately, the guess need not be an uneducated one.

Educated guesses about what the other agent may do next rely upon adopting what Dennett calls, "the intentional stance": "First you decide to treat the object whose behavior is to be predicted as a *rational* agent, then you figure out what beliefs that agent ought to have, given its place in the world and its purpose" (1989, 17, emphasis added). If the theory of mind is often predicated upon the intentional stance—and this appears to be the case—then it would appear that a certain "folk economics" informs folk psychology (Boyer 2018).[10] Rational choice theory, itself the leading theory in contemporary economics, proposes that rational agents operate according to cost-benefit analyses. A rational agent will attempt to maximize its benefits while minimizing its costs.[11] Rational behavior is selfish behavior. Humans are naturally selfish (Ridley 1996).

The theory of mind (ToM) module was selected over evolutionary time to deal with agents and their putatively rational behaviors. That is the module's proper domain. The module's actual domain is an entirely different story. Because the presence of agents in one's surroundings carried immediate fitness benefits or costs, it would appear that the module is calibrated to over-attribute agency. In other words, the human animal tends to see agents, or evidence thereof, everywhere. A classic example has us imagine a twilight walk through the woods (Guthrie 1993). Some distance up the path, one sees an ambiguous shape. Being uncertain of its exact contours, one must make an educated guess as to what the thing could be. The object could either be inanimate or animate.

It is either a boulder or a bear. If the object is a bear and I think it is a boulder, my future reproductive interests may be dashed. I better assume it is a bear. The assumption reflects yet another naturally selected, cognitive endowment. In addition to the theory of mind, the human animal equally possesses a hyperactive agency detection device, or HADD (Atran 2002; Barrett 2004). We are trip-wired to infer the presence of agents. A slight rustle in the grass is much more likely to be assessed initially as the presence of a snake rather than a warm summer breeze. As one might imagine in such a situation, HADD activation has an affective component, fear. A basic emotion (Ekman 1992), "fear is central to mammalian evolution" (Ohman and Mineka 2001, 483). "Fear is a subjective emotion in man," note I. Eibl-Eibesfeldt and C. Sutterlin, "which accompanies escape responses and defensive behaviour" (1990, 381). Fear certainly seems to be the first thing one feels when one detects the potential presence of another agent. The other agent could of course turn out to be a friend in much the same way that the object up ahead may be a boulder, but we adaptively go with foe and fear first. We are adaptively predisposed to Type I errors, that is, false positives.

We attribute agency to objects in the world in much the same way we attribute objects in the world to agency. We tend to see many things in the natural world as products of agential design. Once again, preverbal infants and children demonstrate an innate tendency "to view natural phenomena as intentionally created . . . to construe natural objects as though they are nonhuman artifacts" (Keleman 2004, 295). This is what J. Bering refers to as "teleo-functional reasoning" (2011, 55). Folk physics may tell us that natural objects are one thing and artifacts another, but teleo-functional reasoning tells us a different story. Teleo-functional reasoning motivates perceptions of natural objects as if they were naturally occurring artifacts. Naturally occurring artifacts are produced by nonhuman design. Nonhuman design reflects the mind of god(s). We seem to be intuitive theists (Evans 2001). Perhaps we are all "born believers" (Barrett 2012).

The theory of mind is calibrated to infer the presence of a mind in a physical object. It is not calibrated to process the mind as a product of physical instantiation or mediation. There are modules dedicated to dealing with physical objects, such as bodies, both dead and alive, but they apparently do not affect or influence the module that deals with minds (Boyer 2001; McCorkle 2010). This means that it is cognitively easy for us to divorce minds from bodies. We are, in this regard, cognitively predisposed to adopt a metaphysical position known as dualism, a position made most famous by the seventeenth-century French philosopher, Rene Descartes (Bloom 2004). Dualism holds that there are two fundamental types of things in reality, minds and bodies. "Dualism is not indebted to the philosophical legacy of Descartes or Plato," note Bulbulia and Slingerland, "but rather from panhuman genetic endowment: we are born to believe in ghosts" (2012, 576). The theory of mind is the cognitive basis for beliefs in gods and ghosts (Barrett 2004; Bering 2011). Without it, religion becomes quite difficult to do.[12]

Evolutionary psychology and cognitive science identify naturally selected, pan-human psychological designs responsible for many of the behaviors the human animal performs. When confronted with perceptual ambiguity, for instance, we *all* default to a cautionary position: it is most likely a bear and not a boulder. Some suggest, all the same, that the massive modularity of evolutionary psychology is not exhaustive. It is possible that over time domain general, cognitive adaptations were selected. The control of behavior that Aunger and Curtis identify may in fact rest on the emergence of such domain generalities. "It would simply not be feasible to construct a brain that allocates a specific psychological module to every conceivable event an individual might encounter," write K. N. Laland and G. R. Brown, "domain-general processes are no more incompatible with evolutionary theory than domain-specific processes" (2002: 182–3). This combination of domain specificity and domain generality enables behavioral plasticity. "Selection favors various mechanisms for plasticity, such as individual and social learning, exactly because they allow individuals to acquire locally adaptive behavior strategies over a range of environments" D. Nettle et al. note, "plasticity is ultimately dependent on genotype ... deployed in the service of genetic fitness maximization" (2013, 1032). Here is where the Swiss Army Knife metaphor runs into difficulties. A Swiss Army Knife cannot adjust its assemblage based on environmental feedback. The long blade will forever be a long blade. This is not the case for the human animal's psychological adaptations. Thus, a more apt metaphor for the human mind/brain is a "coloring book" (Kenrick et al. 2010, 268). All neurotypical minds have the same cognitive capacities but the specifics of how those capacities are developed and deployed depend on the colors of the local environment. This allows for a modicum of plasticity when it comes to behavioral responses. If evolutionary psychology is evolutionary biology applied to the mind, human behavioral ecology is evolutionary biology applied to human behavior (Tinbergen 1963).

Human behavioral ecology (HBE) asserts that the human animal organizes and interprets information in the local environment using Darwinian algorithms calibrated to produce adaptive behaviors. Adaptive behaviors are facultative responses (Alexander 1990; Cronk 1991; Winterhalder and Smith 2000; Hames 2001; Laland and Brown 2002; Hayden 2003). The "core assumptions" of HBE are that "context matters when studying the adaptive consequences of human behavior and that behavioral diversity arises because the payoffs to alternative behavioral strategies are ecologically contingent" (Nettle et al. 2013, 1035). Ecological contingencies include, to be sure, both "the physical and social aspects of the environment" (Nettle et al. 2013, 1032). "Our phenotypes are molded by our environments," writes M. J. West-Eberhard, "by our mothers, fathers, schoolteachers, economics, and accidents of history" (2003, 3–4). Ecologically contingent, cultural variance captures the attention of the human behavioral ecologist.

Culture is a codified and thus transmissible collection of prescriptions for adaptive dispositions and behaviors, as well as proscriptions for maladaptive dispositions and behaviors, pertaining to the local ecology. "Behavioral ecologists assume," write Sosis and Bulbulia, "that selection will produce thoughts that justify or motivate optimal behavioral responses to environmental conditions" (2011, 347). As previously noted, human culture is rightly considered part of the human animal's extended phenotype (Dawkins 1982). Culture is, in this regard, as much evoked as it is transmitted (Waller et al. 1990; Tooby and Cosmides 1992; Buss 2001; Fessler and Navarette 2003; Gangestad et al. 2006; Clay et al. 2012), a phenomenon that "has been under-explored as a source of inter-population variation in humans, but its potential importance is high" (Nettle 2009, 227). "Evoked culture arises as a function of specialized, evolved responsivity," write Gangestad et al., "which is adaptively contingent on particular environmental features" (2006, 89). Thus, "[HBE] tends to regard the variability in human society and culture as entities that are . . . evoked by the ecological environment," observe Laland and Brown, "humans are predisposed to learn that which maximizes their inclusive fitness by satisfying various proximal goals, such as to obtain food and mates, and to avoid danger and disease" (2002, 311).

In addition to being a set of ideas, artifacts, and practices, culture is equally a set of psychological dispositions. It is composed of modal personalities. "Regional differences in personality traits may constitute a form of 'evoked culture,'" note M. Schaller and D. Murray, "wherein cultural differences reflect the phenotypic plasticity of the human genome and emerge through mechanisms in which universal human capacities are differentially evoked under different ecological circumstances" (2008, 220). Some personality traits appear better suited than others to handle particular ecological conditions. Schaller and Murray write elsewhere,

> Attitudes, traits, and other dispositional tendencies are influenced by genes. The phenotypic consequences of genes depend, however, on whether (and how)

the genes are expressed during the course of development. Gene expression is profoundly influenced—typically in functionally adaptive ways—by the ecological circumstances within which an individual organism develops. (2011, 137)

How exactly the behavioral strategies and dispositions that interest the human behavioral ecologist arise from a genetic or neural base are issues about which HBE tends to be agnostic. This is known as the "phenotypic gambit" and "behavioral gambit": "The assumptions of no mechanistic constraints coming from the genetic architecture or the neural mechanisms are known, respectively, as the phenotypic gambit . . . and the behavioral gambit" (Nettle et al. 2013, 1032). Although that may be true, Laland and Brown quickly warn that "humans are unlikely to be infinitely flexible and there may well be significant genetic and developmental constraints or predispositions that prevent humans from maximizing fitness under all circumstances" (2002, 147). This may especially be the case today.

The human animal achieved anatomical modernity perhaps as early as "165,000 years ago" (Peoples et al. 2016, 263), in environments quite unlike those we experience today. Certain behaviors that would have been adaptive in the past may no longer be adaptive in the post-industrial present. For instance, humans have a strong preference for foods that are fatty and sweet. Such caloric resources would have been rare treats in the ancient past. It was adaptive to prefer such foods. Today, however, fatty and sweet foods can be purchased on almost every street corner. Our once-adaptive preferences for such foods have now become the source of a maladaptive obesity pandemic. Such an evolutionary lag has also been credited with certain psychopathologies in today's world (McGuire and Troisi 1998). It is quite possible that religion may be one of those features of human life that was once adaptive but is no longer, a topic to which we return in Chapter 6 (Wiebe 2016). To understand the human animal's (mal)adaptive design requires a consideration of the circumstances in which the human animal's limited flexibility was originally selected.

The human animal's mind and behaviors evolved in what has come to be called, the "environment of evolutionary adaptedness," or EEA (Tooby and Cosmides 1992). The EEA is not "a place or a habitat, or even a time period," assert Tooby and Cosmides, "Rather, it is a statistical composite of the adaptation-relevant properties of the ancestral environments encountered by members of ancestral populations, weighted by their frequency and fitness-consequences" (1990, 386–7). Although suggesting that the EEA is not a time period, Tooby and Cosmides all the same associate it with the Pleistocene (*c.* 2.58mya-11,700ya), "because its time depth was appropriate for virtually *all* adaptations of anatomically modern humans" (Tooby and Cosmides 1990, 388, emphasis added). The EEA was not particularly hospitable to early humans.

The human EEA presented several discrete pressures that had to be negotiated. Among the most frequent of such pressures were the need to detect and avoid predators (Barrett 2005; Revonsuo 2000; Shultz et al. 2011), to detect, catch, and consume prey (Barrett 2005; Rosenberg 2011), to locate and retain high-quality mates (Schmitt 2005; Slone 2008; Slone and Van Slyke 2015), to produce and nurture progeny (Bowlby 1969; Ainsworth et al. 1978; Small 1998), and of especial interest for the discussion that unfolds over the following chapters, to detect and avoid pathogens and parasites (Curtis and Biran 2001), and when infected, to survive (Fabrega Jr. 1997). "The initial environment must have been extremely inhospitable and enormous numbers of those early protohumans must have died on the savannas during the drying up of African forests," writes Hayden, "great numbers must have also been killed by the predators" (2003, 25). The EEA was hostile to the human animal's homeostatic goals, presenting as it did separate, dire pressures. There was, however, a common solution. The human animal had to cooperate in order to survive and reproduce. How exactly that came about is "one of the greatest challenges for evolutionary biology" (West et al. 2006, 1103).[13]

Dennett suggested above that as soon as life arose so too did selfish identity. Life is a matter of me against the world. This is not quite right. Insofar as copies of my genes are found in my relatives, it may be better to suggest that life, at least human life, is more about us, genetically related others (i.e., kin), against the world. This is the basis of inclusive fitness theory (Dawkins 1976). Biological success is not calculated solely through one's own progeny. It is also calculated through the progeny of one's siblings and cousins. The gene that is in me, and most likely in my siblings, progeny, and cousins, does not care how it gets a copy into the next generation, nor who is responsible for that copy, just as long as the copy gets there. It's natural to have a modicum of concern about the welfare of kin. This is known as "kin altruism," the ubiquity of which in the animal kingdom may just be "the biological equivalent of the laws of thermodynamics" (Stewart-Williams 2018, 191). Of course, nonkin do not enjoy the same natural solicitude. *This* is the problem of cooperation, "the central problem of social existence" (Greene 2013, 20), "the critical problem early hominins faced" (Rosenberg 2018, 69).

Human survival in the Pleistocene required that "we" cooperate with "them" (Rosenberg 2018). "Humans for a long time have required, for their survival and reproduction, extensive support from kin," note Boyer et al., "but also from nonkin conspecifics" (2015, 435). Getting nonkin conspecifics to cooperate was no easy feat. It remains no easy feat. This is the case because cooperation fundamentally diverges from the selfishness that is endemic to life (Ridley 1996). Taking on a cost the benefit of which *wholly* accrues to a genetically unrelated other is simply not on the cards for any organism. Pure altruism is a nonstarter. The preeminent evolutionary biologist G. C. Williams notes, "As a general rule, a modern biologist seeing an animal doing something to benefit another assumes either that it is being manipulated by the other individual or that it is being subtly selfish" (quoted in Ridley 1996, 18). Greed is good, biologically speaking.

Different selection pressures require different types of cooperation. Might one of these pressures and the accompanying cooperation be primary? Many suggest, yes, but there is disagreement. Rosenberg (2011) suggests that the need to cooperate for the sake of hunting large, calorically rich megafauna was most pressing. Bulbulia et al. propose that "reproduction poses biology's most fundamental cooperation problem" (2015, 51). Other cooperation problems pertain to parents and their progeny as well as between siblings (Palmer and Begley 2015). "The relationships between parents and offspring, or between mates, or between social partners," M. Ridley cynically remarks, "was not one of mutual satisfaction, but one of mutual struggle to exploit the relationship" (1996, 22), writing elsewhere, "the same pattern of conflict within the midst of cooperation is to be found in every other natural collaboration" (1996, 24). If cooperation was vital to our evolutionary forebears' survival in the EEA, and if conflict comes naturally to any collaborative endeavor, then a principal resource to be shared between potential partners would have been trust. To have trust in the other is to believe that the other is going to remain faithful to the collaboration. Signaling such commitments would have been most adaptive in the pursuit of inclusive fitness, the reason for behavior itself. Some believe that this could be religion's primary function. "The most powerful cultural signals of commitment are religious ones," notes W. Irons, "and thus evolution has built into human beings a strong propensity to seek a religious orientation toward life and to hold this orientation to be of the highest value" (2001, 293).

Religion

Degree of sufficiency and necessity are matters of interminable debate when it comes to defining religion. Such difficulties lead some to abandon the task altogether (Kirkpatrick 2005). This will not do. I am inclined to argue, as many others do, that any definition must include some sense of there being non-natural, or, and what amounts to the same, supernatural agents (Guthrie 1993; Horton 1993; Spiro 1994; Stark and Finke 2000; Boyer 2001; Atran 2002; Barrett 2004; Kirkpatrick 2005; Martin and Wiebe 2016; Turner et al. 2018; Smith 2019). A non-natural agent is a disembodied mind (Fales 2013). It is equally a mind improperly embodied. For instance, and according to the preeminent Christian philosopher, R. Swinburne, God is "a person without a body" (1977, 2), that is, a mind without a body. Animist traditions, on the other hand, believe that natural objects, for instance, trees and mountains, are capable of possessing minds (Goldenberg et al. 2000). Trees and mountains do not possess minds (Flanagan 2002). A mind, disembodied or not, with which no human can interact is as good as no mind at all. There are no deistic churches. Religious practitioners thus perceive not only disembodied minds, but also disembodied minds that are capable of interacting with them in meaningful ways.[14] The interactions with gods appear to be illusory extensions of everyday interactions between natural agents. "The origins of religion ultimately are to be found in the interpersonal dynamics that guide each and every interaction among humans," J. H. Turner et al. note, "*ritual worship of the supernatural is very much like regular interaction among individuals*" (2018, 134–5). Regular interactions among individuals often have an economic aspect. Religious practitioners expect a return on their religious investments (Zuckerman et al. 2018).

Religious practitioners turn to their gods when they cannot acquire what they desire on their own (Stark and Finke 2000). Religious behavior is often socioeconomic in nature. "Religion is envisioned as an economic exchange between people and imagined supernatural agents for goods that are scarce (e.g., rain during a drought) or impossible (e.g., immortal life) to obtain in the real world," writes Wilson, "Religious belief is therefore rational in the sense of employing cost-benefit reasoning" (2002, 48). Religion is perceived *socioeconomic intercourse* with non-natural agents. This is close to the mark, but something is still missing. The schizophrenic, after all, is often convinced of his socioeconomic intercourse with non-natural agents. Although the connection between religion and schizophrenia can be made (McCauley and Graham 2020), there is one rather telling difference between the two. Religion enjoys collective sanction (Turner et al. 2018). The schizophrenic does not. Religion is collectively sanctioned perceptions of socioeconomic intercourse with causally efficacious, non-natural agents. This captures the cognitive structure of religion. That said, no religious practitioner thinks of their god in such stark terms. Here is where the coloring book metaphor for the mind may come in handy. Each religion fills in the black and white structure of non-natural agency with specific colors. "From the vantage point of cognitive architecture," Bulbulia writes, "it appears that there is only one human religion with minor but strategically important variation in its conventional expressions" (2005, 72). Variation in conventional expression often reflects ecological contingencies.

No one has ever seen a non-natural agent. Natural agents thus provide the models upon which religious practitioners base their perceptions of non-natural agency. Most often the natural agent is anthropomorphic (Guthrie 1993). Gods are routinely perceived to be either parents or what might be called, an intra-tribal rank superior, for instance, a king (Freud 1927; Ellis 2009). When the god is perceived to be either a father or a king, devotees become progeny or subjects.[15] Both scenarios convey the notion of a god as a protector/provider. Gods, parents, and kings protect and reward their well-behaved devotees, children, and subjects. "Religion can be looked upon as an extension of the field of people's social relationships beyond the confines of purely human society," writes R. Horton, "the human beings involved see themselves in a dependent relationship *vis-à-vis* their non-human alters—a qualification necessary to exclude pets from the pantheon of gods" (1993, 32). Although plausible, Horton's exclusion is mistaken. Gods are not the only entities to populate the non-natural world.

Guthrie's insistence that religion is irreducibly anthropomorphic and Horton's exclusion of pets from the pantheon of deities may be premature. Animals may not be models for the gods. They are, however, models for demons and devils. Demons and devils are routinely theriomorphic in nature.[16] Not just any theriomorphic model will do, however. Seldom do we find images of a devil or demon having the characteristics of a giraffe. "More often than not," notes S. Atran, "supernatural monsters have characteristic features of animal predators, such as fangs, large canines, hooked beaks, claws, and other means of tearing and consuming flesh" (2002, 77). W. Burkert similarly writes, "Demons, in myth and in art, usually take the form of predators" (1996, 42). A certain predation anxiety appears to be part of the human animal's cognitive endowment. "We 'know' about the danger of a predator's attack," Burkert adds, "even before any actual experience, as the chicken 'knows' about the hawk" (1996, 42). Devils appear to be our "ghosts of predators past" (Byers 1998). Atran convincingly concludes: "It is not an infant-mother, infant-father, or infant-family template per se from which God concepts extend, but a more encompassing evolutionary program for avoiding and tracking predators and prey ... *predator and protector*" (2002, 78, emphasis added). Devils are predators. Gods are protectors.

Cognitive science facilitates a definition of religion. Definitions do not, however, identify functions. Perceiving the presence of gods and demons with whom one can interact has functional implications for behavior. Foremost among such implications is perhaps the one pertaining to cooperation. As noted above, cooperation amid genetically unrelated others is no easy feat. In fact, and according to game theory, it seems that it is never rational to cooperate (Axelrod 1984; Rosenberg 2011). This is a problem.

Game theory is a central component of contemporary economics. Its favorite thought experiment is the prisoner's dilemma. The dilemma involves two would-be bank robbers who have been apprehended prior to executing the heist. Wishing to throw the proverbial book at them, the police separate the two for intense interrogation. They want to know what the plan was. Each prisoner has a decision to make. One can either confess (i.e., defect) or stay silent (i.e., cooperate). Disparate penalties hang in the balance. No one wants to go to jail. What is the rational thing to do? If both prisoners remain silent, that is, cooperate with each other, each will be charged with a year of imprisonment for possession of safe-cracking equipment. If, however, both confess, that is, defect from the cooperative strategy, then both will receive a five-year sentence. The third scenario involves only one culprit defecting and the other cooperating. The punishment in this last scenario involves the one who defects receiving a suspended one-year sentence while the other receives a ten-year sentence. If one is seeking to minimize time spent in jail, then "the only rational thing . . . to do is to confess" (Rosenberg 2011, 125). Confessing assures that the maximum penalty will be avoided. Rational choice theory thus favors defection in the prisoner's dilemma. Economists identify this as the dominant strategy. Some nuance is warranted, however. Defection is the rational thing to do in a *one-off* prisoner's dilemma. It is rational to defect if one is never going to see the other again. Such opportunities characterize primarily modern, urban environments, "an evolutionarily novel circumstance" (Stewart-Williams 2010, 214). The dominant strategy is not so dominant should the dilemma be iterated. "Prisoners" in the EEA were bound to see each other again.

"Always defect" was not the dominant strategy in the EEA. Tit-for-tat was. Tit-for-tat is the logic of reciprocal altruism. "Tit-for-tat is a mechanism for generating cooperation between unrelated individuals," writes Ridley, "the principal condition required for Tit-for-tat to work is a stable, *repetitive* relationship" (1996, 63, emphasis added). The logic that would compel cooperation in an iterated prisoner's dilemma is the same logic that would lead to the emergence of reciprocal altruism in the wild. At the heart of this logic is non-zero-sumness. Wright summarizes, "The essential feature of non-zerosumness is that, through cooperation, or reciprocation, *both* players can be better off" (1994, 194). For instance, success may not be evenly distributed among a group of hunters. I may or may not enjoy success on any given day. Likewise, on any given day, you may or may not enjoy success. There will be days where we will both be successful. Far more likely, however, is that both of us will either fail or that only one of us will succeed. Things are truly dire in the former situation. In the latter situation, should the lucky one decide to share some of the kill, then both of us are better off. A decision to share is based on the expectation that should the roles be reversed in the future, the same mutual benefit will be enjoyed. Should I be the lucky one who shares, and you are the lucky one who hoards, then I lose. In such a situation, and expecting another iteration of "who got lucky today," it would be foolish for me to continue to cooperate with you if you continue to hoard. I will not share with you the next time I'm lucky. Similarly, if I put in all the work and you only pretend to do so in order to enjoy what I reap, then I will tend to see you as a cheater, that is, a free rider. One would be foolish not to join the free rider in his indiscretion. Cheating appears contagious. "Reciprocity violations are different from other sorts of moral wrongs in that they have the potential to pollute and circulate," V. Kumar notes, "where there is an expectation of trust and reciprocity, spoiling these interactions (pollution), and their behavior often leads others to do so as well (circulation)" (2017, 10). Contagious indiscretions evoke disgust. "Disgust is . . . a fitting response to reciprocity violations in part because the empathic nature of disgust recognition facilitates collective punishment," Kumar further argues, "and collective punishment is an appropriate response to reciprocity violations that pollute social interaction" (2017, 11).

Many game theorists suggest that the dominant strategy in an iterated prisoner's dilemma is to start out cooperating. The first Tit is a trusting one. After my initial cooperation, my next move will mimic your first move, and so on. But should one be so cooperative at the start? Should one be so trusting? Resource scarcity, after all, characterized the EEA. Anyone who was too trusting was most likely at a disadvantage. According to Wilson, "the spirit of communitas" which characterizes "the mind of the hunter-gatherer" reflects a willingness "to work for the common good but ever-vigilant against exploitation" (2002, 224). Suspicions regarding the other's fidelity never truly abate (Ridley 1996). The trust that informs tit-for-tat's first cooperative move ought to be earned, not assumed.

There were perhaps two primary situations in the EEA in which the opportunity for a stable-yet-vulnerable repetitive relationship would have presented itself. The ever-present need to hunt collectively calorically rich megafauna would have presented such a repetitive dilemma. The need for mate acquisition and retention, not to mention ensuing parental investment in progeny, likewise presented another. Rosenberg (2011) suggests that the former problem was primary. Bulbulia et al. (2015) suggest the latter. In the competition for scarce economic and reproductive resources, it was best to search for signals of commitment, the value of which surpasses mere assertion. Talk is cheap. One must show that one can walk the walk as well. Certain gaits are easier than others.

Trust and Cooperation

Many in the biology of religion argue that religion's primary function is to foster trust in economic and reproductive exchanges. It can do this by affording opportunities to demonstrate one's commitment to cooperation through what are called costly and hard-to-fake signs (Irons 2001). This is the costly-signaling theory of religion, or CST (Sosis and Alcorta 2003). Costly signals are strategically irrational signals. The rational actor is, after all, the selfish actor. "Religion fosters co-operation by enabling individuals to reliably predict and secure social exchange where there are rational incentives to defect" (Bulbulia 2005, 85). There are generally two types of irrational signals. One type is theological knowledge, the other ritual behavior. Regarding the former, A. Mahoney notes, "the acquisition of biologically non-strategic information is useless in an evolutionary context" (2015, 192), writing elsewhere, "so much theological knowledge is maximally counterintuitive because if it were not so, theology would not perform a costly signaling function" (2015, 199). The irredeemable futility of theological knowledge on a philosophical and market register may be utterly practical on a biological one (Berman 2009). "Requiring potential members of a religious organization to commit to a god that has no verifiable existence—which is to say, require them to make a costly and useless commitment," argues Slone, "is a good trick for discovering who is and who isn't thoroughly committed to the group and its principles" (2008, 184). Only the committed can believe that three is one.

Religion equally provides opportunities to behave irrationally (Irons 2001). There are two types of irrational behavior. The first type involves physical costs and is often associated with initiation rituals. A would-be tribe member must prove his willingness to cooperate by undergoing a harrowing ordeal. One rather widespread harrowing ordeal is genital mutilation. By undergoing such an ordeal, you earn my trust. Hardship rituals are calibrated precisely for that function. Let the tit-for-tat games begin.

The second display of commitment involves resource costs and is often associated with religious indoctrination, an indoctrination "sufficiently complex to be difficult for an outsider—one who has not spent years learning the tradition—to imitate" (Irons 2001, 298). "At one end of the spectrum, we find extraordinary risky and painful ordeals—trials by needles and fire, teeth punching, nonsterile circumcisions, practices of leaping from great heights, soul quests in hostile environments, potent drug use, lifelong celibacy, and much else," Bulbulia writes, "At the other end, we find apparently fruitless investments of time and energy through long, tedious rituals for which agents incur massive opportunity costs" (2006, 108). Those unwilling to pay such costs self-identify as potential free riders. These individuals are avoided. "Those who are uncommitted," Sosis and Alcorta conclude, "can be avoided as partners in collective action because they will find it too expensive to pay the costs of religious behavior" (2003, 267). Irons similarly remarks, "religious ideologies are more effective than secular ones at the difficult task of persuading human beings to live in a community where property is held in common and where the risk of being exploited by free riders is great" (2001, 303).

The one-off prisoner's dilemma counsels defection. It is irrational to cooperate with someone whom you will never see again. Such was not the reality for most of human evolution. There was plenty of time for tit-for-tat to evolve as the dominant strategy within hunter-gather groups because one could count on seeing one's exchange partner over and over again. One ought to inhibit one's selfish impulses lest one be ostracized from the tribe, a death sentence if ever there was one in the Pleistocene. This problem became quite grave with the evolution of language. Language facilitates gossip (Bering 2011). Gossip is strategic information shared between at least two parties regarding an absent third. This becomes problematic for the would-be free rider. Should one defect from the cooperative bond, one can expect that the cheated will go and report the indiscretion to others. Sticks and stones break bones. Words ruin reputations in perpetuity. A ruined reputation would not have been in anyone's inclusive fitness interests. The possibility of gossip in a hunter-gather tribe was a strong incentive to behave morally. "HGs gossip endlessly . . . it's mostly about the usual: norm violation by high-status individuals" (Sapolsky 2017, 324). Gossip facilitates "reverse dominance" (Boehm 1993). Reverse domination occurs when a group polices itself, "ranging in intensity from gossip, to ridicule, to ostracism, to assassination" (Wilson 2002, 21). Reverse domination can only take place within certain demographic limits. It is not effective in large groups of anonymous others. Such groups afford opportunities for one-off prisoner's dilemmas. One's defections are no longer so perilous in large groups. Defection eventually became the rational choice. This provided a selection pressure for religion to evolve. What evolved? The size of the gods.

Hunter-gatherer groups were often small enough to allow reverse domination. The gods of such groups were not generally seen as morally interested agents (Peoples et al. 2016). They may have been powerful forces in need of appeasement, but they didn't seem terribly concerned with moral violations amid the tribe. "A startling fact about the spirits and deities of foraging and hunter-gatherer societies," A. Norenzayan points out, "is that most of them do not have wide moral concerns. . . . The gods may want to be appeased with sacrifices and rituals . . . [but] they are typically unconcerned about moral transgressions such as theft and exploitation" (2013, 7). Once a tribe got so large that it became impossible to monitor each other's behaviors, however, there was a new pressure to facilitate cooperation among *anonymous* others. The result was the evolution of what Norenzayan calls, "Big Gods." A god's size reflects the depth and scope of his/her/its interest in the moral interactions of exchange partners.

Big Gods always know one's intentions and motives. Even when no one else is around to detect defection, a Big God is. C. P. Weingarten and J. S. Chisholm note, "Defection (non-cooperation) is not a good alternative for the religious individual who believes in a deity who always knows the truth about whether one is cooperating and who can supranaturally [sic] reward or punish in response" (2009, 761). "The very point of supernatural monitoring," adds Norenzayan, "is the outsourcing of social monitoring duties to gods so that moral concern can be extended writ large—to watch even when no one is watching, to care when no one cares, to threaten when no one can threaten" (2013, 27). Perceiving that a pair of eyes is watching motivates cooperative behaviors (Bering 2011). Big Gods facilitate economic cooperation amid anonymous others, a feat no one human seems capable of performing either alone or collectively. Big Gods are an adaptation for big groups.

Costly-signaling theory suggests that religions provide opportunities for individuals to demonstrate their commitment to fair economic exchange by irrationally incurring hard-to-fake costs in the short term. Costly and hard-to-fake signals promote trust. This may not be the only thing they do. Such signals may equally increase the credibility of the religion itself. This is what Norenzayan calls a credibility-enhancing display, or CRED. Employing immunological language, he writes, "the CRED framework predicts that witnessing extravagant religious displays *causes* cultural contagion of religious beliefs.... CREDs have the power to induce greater belief and commitment among observers ... witnessing was as potent as participating" (2013, 102–3). Costly and hard-to-fake performances encourage others to raise their cooperative game as well. Psychologists refer to this as "moral elevation." "People who witness or learn about individuals who perform such costly acts tend to describe them as inspiring moral exemplars," write C. Palmer and R. O. Begley, "and, through an aspect of evolved human psychology labeled 'moral elevation' . . . have been shown to respond to such acts by making similar sacrifices of their own" (2015, 100). One's sacrificial behaviors for the group often motivate others to sacrifice for the group as well. It is a good thing, economically speaking, for everyone in a group to witness and occasionally participate in self-sacrificial acts (Powell and Clark 2012). The selection pressure to cooperate economically contributed to the emergence and evolution of religion. There were other pressures equally pressing.

Economic success is not biological success. Biological success is not measured in calories or dollar signs. It is measured in the number of one's genes that are represented in future generations. Biological success requires progeny and kin. It requires reproductive cooperation. Cooperating reproductively is never a guarantee. This is the case because potential partners tend to have different reproductive interests and strategies. True, both partners "want" genetic representation in the next generation. The problem is that the scope of such representation is unequal between the sexes. A man can potentially have the same number of children in a month that a woman can have over the entire course of her reproductive career. This is a reality ripe for reproductive conflict. Sexual selection theory addresses such concerns.

Sexual selection theory proposes that some phenotypic traits were selected because they were advantageous in the competitive market of reproductive resources (Slone and Van Slyke 2015). Such competition could either be intrasexual or intersexual. Intrasexual competition led to the emergence of sexual "weapons." A sexual weapon is a trait with which one outcompeted a same-sex competitor. Intrasexual competition accounts for such things as antlers, tusks, and horns. Such appendages can grow so large that they become a survival disadvantage. This raises the important point that evolution is not really about the survival of the fittest. It's about the reproduction of the fittest (Stewart-Williams 2018). A sexual advantage can be a survival disadvantage. Consider the longhorn ram. While the horns are surely sexual weapons in the fight against other rams for access to ewes, and perhaps ewes see bigger horns as honest signals of fitness, the horns, all the same, can grow so large as to pierce the ram's flesh, an eventuation not in the ram's survival interests. Intersexual competition, on the other hand, led to the emergence of sexual ornaments. Ornaments were traits favored by a potential mate (Stewart-Williams 2018, 22). A stock example is the peacock's tail (Zahavi and Zahavi 1997). The magnificent plume is a proverbial bull's eye for a predator. It is a costly and hard-to-fake sign of fitness. Only the most fit and thereby attractive peacocks could survive in the wild with such extravagant, phenotypic traits. It has been suggested that religion affords opportunities to develop sexual ornaments and weapons (Slone and Van Slyke 2015).

Religion can be sexy. It affords the opportunity for a man to display his peacock's tail, that is, his "'cognitive' plume" (Bell 2015, 182). Cognitive plumes are peacocks' tails in the cognitive niche. "What would a cognitive ornamentation look like?" asks Bell, "Mnemonic ability and social intelligence are highly rewarded traits today, which are prized by females when selecting a mate" (2015, 182). The ability to demonstrate cognitive sophistication through the performance of intricate rituals with baroque formulas signals a certain genetic fitness to a would-be sexual partner. It is similarly weaponized insofar as not every male enjoys the same cognitive capacities. "Male-dominated rituals were essentially ornaments to attract mates," Bell writes, "the signaling exhibited cognitive ability . . . a practice by men to signal to women their cognitive 'plume'" (2015, 182). To this day, it would seem that women tend to be attracted to men who can display cognitive plumes (Blackmore 1999).

Religion equally affords the possibility for a man to demonstrate his irrational commitment to one woman. By participating in a religion, a man adopts a set of behaviors and beliefs that signal his willingness to restrict his sexual opportunities. He signals his willingness to refrain from becoming a promiscuous rider. "We expect religious signals," notes Bulbulia et al., "to be honest indicators of cooperative parenting" (2015, 42). What is more, "by being committed to a religious system (as evidenced by being willing to engage in its costly and apparently useless behaviors) and its ethical demands, which typically include prohibitions against selfish, anti-social behavior," Slone writes, "a man signals that he possesses the types of characteristics that a woman would find desirable" (2008, 183). Religion thus provides an opportunity for the male to demonstrate his willingness to forego multiple, sexual interactions in preference for a committed relationship with the attendant investment of limited resources, the very traits women generally tend to prefer.[17] The return on investment for the male cashes out in terms of the quality as opposed to the quantity of children. The former appears inversely proportional to the latter.

The quality of a child reflects the ability and/or willingness of the parent to invest in their development. In harsh ecological circumstances such as the EEA, it would often have been genetically beneficial to have more children rather than fewer children. The more children one has, the more likely some will survive. This is often referred to as a fast, reproductive strategy. The fast strategy entails earlier mating, multiple partners, less parental investment, and more defection (Baumard and Chevallier 2015). The slow strategy, on the other hand, focuses more on the quality of the child and not the quantity. The slow strategy correlates with affluence, commitment to one partner, and the greater provisioning of progeny (Sanderson 2018). It equally correlates with religion. Religion has been shown to correlate with lower levels of sociosexuality and short-term mating interests (Schmitt and Fuller 2015). Some authors suggest that the desire to engage in slow strategies actually motivates the adoption of religion (Kirkpatrick 2005; Blume 2015; van Slyke 2015). Baumard and Chevallier report, "Longitudinal studies suggest that people's strategy appears to cause religiousness, rather than religiousness causing people's strategy" (2015, 4). Those desiring long-term, slow strategies would do well to adopt a religion.

Inclusive fitness interests are apparently best served when parents cooperate and jointly raise and provision children. But such provisioning needs to be discriminative, especially for the father. Whether or not parents invest in children depends largely on whether the children were their own. Most adult males want to provide only for their genetic offspring. Doing otherwise amounts to cuckoldry, a genetic dead end. "Contemporary estimates of worldwide cuckoldry (ranging from 1–30 percent; Goetz et al. 2008) suggest that cuckoldry occurred often enough throughout our evolutionary history to have imposed strong selection pressures on men" (Sela et al. 2015, 116). The same cannot be said for the cuckquean; women, after all, have a direct knowledge of which children are theirs. All of this relates to the problem of paternity certainty (Geary 2005). Absent genetic testing, a man simply cannot know for sure which children are his because he cannot know for sure that his sexual partner did not in fact have multiple partners prior to showing signs of pregnancy. It is always possible that the woman cheated. Men and woman are equally capable of being promiscuous riders. "Men valued chastity significantly more highly than women did," Nesse and Williams note, "while there was no culture in which the reverse was true" (1996, 189). Rosenberg adds, "there is always strong selection—genetic or cultural—for . . . practices that maximize the probability that the children the male is supporting are actually genetically his own" (2018, 227). Cultural selection led to many religions adopting practices and/or beliefs that would reduce the uncertainty of paternity (Slone and Van Slyke 2015; Baumard and Chevallier 2015; Schmitt and Fuller 2015). For instance, the Dogon of sub-Saharan Africa make use of menstrual huts and the notion of menstrual pollution as "the supernatural enforcement mechanism" (Strassman et al. 2012, 9781). These huts serve as a signal to the father and his patrilineage that the woman is once again fertile and as such the risk of cuckoldry is high. In such cases, the husband duly initiates post-menstrual copulation and the patrilineage's vigilance is raised. Strassman et al. also report that the odds of nonpaternity are five times higher for the local Catholic population that does not enforce visits to menstrual huts. They also note that many religions have various ways of assuring paternity. In addition to the Dogon and their menstrual huts, the Jewish tradition observes menstrual purity laws; a Muslim man will only marry a divorced Muslim woman after three menstrual cycles; the *Laws of Manu* in the Hindu tradition discourage any extra-pair copulation; while in Buddhism and the Bible, there are injunctions against bastards (Strassman et al. 2012). The great Indian epic, the *Ramayana*, has as one of its central themes the chastity of Sita. To this day, Hindu mothers are known to encourage their daughters to be as chaste as Sita (Kakar 1981). Lastly, there is another reason for the hardship ritual of circumcision. Despite the fact that "it is unlikely that damaging or removing mechanically, neurally, and endocrinologically specialized, healthy sexual tissue is neutral with respect to *its* evolved function" (Sela et al. 2015, 120, emphasis added), from a certain social perspective there may have been some benefits. Sela et al. argue, "genital mutilations may impair the evolved capacity for extra-pair fertilizations, thereby decreasing paternity uncertainty and reproductive conflict, and that the benefits of trust and social investment from powerful married men outweigh the costs of mutilation" (2015, 121). Circumcisions facilitate both economic and reproductive cooperation. A similar claim can be made about monogamous relationships. "Monogamy has a calming influence on within-group functioning," note D. P. Schmitt and R. C. Fuller, "because most men seek out long-term mates" (2015, 316). Religiously sanctioned, sexual unions, that is, marriages, serve to assure the father that the children his wife, or wives, has are his. Schmitt and Fuller conclude, "religion can . . . be viewed as a cultural expression of genetically evolved mechanisms . . . guiding optimal (and environmentally contingent) mating strategies" (2015, 322), noting elsewhere, "sexual behavior is quite possibly the facet of social life most ubiquitously targeted for regulation by religious beliefs" (2015, 315). There is yet another adaptive function of marital unions, and it has everything to do with immunology.

There are five types of marital union—monogamy, two types of polygyny (i.e., sororal and non-sororal), and two types of polyandry (i.e., fraternal and non-fraternal). Religions tend to promote monogamy, sororal and non-sororal polygyny, but only fraternal polyandry. Non-fraternal polyandry involves the sexual sharing of a woman among genetically unrelated men. Colloquially, not to mention derisively, a woman who has multiple, genetically unrelated sexual partners is often referred to as a "whore," as opposed to a Madonna. The former often evokes disgust. Curtis and da Barra (2018) report a study in which test subjects found a woman disgusting because she had had sex with seven people in one day. The same level of disgust would most likely not be directed at a man who had the same experience. Why might this be the case? Non-fraternal polyandry is singularly suboptimal among the possible sexual unions. Suboptimal, sexual behaviors such as incest elicit sexual disgust. "Given that many aberrant sexual behaviors are fitness reducing," Fessler and Navarette write, "we propose that sexual disgust is an adaptation that functions to inhibit participation in biologically suboptimal sexual unions" (2003a, 407). No religion promotes suboptimal, sexual behaviors and unions (Sanderson 2018). No religion promotes non-fraternal polyandry. Why is non-fraternal polyandry singularly suboptimal?

Disgust sensitivity is heightened for a pregnant woman. This is especially the case during the first trimester. Heightened disgust sensitivity compensates for the woman's suppressed immune system (Miller and Maner 2011). It is the essence of morning sickness. The reason for such immunosuppression is that the developing fetus, or allograft, has a unique genetic signature. The fetus is semi-allogenic, the direct result of sexual reproduction. Because the fetus is genetically unique, the would-be mother's physiological immune system, if not suppressed, would in all likelihood treat the fetus as an aberrant growth. Aberrant growths are spontaneously aborted. This presents a classic selection pressure. "If rejection of the conceptus is to be precluded, maternal tolerance must begin prior to implantation and subsequent development," note Fessler and Navarrete. "The elevation of progesterone levels, and the accompanying immunosuppression, therefore begins during the luteal phase of the menstrual cycle" (2003a, 408). Natural selection favored a menstrual cycle that involved a "voluntary" suppression of immune function in anticipation of a possible pregnancy. A suppressed immune system is not, however, the only thing contributing to successful implantation and gestation of the semi-allogenic conceptus. There is another mechanism for inducing maternal tolerance.

Studies show that repeated exposure to one man's seminal fluid familiarizes the woman's immune system to the genetic markers of the would-be father

(Robertson et al. 2013; Schjenken and Robertson 2014; Roberston and Sharkey 2016). Upon repeated exposure to allogenic markers in seminal fluid, the would-be mother's immune system can better identify and therefore tolerate the ensuing conceptus that bears the genetic markers of both the father and herself. S. A. Robertson and D. J. Sharkey write, "the observations of partner specificity and the cumulative benefit of semen exposure imply that immunological 'memory' of a partner's antigens is programmed and boosted at insemination" (2016, 516). This partially accounts for religious counsel regarding appropriate marital unions. The marital unions of monogamy and both types of polygyny involve only one man's seminal fluid, with its unique genetic signature, being "introduced" to genetically dissimilar women. The case of fraternal polyandry is similar insofar as the brother-husbands share genetic signatures. One woman having sex with multiple brothers accomplishes the same familiarization. It is only non-fraternal polyandry that would seem to be a problem. A woman who is "married" to unrelated men presents the problem of paternity certainty. She also runs the risk of engaging in suboptimal sexual relations insofar as her immune system could reject the "unfamiliar," semi-allogenic conceptus. Moreover, seminal fluid contains different types of sperm, some of which are charged with a search and destroy mission. "Human sperm in a single ejaculate are of several different kinds, some of which are incapable of fertilizing an egg," note Nesse and Williams, "many of these sperm are designed . . . specifically to find and destroy any sperm from other men" (1996, 193–4). Mating with genetically unrelated men is suboptimal and thus evocative of disgust, as Curtis and da Barra's test subjects evinced. One simply does not find many religions—if any—promoting non-fraternal polyandry.[18] "There is direct evidence that religion does promote reproductive success," Sanderson writes. "All of the major world religions have been pronatalist to one extent or another" (2018, 153; Schmitt and Fuller 2015). Sapolsky adds, "Most cultures have historically allowed polygyny, with monogamy as the rarer beast. Even rarer is polyandry—multiple men married to one woman. This occurs in northern India, Tibet, and Nepal, where the polyandry is 'adelphic' (aka 'fraternal')" (2017, 339). Slone and Van Slyke conclude, "(religion) helps to manage the suite of adaptive problems related to reproduction via the costly signaling of strategic information useful for attracting, acquiring, and retaining mates, ensuring paternity certainty, prevent mate defection and infidelity, encouraging parental investment, and more" (2015, 3).

Assuming the female's physiological immune system does not reject the semi-allogenic conceptus and that the male is certain that he is responsible for the pregnancy, the pair can expect the arrival of an infant in due course. This is a good thing for inclusive fitness. As previously noted, the metric by which biological success is measured is by assessing the number of copies of one's genes that are in the next generation. This may, however, be a bit myopic. S. Stewart-Williams suggests that "the ultimate benchmark of evolutionary success is not the number of babies an organism has, but rather the number of *grandbabies*" (2018, 24). The human animal is not only interested in producing viable progeny. It is equally interested in raising its viable progeny to become themselves viable parents. Three generations of biological success would seem to be the upper limit on an organism's strategies for flooding future generations with its genetic copies, that is, while it is still alive. The descendant-leaving (DL) hypothesis suggests that Stewart-Williams's metric may be equally myopic. According to Palmer and Begley, biological success ought to be measured beyond "the one or two generations where it is typically measured . . . that is, the superiority of measuring 'descendant-leaving success' instead of 'reproductive success'" (2015, 103). It is one thing to have one's genes represented in the following two generations. It is another to have one's genes represented in the many generations thereafter. How might religion facilitate such multigenerational success? By inculcating the Golden Rule.

Palmer and Begley suggest that the costly-signaling theory of religion misses the real benefit of costly behaviors. These costs are ultimately cashed out not just in terms of cooperation in the here and now. Religions inculcate cooperative attitudes in many generations to come. According to the DL hypothesis, if I can get future generations of my co-descendants to treat each other with kindness and consideration, my genes stand to win evolution's genetic jackpot. Once again, this is no easy feat.

It is true that siblings share genetic material. They do seem to come into the world predisposed to have a modicum of concern for the welfare of their brothers and sisters. A modicum of concern is not full concern. Siblings are wholly related only to themselves. Sibling rivalry inevitably ensues. The key to the DL hypothesis is the parental manipulation of kin altruism. Parents "want—or, at least, their genes 'want' them—to extract from the child more kin-directed altruism and sacrifice, and thus to instill in the child more love, than is in the child's genetic interest" (Wright 1994, 168). Similarly, "parents, grandparents and other sets of kin gain inclusive benefits from increased cooperation among their descendant (as well as collateral) relatives, because copies of their alleles are thereby interfering with each other's transmission to a lesser extent" (Crespi and Summers 2014, 315). Palmer and Begley suggest that parental manipulation is not only effective in the present. It can remain effective even when those parents are dead and *long* gone. This is especially the case should such parental manipulation become codified in a religious tradition. "Parental manipulation could hypothetically produce altruistic behavior through an infinite number of generations of descendants if the manipulative behavior became tradition" (Palmer and Begley 2015, 106). This appears to be the evolutionary basis for the Golden Rule, the first iteration of which may not have been so golden. The original Golden Rule (*c.* 200,000–100,000 years ago) most likely pertained to loving one's co-descendant as much as one loved oneself. It was a rule intended to mitigate sibling rivalry. Palmer and Begley suggest that the more familiar rule to love your neighbor as yourself most likely emerged much later. This more familiar rule may have emerged as recently as 7,500 years ago when "people had to learn for the first time in history, how to encounter strangers regularly without attempting to kill them" (Diamond 1997, 273). Not killing the stranger is itself a form of cooperation (Greene 2013). The Golden Rule was eventually expanded to include one's neighbor, that is, a tribal mate. "Religious stories," note Crespi and Summers, "should focus mainly on kin and group-based moral inculcation and enculturation" (2014, 316), writing elsewhere, "One human phenotype, religious behaviour, stands apart from all others with regard to its dominating emphasis on altruism and prosociality" (2014, 313). Blume similarly notes, "Empirical observations as well as model calculations are conclusively showing that higher fertility of the religious is able to drive genetic as well as cultural evolution by demographically reinforcing commandments to be fruitful and to cooperate with co-believers" (2015, 68). This is what accounts for religion's esoteric consanguinity, or fictive kin. By believing we are all brothers and sisters in Christ, for instance, we manipulate our disposition toward co-descendant altruism.

Religion's capacity to facilitate cooperation amid genetic kin and non-genetic, anonymous strangers has been mostly adaptive throughout human evolution. It has facilitated the exchange of scarce resources rich in usable energy, the only stuff capable of thwarting temporarily the onset of entropy, that ultimate fate given to us by the second law of thermodynamics. Religion equally facilitates the acquisition and retention of reproductive resources, both sexual partners and progeny. "Religious societies have been shown to out-persist . . . produce more individual offspring (due to reproductive norms and the link between religiosity and fertility) . . . and cooperate more effectively than comparable non-religious societies" (Powell and Clarke 2012, 476; Blume 2015). Economic and reproductive pressures combined account for only one side of the survival and replication coin. The other side is the one that reminds us that we, too, are a source of usable energy for an acquisitive other. Throughout evolutionary history, acquisitive others were either macropredators, for instance, big cats and conspecifics, or micropredators, for instance, pathogens and parasites. It is the contention throughout the remaining chapters of this volume that religion played a significant role in managing the threats issuing from the latter. This is not an entirely new proposal. "Although religion apparently is for establishing a social marker of group alliance and allegiance," note C. Fincher and R. Thornhill, "at the most fundamental level, it may be for the avoidance and management of infectious disease" (2008b, 2593). All forms of cooperation—economic, reproductive, parental, and co-descendant—presuppose the health of those involved. Solving the riddle of infectious disease was perhaps the human animal's foremost chore, both individually and collectively. Religion solved the riddle. In advance of modern medicine, it was religion's task to manage the transmission, contraction, and eradication of infectious diseases. How it did so is the topic to which the discussion turns in the next three chapters.

3

Religion's Tribalism

The Behavioral Immune System

Modern evolutionary biology has generated a number of new perspectives on the origin and functions of religion (Bulbulia and Slingerland 2012). The previous chapter considered some of these. Particular attention was given to the psychological adaptations the human animal came to possess in order to navigate successfully the cognitive niche. The cognitive niche is populated with conspecific agents. Conspecific agents were one of the pressures that led to the emergence of the theory of mind. Theory of mind enables the attribution of intentions and desires to physical objects, including human bodies. It is a psychological adaptation for interpreting and predicting agential behavior. Theory of mind equally enables us to imagine disembodied minds, that is, gods. The human animal couldn't be religious without it.

The previous chapter similarly paid attention to the widely held view that religion was the answer to the selection pressure for cooperation. Naturally selected to care about its inclusive fitness, the human animal has a particular penchant for cheating on genetically unrelated others for scarce resources acquired through collective action. The human animal is disposed to free riding. Cooperation problems equally attend sexual reproduction and parental investment. The human animal is similarly disposed to promiscuous riding. Religion's answer to these collective action problems is costly and hard-to-fake signs of commitment. Such signs often involve the learning and endorsement of practically useless theologies as well as the performance of prodigal rituals. Such self-incurred, irrecuperable costs communicate trustworthiness. The severity of the cooperation problems attending economic and reproductive interests notwithstanding, there was yet another cooperation problem to be solved. Religion had to solve the problem of infectious disease (Van Blerkom 2003; Crawford 2007; Schulenburg et al. 2009; Neuberg et al. 2011; Thornhill and Fincher 2014a).

Economic and reproductive efficiency presuppose sound bodies and sound minds. A sick population is, after all, a population on sick leave. This chapter considers how religion maintains a sound body. In the following chapters, we will consider how religion maintains a sound mind.[1] Because infections are transmissible, maintaining a sound body requires both individual and collective effort. Individually, maintaining a sound body requires practising sound hygiene. Religions are routinely associated with counsel regarding the body's cleanliness (Reynolds and Tanner 1995; Curtis 2007a). Collectively, maintaining a sound body requires a public health policy. Public health is cooperative hygiene. "The basic premise of public health," notes V. Curtis et al., "(is) a social group acting together . . . in a wide range of cooperative strategies to reduce the transmission or the virulence of pathogens" (2011, 394). One such strategy was, and perhaps remains so in certain parts of the world, religion. Religion's public health strategy is primarily manifest in its ubiquitous purity and pollution codes (Douglas 2010 [1966]; Curtis 2007b). "Many religious rituals and behavioral taboos," notes D. P. Clark, "functioned originally as pre-scientific public health" (2010, 157). H. Fabrega Jr. adds, "Most conventions pertaining to subsistence and social behavior operate as prescriptions to avoid illness" (1997, 81). Prior to the modern period, most conventions pertaining to subsistence and social behavior were religious conventions.

Infectious disease is the primary selection pressure against the human animal. This pressure presents perceptual problems. Without the aid of prosthetics, the human senses are simply incapable of perceiving directly the presence of infectious microorganisms. Accordingly, and in keeping with what evolutionary psychology would predict, natural selection appears to have selected yet another cognitive module trip-wired for cues to the presence of infectious material or agents. A hyperactive pathogen detection device (HPDD) complements our hyperactive agency detection device (HADD). Both devices have their affective components. HADD evokes fear. HPDD evokes disgust. Disgust is the affective component of the behavioral immune system.

The behavioral immune system (BIS) is the first arm of the integrated immune system. It was naturally selected to forestall the contraction of a calorically expensive and debilitating infectious disease. The BIS promotes prophylactic behaviors. Counsel concerning such behavioral prophylaxis is often expressed through religion's purity and pollution codes. These codes pertain not only to the individual's state of cleanliness. They equally pertain to how one interacts with others. Hygiene is as much a private affair as it is a public one. Regarding the public dimension, infectious disease accounts for what some suggest "may ultimately prove to be the most important dimension for capturing cultural variation" (Heine, quoted in Schaller and Murray 2010, 250), that is, individualism and collectivism (Triandis 1995; Hofstede 2001; Gelfand et al. 2004). The BIS promotes collectivist values and behaviors in robust disease ecologies. Religion's tribalism is collectivism.

For most of its history, religion has reflected and promoted some form of collectivism, that is, tribalism. Religion's tribalism is associated with assortative sociality and its attendant xenophobia and ethnocentrism, all of which are uniquely calibrated to forestall contact with the extra-tribal other. Until the advent of modern medicine, the extra-tribal other was rightly viewed with suspicion. The extra-tribal other was a potential source of a novel infection. Religion's tribalism has been, for this reason, particularly successful at promoting health and survival (Fincher and Thornhill 2008b; Fincher and Thornhill 2012). Religion's tribalism is an instance of evoked culture.

Evoked cultures are facultative responses to local, ecological pressures. Local ecological pressures include not only the flora and fauna of the local environment. They also include the personality profiles of the population in question. "The *reverse causation* hypothesis" (Hofstede and McCrae 2004, 75) proposes that cross-cultural differences correlate with differences in the predominant personality profiles (Schaller and Murray 2008, 2010). "The *reverse causation* hypothesis suggests that culture may be shaped by the aggregate personality traits of its members," note G. Hofstede and R. R. McCrae, "and that the value systems and their associated institutions can be seen as social adaptations to the psychological environment that a distribution of personality traits represents" (2004, 75–6). "It seems comparably plausible," K. D. Lafferty adds, "that the modal personality of a populace can help shape culture from the bottom up" (2005, 281; Hofstede 2001).

The modal personality of a populace is due in large part to the predominant childhood experiences of that populace (Chishom 1996; Small 1998; Kirkpatrick 2005). Such experiences are profoundly influenced by the prevailing childrearing strategy (Bowlby 1969; Ainsworth 1969). The prevailing childrearing strategy often reflects the degree to which the populace is exposed to the threat of infectious disease (LeVine 1977; Levine et al. 1994; Small 1998). Robust disease ecologies often evoke the pediatric strategy of childrearing (LeVine 1977). This strategy tends to foster insecure-anxious attachments (Cassidy and Berlin 1994).[2] Such attachments produce adult personality profiles particularly suited for collectivist living, for religion's tribalism (Schmitt et al. 2004). Accordingly, "you cannot fully understand humans as a species, the course of our history, the natures of our societies and cultures, or our relationship to the world around us," observes M. Singer, "without considering pathogens" (2015, 100).

Infectious Disease: A Primary Selection Pressure

The theory of evolution by natural selection asserts that selection pressures cause differential success in reproductive fitness. There are three general types of pressure, "physiological (scarcity of food, salt, or water), physical (wounding, infection), or psychological (threat, aggression)" (Dhabhar and Viswanathan 2005, R738). All organisms face such pressures throughout their lifetimes. The extent to which a pressure causes differential success depends on the organism's stage in life. There are three such stages in a sexually reproducing organism's life. The first stage concerns prereproductive maturation. The second stage involves reproductive behavior. The final stage is postreproductive senescence. Pressures that affect postreproductive organisms will not selectively move a population in any cumulative direction, the grandmother hypothesis notwithstanding (Voland 2005). It is the first stage, and perhaps surprisingly not the second, that appears most pressing in terms of selection. "Prereproductive pressures," argue A. A. Volk and J. A. Atkinson, "may, all else being equal, trump ensuing reproductive pressures" (2008, 104). The primary, prereproductive pressure throughout most of prehuman and human history was infant and child death, "the greatest disaster that can befall any parent" (Spilka et al. 2003, 505) and "one of the most enduring features of the human EEA" (Volk and Atkinson 2013, 182). Estimates based on both Paleolithic and hunter-gatherer data suggest that the chances of surviving to reproductive age in the EEA may have been around 50 percent (LeVine 1977; Small 1998; Gangestad et al. 2006; Oaten et al. 2009; Thornhill et al. 2009; Perlman 2013; Ellis and Del Giudice 2019). A 50 percent chance of failing to reproduce is a dire statistic. Alas, "the history of childhood is a history of death" (Volk and Atkinson 2013, 182).

There are several threats to infant and child survival. The last chapter documented some of these. For instance, the cooperative acquisition and distribution of calories extracted from scarce resources would have been of great concern; malnutrition remains a prominent cause of infant and child morbidity and mortality in many parts of the world (Black et al. 2008). Predators are of equal threat to any organism, especially in its developing years (Ohman and Mineka 2001). Volk and Atkinson (2008, 2013) identify threats issuing from conspecifics, for instance, infanticide, as well as sheer accidents, falling from a height, for example. There is yet another pressure that appears equally pressing. "The existence of disease-causing viruses, bacteria and parasites," observes B. L. Hart, "represents a major force shaping behavior that is, arguably, as profound as the forces having to do with predator avoidance or resource utilization" (2011, 3406; May and Anderson 1979; Hart 1990). Many agree (Curtis 2007a; Schaller and Murray 2011; Barrett 2015; Coyne 2015; Pinker 2018; Sarabian et al. 2018). The persistent and ubiquitous pressure issuing from parasites and pathogens had a pronounced influence on the development of human behavior and culture. It influenced the development of religion.

The pronounced influence of infectious disease on the development of personality and the construction and propagation of culture has become abundantly clear over the past couple of decades. The threat of infectious disease affects mate preferences (Gangestad and Buss 1993; Gangestad et al. 2006; Lee et al. 2015); sociosexuality, extraversion, and openness to experience (Schaller and Murray 2008); marriage systems (Low 1990); hygiene codes (Curtis and Biran 2001); food preparation and preference (Sherman and Billing 1999; Fessler and Navarrete 2003b); musical preferences (Pazhoohi and Luna 2018); moral systems (Van Leeuwen et al. 2012); civil war (Letendre et al. 2010); democratization and liberalization (Thornhill et al. 2009); fairy tales (Schaller 2006); xenophobia and ethnocentrism (Schaller et al. 2003; Faulkner et al. 2004; Murray et al. 2011); cognitive ability (Eppig et al. 2010); linguistic diversity (Fincher and Thornhill 2008a); ritualized physical contact (Murray et al. 2016); individualism and collectivism (Schaller and Murray 2010); and yes, finally, religion (Fincher and Thornhill 2008b; Fincher and Thornhill 2012; Terrizzi et al. 2012). We will have ample opportunity to return to some of these studies in what follows. For now, we can take stock of the fact that infectious disease was, and remains, "one of the strongest selective pressures known in evolution" (Schulenberg et al. 2009, 4). In fact, "fast-evolving viruses, bacteria, and other pathogenic microorganisms are our only remaining serious predators" (Silver 2006, 180). Infectious disease is "public enemy number one" (Herz 2012, 78).

Infectious disease is a public enemy precisely because it is, by its very nature, communicable. Whereas a free rider absconds with economic resources and a promiscuous rider cuckolds a partner, an infected rider transmits infectious disease. Infectious disease can proverbially rob you of the one resource you must possess in order to worry about being cheated out of economic and reproductive opportunities in the first place, that is, life (Pinker 2018). For this reason, infected riders are more costly than free and promiscuous ones. "Disease and injury," notes H. Fabrega Jr., "undermine the necessary cooperation and deliberateness needed to pursue survival tasks (undertake and carry out basic subsistence and survival activities)" (1997, 33–4). Our evolutionary ancestors had to devise strategies to stay healthy amid an endless onslaught of infectious pathogens and parasites. Religion was one such strategy.

Pathogens are a primary selection pressure against all species of animal (Schaller and Murray 2011; Hart 1990). A need to avoid infectious matter arose with the emergence of life itself. Even a bacterium can catch a cold. The prevailing trouble with such micropredation is that the would-be host, for instance, a human animal, cannot detect directly the presence of such microorganisms. The world of microbiology is invisible to the unaided senses. This is a grave problem about which natural selection could not remain silent. It didn't remain silent. Natural selection selected the hyperactive pathogen detection device (HPDD). The HPDD is a device calibrated to "inform the avoidance of contaminants" (McCauley and Graham 2020, 14). Natural selection thus endowed us with yet another domain of folk science. It endowed us with an "intuitive microbiology" (Pinker 1999, 383), an "implicit germ theory" (Oaten et al. 2009, 312). "We could evolve pathogen detection systems," note J. M. Tybur and D. Lieberman, "that treat certain stimuli as *information* regarding the statistical likelihood that pathogens are present . . . even if they are, in fact, not" (2016, 6–7). M. Oaten et al. similarly observe, "disease avoidance should be both automatic and fairly impenetrable to cognition, to ensure that all disease signals, *false or real*, are acted upon" (2009, 305, emphasis added). As it is with anything hyperactivated, the HPDD is vulnerable to Type I errors (Thornhill and Fincher 2014b).

In repeated experiments, test subjects routinely treat certain objects as if they were infectious even when they *know* they are not. For instance, most people tend to decline the offer of a piece of chocolate when it is molded to look like dog feces (Rozin and Fallon 1987). Test subjects are similarly reluctant to consume a glass of juice if a sterilized cockroach has been recently removed (Hejmadi et al. 2004; Rozin et al. 2000). The subjects clearly *understand* that the chocolate and the juice are wholly sanitary, and yet they are still reluctant to accept the offers. Disease avoidance appears impenetrable to cognition. The subjects' cognition simply could not override what their "guts" were telling them. And what, precisely, were their guts telling them? "Yuck!" (Kelly 2011).

Chapter 2 indicated that fear often accompanies the activation of the hyperactive agency detection device (HADD). A second type of fear accompanies HPDD activation (Herz 2012). This second type is disgust (Olatunji and McKay 2009). Disgust is a universal, basic emotion that is unique to the human animal (Ekman 1992; Goldenberg et al. 2000). It is unique because only the human animal lives long enough for disgust to be adaptive. "The reason humans needed to evolve the emotion of disgust from the more basic reaction of fear is because we are unique among mammals in how long we can live," R. Herz observes, "animals with short life spans don't need the emotion of disgust . . . because they are far more likely to meet a fast, fear-based death—by being eaten—than to die slowly—from disease. . . . Given our exclusive position of longevity and dominance in the animal kingdom, humans needed an emotional system that could warn us of our foremost killer, pathogens, and therefore we evolved the emotion of disgust" (2012, 83).

As it is with disgust, so too is it with religion, both are unique and universal to the human animal. This is no coincidence. The connection between disgust and religion is not arbitrary (Terrizzi Jr et al. 2012). "If we had no sense of disgust," J. Haidt proposes, "I believe we would also have no sense of the sacred" (2012, 173–4). Disgust is "a central component of the human behavioural immune system" (Tybur et al. 2018, 2). "Religiosity functionally is a component of the behavioral immune system" (Thornhill and Fincher 2014b, 237).

The historical record indicates that human groups grew in size over time (Harari 2015). Such population growth greatly increased the chances of contracting and transmitting infectious diseases.[3] Contracting an infection is both calorically expensive and life-threatening. Calories spent fighting an infection are calories not spent on development, foraging, predation defense, and reproduction (Hill 1993; Kaplan et al. 2000; McDade 2003). If there were things human animals could do and feel to prevent contracting an infection, natural selection surely would have found them. It found them. Natural selection selected the behavioral immune system (BIS). The BIS is a suite of prophylactic behaviors and dispositions the human animal often adopts in order to mitigate the primary selection pressure that is the transmission and contraction of infectious disease (Schaller and Park 2011; Schaller and Murray 2011; Clay et al. 2012; Terrizzi Jr. et al. 2013; Neuberg 2014; Thornhill and Fincher 2014a; Hruschka and Hackman 2014; Lieberman and Patrick 2014; Tybur and O'Brien 2014; Schaller 2014). It is "a set of mechanisms that allow individuals to detect the presence of parasites in the objects and individuals around them, and to engage in behaviors that prevent contact with those objects and individuals" (Schaller and Duncan 2007, 295).

An infection is an affair of the individual's body. It is simultaneously a social one (Fabrega Jr. 1997; Clark 2010; Singer 2015). The few exceptions notwithstanding, no one is born infected. Infections are acquired from another. Maintaining a sound body thus requires both individual and collective effort.

The previous chapter documented how economic and reproductive efforts are vulnerable to free and promiscuous riders. The same applies to public health. "Public health is a common good: individuals who defect from paying the costs of contributing can still enjoy the benefits," notes V. Curtis et al. "Public health problems are, therefore, subject to free riding" (2011, 395). Free riders may enjoy the benefits of herd immunity, but they are all the same most capable of contracting and transmitting new infections (Curtis et al. 2011). It is, for this reason, incumbent upon everyone to uphold their end of the hygienic bargain. In much the same way that religion is capable of solving the cooperation problems associated with the free and promiscuous riders, it similarly solves the infected rider problem. Religion promotes tribalism. Religion's tribalism is collectivism. Collectivism is the most pronounced manifestation of the behavioral immune system. "Collectivism is fundamentally antipathogen psychology" (Fincher and Thornhill 2008b, 2588).

Collectivism[4]

Collectivism is a system of values and practices that promotes interdependence amid the ingroup (Triandis 1995; Triandis 2001; Hofstede 2001; Gelfand et al. 2004; Thornhill and Fincher 2014b; Sapolsky 2017). Collectivism manifests in a number of ways. For instance, collectivist interdependence is often linguistically expressed through a phenomenon known as "pronoun drop" (Clay et al. 2012). Pronoun drop pertains specifically to "the practice of omitting the first-person singular pronoun (*I*) from a sentence" (Hofstede 2001, 233). In addition to being dropped, the pronoun can also be positively vilified. There is an emotive Arab saying, "The satanic term 'I' be damned!" (Hofstede 2001, 233). Collectivist cultures privilege in this way the "We-self" at the expense of the "I-self" (Roland 1988).

Collectivist cultures also tend to nurture a particular cognitive style. This style is holistic (Clay et al. 2012). R. E. Nisbett (2003) reports a study in which test subjects in the individualist United States and collectivist China both observed a picture of a fish tank. When asked to describe what they saw, the American subjects tended to describe the big fish in the middle of the picture, whereas the Chinese subjects tended to describe the various objects surrounding the big fish. Sapolsky (2017) similarly reports an experiment in which test subjects are shown a picture of a social scene with multiple people present. The frontal cortex of collectivists works much harder when tasked with focusing solely on the individual standing out front rather than the whole scene. Sapolsky also reports an experiment where test subjects were presented with a monkey, a bear, and a banana. The subjects were asked to group the objects. Individualists grouped the monkey and the bear. Monkeys and bears belong to the same biological taxon. Collectivist subjects, on the other hand, grouped the monkey and banana. Monkeys and bananas are naturally "related" to one another. In another experiment, when collectivists were asked to think about a time when they, as individuals, influenced someone else they secreted glucocorticoids, a hormone directly related to stress. Alternatively, when collectivists see a picture of a calm face, they tend to activate their mesolimbic dopamine system, a system involved in positive responses. The opposite was true for the individualists. Individualists felt a rush of good feeling when seeing a single, excited face (Sapolsky 2017).

Collectivist cultures tend to be conservative cultures. Innovation is the result of dangerous, individual initiative (Nettle 2006). Collectivism promotes in this way "tightness." Tightness is a measure of how unwilling a culture is to tolerate deviance and nonconformity (Schaller and Murray 2011). Positively stated, D. S. Wilson et al. note that "tightness promotes solidarity, coordination, and the perpetuation of tradition" (2017, 143). Infectious disease is directly related to tightness. "Predictors of cultural tightness," Sapolsky notes, "include having high historical incidence of pandemics, of high infant and child mortality rates, and of higher cumulative average number of years lost to communicable disease" (2017, 302). Such "predictors" were ubiquitous throughout the EEA. Prior to the modern period, "loose cultures" would have been the exception. This partially accounts for why cultural progress was so slow when compared to recent history. A tight culture fails to take note of the other culture's accomplishments. Innovation stalls. Cultural tightness reflects and promotes ethnocentrism.

Tightness correlates with ethnocentrism. Ethnocentrism is the tendency to see one's own traditions and values as the only ones worth abiding. The complement to ethnocentrism is often xenophobia and neophobia (Murray et al. 2011; Sapolsky 2017). Those living in collectivist cultures tend to be suspicious of the foreign and the new, choosing to stick with time-honored, prophylactically vetted local traditions. C. Fincher and R. Thornhill observe, "There is ample evidence that the psychology of xenophobia and ethnocentrism . . . is importantly related to avoidance and management of infectious disease" (2008b, 2588). Intolerance regarding deviance and nonconformity also correlates with a respect for and acceptance of authority. This is known as right-wing authoritarianism, or RWA. Collectivist cultures expect one to adopt the local traditions and abide the local authorities. Right-wing authoritarianism thus characterizes those who value conventionalism, submission to authority, and often display hostile reactions to those who do not belong to one's group (Weber and Federico 2007). Significantly, right-wing authoritarians are "particularly afraid of disease" (Hodson and Costello 2007, 696). Social dominance orientation (SDO) also characterizes those who tend to devalue other groups. SDO equally endorses dealing with other groups in a hostile manner, if necessary. RWA and SDO are "examples of socially conservative value systems" (Terrizzi et al. 2013, 100). Tybur et al. write, "Nations with greater infectious disease burdens (i.e., parasite stress) are governed by more authoritarian regimes and are more religious, more collectivistic, and less open to experience, all of which are hallmarks of conservative ideology" (2016, 12409; Terrizzi Jr. et al. 2013).

All of the foregoing values and dispositions are associated with assortative sociality. Assortative sociality counsels tremendous discrimination in choosing with whom one will interact. Regions burdened with greater pathogen stress tend to promote assortative sociality. This sociality often finds expression through religion. Robust disease ecologies tend to have more religions with higher degrees of collectivism and the accompanying lower openness to experience, lower extraversion, lower sociosexual orientation, greater conformity pressure, greater restriction of rights and civil liberties, and lower democratization (Cashdan 2001; Duncan et al. 2009; Schaller and Murray 2011; Murray et al. 2011; Tybur et al. 2016, 2018). Religion's tribalism curtails in this way exposure to novel ideas, individuals, populations, and pathogens. It is a manifestation of the behavioral immune system and as such serves an "antipathogen defense function" (Fincher et al. 2008, 1279). "The relationship between the BIS (e.g., disgust and fear of contamination) and religious conservatism (e.g., religious orthodoxy and fundamentalism) may be functional and not merely symbolic" (Terrizzi Jr. et al. 2012, 116).

Religion's Purity and Pollution Codes

Religion has always trafficked in purity and pollution codes (Douglas 2010 [1966]; Curtis 2007a, 2007b; McCauley and Graham 2020). The nature and function of such codes have been of great interest not only to the religious studies community but to the anthropological one as well. Perhaps no other text has been quite as influential to both as Mary Douglas's *Purity and Danger* (2010 [1966]). Douglas (in)famously argues that religion's concerns with purity and pollution were not concerns with parasites and pathogens. They were veiled concerns regarding the precarity of the local cosmology. Cosmology, in the folk sense of the term, is any system of symbols that imposes order on an otherwise seemingly chaotic reality. Folk cosmologies tend to set up systems of meaning and order through binary oppositions (Leeming and Leeming 1994). Such systems ostensibly enable the possibility of dirt and its attendant pollution. According to Douglas, things and behaviors that do not find their proper place in binary classifications make trouble for the system. For instance, viscous substances do not admit of being either liquid or solid. Such anomalies fall outside the classificatory structure. They are matter out of place. This makes them dirty.

> If we can abstract pathogenicity and hygiene from our notion of dirt, we are left with the old definition of dirt as matter out of place.... It implies two conditions: a set of ordered relations and a contravention of that order. Dirt then, is never a unique, isolated event.... Dirt is the by-product of a systematic ordering and classification of matter.... This idea of dirt takes us straight into the field of symbolism and promises a link-up with more obviously symbolic systems of purity. (Douglas 2010 [1966], 44)

For Douglas, and those who follow her lead, there is nothing inherently dirty in the world. "Our pollution behavior," Douglas asserts, "is the reaction which condemns any object or idea likely to confuse or contradict cherished classification" (2010 [1966], 45).

Concerns regarding the precarity of one's cherished classifications are ostensibly expressed through concerns regarding the boundaries of the body. Insofar as the body is a source of things moving in and out, it is apparently an apt symbol for all concerns regarding breached boundaries, confused classifications. "Even more direct is the symbolism worked upon the human body," Douglas argues, "The body is a model which can stand for any bounded system. Its boundaries can represent any boundaries which are threatened or precarious.... We cannot possibly interpret rituals concerning excreta, breast milk, saliva and the rest unless we are prepared to see in the body a symbol of society, and to see the power and dangers credited to social structure reproduced in small on the human body" (2010[1966], 142). Perhaps this is the case. Perhaps religious cultures of the past were concerned with the body's boundaries because they were ultimately concerned with, for instance, keeping free riders out of society. The previous chapter made it clear that tribes are seemingly most interested in who is in the ingroup and who is not. Such policing was necessary to maintain the *economic* health of the collective. If there are concerns about the dangers of things passing back and forth in the individual's body, then maybe they are ultimately concerned with what will transgress the political borders of the religious tribe. The biological body is in this way a symbol for the body politic. Perhaps. There is, all the same, good reason to doubt.

Douglas's influential dismissal of hygiene concerns from religion's purity and pollution codes hangs on a rather dubious conditional. Recall, "*if* we can abstract pathogenicity and hygiene from our notion of dirt, we are left with the old definition of dirt as matter out of place" (2010 [1966], 44, emphasis added). Clearly, we *can* make such an abstraction. The pressing issue must be, *should* we? Douglas gives us her reason why we should:

> The bacterial transmission of disease was a great nineteenth-century discovery.... So much has it transformed our lives that it is difficult to think of dirt except in the context of pathogenicity. Yet obviously our ideas of dirt are not so recent. We must be able to make the effort to think back beyond the last 150 years and to analyse the bases of dirt avoidance, before it was transformed by bacteriology. (2010[1966], 44)

Douglas claims that religion's ubiquitous purity and pollution codes could not have been concerned with issues of pathogenicity because such rules and observations predate germ theory. If one is consciously unaware of bacteriology, then one's behaviors cannot have anything to do with combating bacteria. Such privileging of conscious awareness is a mistake (Dennett 1991; Rosenberg 2011, 2018). Douglas is mistaken. "It is not necessary that people be aware of the benefit of a practice," note L. J. Weaver and A. C. Hibbs, "so long as its benefit is potent enough to affect their actual survivorship" (2012, 5). The same can be said for nonhuman animals. Lacking a knowledge of bacteriology, nonhuman animals engage in behaviors that are hygienic in nature (Hart 1990). It is quite plausible that Paleolithic cultures hit upon efficacious practices to which they misattributed the cause. This is, in fact, what an evolutionary perspective would lead one to believe. "Evolutionary explanations," note Curtis and Biran, "have an advantage over their predecessors ... a means by which beneficial behaviors can arise without the need for a conscious understanding of the link between behavior and benefit" (2001, 26–7; Sweek 2002).

The human animal's evolutionary forebears simply did not need to understand infectious disease and its transmission routes in order to abide prophylactic counsel, no matter in which idiom it was couched. Curtis provides the appropriate reply to Douglas and those who continue to follow her lead:

> Douglas has the local cosmology, or world order, coming first, with dirt as its product.... Cultural commentators on filth ... continue in the Douglasian

tradition, puzzling over the same paradox . . . how can something as visceral as disgust be produced by history and culture? Yet if the dirty is what disgusts us, then this is surely wrong: dirt arose before culture and history, and therefore cannot just be its product. (2007a, 663)[5]

M. Tadd similarly writes, "Contrary to Douglas' argument, it is not the ambiguity of symbols that causes fear of certain substances, but innate, biological programming" (2012, xiv), noting elsewhere, "disgust and un-cleanliness are not just brought about by the disruption of symbolic categories: they derive from the interaction between tangible invasion and pain and cultural and religious values" (2012, xiii–xiv). "There is a link between dirt, disgust, hygiene and disease, but it is a link that predates history, that predates science and culture, that even predates *Homo sapiens*," Curtis concludes, "Disgust has a long evolutionary history; the reason it is part of our psyche is neither primarily cultural nor historical, but biological. . . . [It] is a part of human nature" (2007a, 660).

The need to survive the selection pressure parasites and pathogens posed could not wait for the advent of modern germ theory. The evolution of disgust did not wait. Disgust evolved to expedite hygienic behaviors, to protect us from the risk of infection (Curtis et al. 2004). This is the ultimate explanation for religion's purity and pollution codes. Hygiene counsel is clearly found in Mesopotamian, Jewish, Hindu, Christian, Muslim, and Greek texts (Curtis 2007a, 2007b). Similar counsel can be found in ancient Chinese texts (Arthur 2013). In addition to such historical, textual data, recent experimental evidence similarly attests to the connection between disgust and religious hygiene.

J. L. Preston and R. S. Ritter (2012) tested to see if subjects connect notions of religious purity with actual physical cleanliness. Their results were positive. For instance, in a word-stem task, test subjects primed with religious subject matter tended to complete the word-stem such that it spelled a cleaning product.[6] Similarly, religious primes raised the desirability of cleaning products, for example, soap, over a control product, for example, a battery. What is more, cleaning primes increased the self-reported value of one's faith. C.-b. Zhong and K. Liljenquist (2006) report that feeling personally clean enhances one's sense of personal righteousness. This association may account for the various ablution rituals people from all sorts of religious traditions engage prior to entering sacred spaces such as temples and mosques. Equally, clean smells promote morally righteous behavior, while disgusting ones promote harsh moral judgments. Preston and Ritter conclude,

> Religion and cleanliness have both been connected to the pursuit of purity, and many religious rituals center on physical cleanliness as a part of religious devotion. Likewise, the present findings may suggest another important function of religion, to foster hygiene and cleanliness among its followers.... The present research demonstrates a mutual association between cleaning and religion, the first experimental evidence that the two are conceptually and motivationally linked. (2012, 1368).

V. Saroglou and L. Anciaux similarly observe, "Rituals of purification in many religious traditions suggest a high concern in religion with cleanliness and purity, and many studies confirm that the religious personality is marked by (obsessive) traits of orderliness-cleanliness" (2004, 261). Religion's concerns with moral righteousness may equally motivate prophylactic hygiene practices.

To be physically clean is to feel morally pure. To want to be morally pure, one can get physically clean. The latter is the famous "Macbeth effect." "The Macbeth effect: Exposure to one's own and even to others' moral indiscretions poses a moral threat and stimulates a need for physical cleansing" (Zhong and Liljenquist 2006, 1452). To be reminded of one's moral impurities, for instance, that one is a sinner, promotes physical purification. Although the former is psychologically averse, the physical benefits of the latter compensate. Sapolsky (2017) reports experimental results indicating that if one has engaged in lying, the medium by which one lied will affect the process of restitution. If one has lied with one's mouth, then one will more likely reach for mouthwash. If one wrote down a lie, one will reach for soap. Similarly, if one has been asked to remember a moral indiscretion, one will choose as a "parting gift," for participation in an experiment, a box of antiseptic wipes as opposed to a pack of pencils. "Literal cleanliness and orderliness," Sapolsky writes, "can release us from abstract cognitive and affective distress" (2017, 563). Religion can thus foster concerns with physical cleanliness by reminding practitioners of their moral shortcomings. Moral impurity motivates physical purity. Those who wish to continue in the Douglasian tradition would thus be well advised to consider such experimental results moving forward. There is, indeed, "a deeply rooted connection between religion and cleanliness" (Preston and Ritter 2012, 1365).

Asserting that what disgusts is what disturbs the local cosmology wasn't Douglas's only mistake. She also suggests that concerns with the body's envelope are a symbolic concern with the body politic's envelope. Concerns with what goes in and out of the body are ostensibly a symbolic concern with what crosses the boundaries of the local group. This too is mistaken. In fact, it's just the opposite. A concern with what crosses the political border is ultimately a concern with what might eventually cross the body's border (Fessler and Haley 2006). It is this concern that accounts for religion's tribalism. Religion's tribal members share a common set of purity and pollution codes intended to promote locally effective hygiene practices in the domains of personal cleanliness, food preparation, intimate interpersonal contact, and childrearing (Curtis and da Barra 2018, 2). Outgroup members abide by a different set of codes. Outgroup members are "more likely to engage in practices that violate local cultural rules adapted by a process of cultural evolution to protect in-group members from locally prevalent pathogens" (Navarrette and Fessler 2006, 271). C. D. Navarrette and D. M. T. Fessler identify here an essential component of what has been called, "intergroup vigilance theory" (Schaller et al. 2003, 112).

It is often adaptive to be wary of an outgroup other. "Members of other groups can be both dirty (because they are likely to harbor unfamiliar diseases) and impure because they do not follow the same cultural prescriptions," Curtis et al. write, "such xenophobia motivates solidarity within the group" (2011, 395). Different groups adopt different practices. What is good for them may not be good for us. Such perceptions often lead to what has been called, "pseudospeciation" (Sapolksy 2017, 372). To pseudospeciate is to treat another group or tribe as a monolithic aggregate of subhuman organisms. Pseudospeciation is dehumanization (Sapolsky 2017). The animals to which dehumanized groups are often reduced are typically those with an association with disease.[7] For instance, the other is often thought to be vermin or cockroaches. Accordingly, the other can elicit the two emotions of the two threat management systems, that is, the self-protection system and the disease-avoidance system. "Other people not only pose direct threats to human survival via their potential for violence, but also pose indirect threats via their role in transmitting disease" (Neuberg et al. 2011, 1045). While we can certainly fear the other, we can equally find the other disgusting (Sapolsky 2017). The number of different groups capable of disgusting us appears to follow a latitudinal gradient. "The fact that species diversity increases from the polar regions to the tropics is a pattern that has long fascinated biologists and begs for an explanation," write D. S. Wilson et al., "Intriguingly, human linguistic and cultural diversity exhibit the same pattern, suggesting that biological and cultural diversity do have a common set of explanations" (2017, 141; Thornhill and Fincher 2014b). The species diversity of which Wilson et al. write equally pertains to species of infectious diseases. Infectious disease diversity correlates with religious diversity. Regions burdened with robust disease ecologies are regions with the greatest number of religions (Fincher and Thornhill 2008b). "When diseases pose an especially substantial problem (and ritualized behavioral practices provide a more consequential buffer against that problem)," note M. Schaller and D. Murray, "religiosity will be more prevalent as well" (2010, 251).

Religion's Tribalism and the Geography of Immunocompetence

Pathogen prevalence and diversity follow "the latitudinal species diversity gradient" (Guernier et al. 2004, 0740). As one approaches the tropics—by which is meant the thirty degrees both north and south of the equator—one tends to find more robust disease ecologies (Low 1990; Cashdan 2001). Perhaps to be expected given our discussion of the second law of thermodynamics in the previous chapter, and according to "the climatically-based energy hypothesis," "energy availability generates and maintains species richness gradients" (Guernier et al. 2004, 0743). The availability of usable energy increases with proximity to the equator. This is the case because equatorial latitudes enjoy relatively high, annual mean temperatures as well as consistency of rainfall. Such conditions are conducive to the flourishing of disease ecologies (Schaller and Murray 2011; Van Blerkom 2003). As infectious disease ecologies become more robust and varied, so too do linguistic, cultural, and religious traditions. There are simply more languages, cultures, and religions in the tropics (Fincher and Thornhill 2008b; Thornhill and Fincher 2014b). This is no accident. Fincher and Thornhill call this the "parasite-driven wedge" (2008a, 1290). Differential success in adapting to the pressures of infectious disease ecologies is what ultimately accounts not only for the variety of species on the planet but for the variety of cultures and religions as well. Infectious disease diversity is the common explanation for both biological and religious diversity.

Pathogen prevalence is geographically specific. A pathogen that is locally prevalent in one area may not be prevalent in another. Groups of organisms are thus differentially exposed to disease ecologies. What is more, groups can become adapted to their local disease ecologies. Although locked in a Red Queen's race with local pathogens (Ridley 1993), groups, all the same, tend to enjoy a certain lowered pathogen virulence within the local ecology.[8] "Parasite-host coevolutionary races are spatially variable," Fincher and Thornhill observe, "generating spatial variance in the immunobiology of human host populations and groups" (2008b, 2587). Hart similarly notes, "The immune system is 'personalized' according to the particular environment" (2011, 3410).

Religion's tribalism and its ethnocentrism and xenophobia protect in this way locally adapted populations. Religion's tribalism reflects the geography of immunocompetence.

Organisms enjoy a degree of immunocompetence within their local niche. A change in location could therefore be hazardous. Entering another's territory exposes one to a host of new diseases. The complement to such exposure is that one exposes those in the new context to one's own pathogen load. The historical record is replete with instances of travelers encountering deleterious pathogens along their journey while simultaneously exposing their hosts, if such a term can be used here, to the diseases to which they have developed immunocompetence (McNeil 1976). One of the more striking of such cases concerns Hernan Cortes and his men exposing the Aztecs to "old world" diseases. The result was sheer devastation (Diamond 1997). The need to protect the immunocompetence of human hosts from foreign pathogens, that is, immunologically locally adapted individuals, accounts for the varieties of religious traditions. "Religions emerge," conclude Fincher and Thornhill, "from intergroup cultural boundaries that form in response to the spatial variation of infectious disease stress and associated assortative sociality and limited dispersal" (2008b, 2587). A concern with the maintenance of boundaries is thus a concern with prohibiting novel infections residing in ambulatory strangers from entering one's community (Freeland 1976; Loehle 1995; Villarreal 2008; Sarabian et al. 2018). Douglas had it exactly backwards. What is more, religious tribalism's geography of immunocompetence presents an alternative reading of costly and hard-to-fake signs of commitment.

Costly-signaling theory proposes that rites of initiation often entail putting the candidate through a rigorous ordeal in order to allow the candidate to prove his economic sincerity. There's something else the candidate proves—his health status. Should an individual wish to join a new group—for economic or reproductive reasons—that group is right to worry that the candidate may harbor a novel infection. If collectivist groups share a common immunity to the local pathogen ecology, then any new member coming from another group may be akin to a proverbial Trojan Horse. Like the destructive army jumping out of the wooden gift, an infectious disease may jump out of the newcomer, wittingly or not. The novel infection could wreak havoc on the immunologically naïve, local group. Religion's hardship rituals may prove prophylactically effective. Placing a candidate under stressful conditions lowers that candidate's constitution. A compromised constitution allows any latent infections to become manifest. This may, in fact, be the original function of hardship rituals. This is quite possibly the case because such rituals are not unique to the human animal. They have been documented among nonhuman primates. W. J. Freeland writes, "the final 'decision' on whether or not the strange individual should be admitted is likely to be made after the stranger has been subjected to a stressful, peripheral social status" (1976, 14), noting elsewhere, "behavioral and nutritional stress lowers resistance to, and exposes, latent and immunologically controlled diseases (e.g., herpes)" (1976, 13; Sapolsky 2004; Glaser 2005). "The introduction of new individuals into the group, which typically takes weeks or months, has a disease avoidance function," Hart adds, "such peripheralization, together with behavioral and nutritional stress to which the intruder is often subjected, make it likely that if the intruder is harboring a latent infection it will become visibly sick; the stranger may then not be allowed in the group at all or may die" (1990, 281). Religion's stress-inducing hardship rituals thus amount to hard-to-fake signs of health or, for that matter, illness. There is yet one more biological aspect to religious tribalism's geography of immunocompetence.

Species are populations of genetically unique individuals. What ultimately distinguishes one species from the next is reproductive isolation (Campbell 1987; Mayr 2001). If two organisms cannot successfully reproduce, they are reproductively isolated and thus belong to separate species. Reproductive isolation can result from either prezygotic or postzygotic mechanisms. In other words, the isolation takes place either prior to (pre) or after (post) sexual intercourse. Religion's tribalism functions as a prezygotic isolating mechanism.

Mayr (2001) identifies five prezygotic isolating mechanisms.[9] There is a sixth, propositional isolation (Munz 1985). Propositional isolation occurs when, for instance, one's set of religious beliefs counsel preclusion of interaction with outgroup others, especially sexual interaction. Most religious tribes have throughout time counseled some form of tribal endogamy. Endogamy pertains to reproducing only with those who belong to one's tribe. Such counsel is routinely associated with collectivism. "Geographic isolation is a major cause of reproductive isolation in humans as it is in most species," writes R. L. Perlman, "but our species is unusual in that it has many reproductively isolated populations whose isolation is based on religion . . . rather than geography" (2013, 39). Wilson et al. suggest that there are "various ways in which human cultural groups may legitimately be viewed as functionally equivalent to biological species" (2017, 138). Whether physical, behavioral, or propositional, as long as the mechanism prevents sexual intercourse between two groups, we are dealing with different species. Of course, a propositional barrier may be the most permeable of the isolating mechanisms; all the same, and at least for some time, it is such a barrier.

Jealously guarding and promoting the propositional claims of the local religion can "reduce or eliminate gene or cultural information flow" (Fincher and Thornhill 2008a, 1290). It can equally act as "an engine of speciation and of ethnogenesis in humans" (Fincher and Thornhill 2008a, 1293). M. E. Hochberg et al. propose that such dynamics can in fact produce "protospecies" (2003, 154). "Just as specific kinds of physical barriers (waterways, mountain ranges) create island biogeographies," note Schaller and Murray, "specific kinds of psychological traits (low levels of extraversion, low levels of openness to experience) and specific kinds of value systems (collectivism) create insular social geographies" (2011, 129). We are not trafficking in hyperbole here. Insular social geographies produce genetic signatures. These signatures are most associated precisely with the physiological immune system. "Because there is considerable geographic variation in the distribution of disease, it is no surprise that we find important geographic variation in the genes that defend us from these diseases," L. L. Cavalli-Sforza writes, "among the genes that show the greatest geographic variation are the immunoglobulin genes" (2000, 50; Prugnolle et al. 2005). Immunoglobulin genes code for the Human Leukocyte Antigen (HLA) complex, an essential component of the physiological immune system. There is perhaps no better example of such prezygotic, propositional speciation than the Hindu caste system, the most baroque social system on the planet (Milner Jr. 1994).

The south Asian subcontinent is a region of great pathogen and parasite stress and diversity (Malhotra 1990; Deodhar 2003; Berger 2012). Of 230 geopolitical regions recently examined for the historical prevalence of nine virulent, infectious diseases, for instance, leprosy, India was one of only seventeen regions (7 per cent) that scored above 0.9, with 0 as the mean (Murray and Schaller 2010).[10] Another study reports that of the 348 generic infectious diseases in the world today, "246 of these [approximately 70 percent] are endemic, or potentially endemic, to India."[11] The robust disease ecology of south Asia accounts for the region's signature social institution, caste. "The taboos on personal contact across caste lines, and the elaborate rules for bodily purification in case of inadvertent infringement of such taboos," writes W. H. McNeil, "suggest the importance fear of disease probably had in defining a safe distance between the various social groups that became the castes of historic Indian society" (1977, 91). J. Mattausch similarly observes, "caste developed as a health strategy, to keep healthy in an environment of mysterious, virulent diseases and dangers" (2012, 28). This would make imminent sense of one of the most sanctioned behaviors associated with caste.

The Hindu caste system, and its robust purity and pollution codes, submits a range of behaviors to sanction. One such behavior is sexual intercourse. One is to marry within one's caste. "Castes are endogamous groups," Cavalli-Sforza et al. note, "purity of caste is essential, and violation of the endogamy rule involves pollution and punishment" (1994, 211). The Hindu caste system is, precisely for this reason, a prezygotic isolating mechanism. "Each caste is a breeding isolate" (Pitchappan 2002, 158). What is more, castes are equally eating isolates. In addition to caste endogamy, Hinduism endorses caste commensality. One is to eat with those who belong to the same caste. Sharing a bed and a meal are, after all, the two greatest means for spreading nonzoonotic infections (Tybur et al. 2018). Given the pronounced disease ecology of equatorial south Asia, it makes good hygienic sense that the social groups of the subcontinent would be particularly concerned with caste endogamy and commensality.

Caste Hinduism is collectivist Hinduism. Empirical evidence bears this out. Of eleven culture clusters studied, south Asia is the highest in "in-group collectivism practices" and second highest in "in-group collectivism values" (Gelfand et al. 2004, 479–80).[12] South Asia is also home to the greatest linguistic and religious diversity (Fincher and Thornhill 2008a). Where collectivists groups proliferate, so too do languages and religions. Different languages and religions establish propositional isolation. As Cavalli-Sforza would predict, this isolation has a genetic signature (Basu et al. 2003; Ayub and Tyler-Smith 2009; Bamshad et al. 2001).

The genetics of one caste grouping may not be the same in another. These genetic distinctions appear most pronounced when it comes to the genes coding for the physiological immune system. Regarding south Asia, "the sympatrically isolated caste and sub-caste populations of southern India . . . differ significantly in the HLA and other immune repertoire" (Pitchappan 2002, 157). Elsewhere, Pitchappan et al. note that "the frequencies of various HLA alleles are also quite different in various parts of India and in various linguistic and caste groups" (2008, 151). Thornhill and Fincher have similarly observed "the caste-specific infectious diseases and associated caste-specific genetic immunity among Indian castes in the same geographic locale" (2014a, 258). Propositional isolation maintains the geography of immunocompetence. T. Zerjal et al. argue that "despite its very large size, the Indian Hindu population is better regarded as a highly substructured set of separate populations with limited gene flow among them than as a single population" (2007, 143). The efficacy of Hindu purity and pollution codes is thus on display in the human genome. Such variation in immunoglobulin genes has been identified elsewhere. For example, Thornhill and Fincher point to "the village-specific immune defenses against leishmania parasites in adjacent Sudanese villages, and the variation in virulence of human African trypanosomiasis in northern versus southern populations in East Africa" (2014a, 258). E. N. Miller et al. (2007) similarly found that in adjacent villages in the Sudan you will find different genetic resistances to leishmaniasis. D. Modiano et al. (1996) observed different genetic resistance to malaria among sympatric ethnicities in Africa. Tybur et al. (2018) note that the Tsimane of the Amazonian rainforest present varying genetic signatures for antipathogen defense. Finally, W. C. Eveland et al. (1971) found that in the Amazon, tribes vary in their immunological defenses against spatially diversified parasites. Religion's prezygotic, propositionally isolating mechanisms truly reflect and protect the geography of immunocompetence.

The tribalistic conformity to one's own religious traditions coupled with xenophobia reflects the geography of immunocompetence. The geography of immunocompetence results from the fact that pathogen ecologies vary both spatially and temporally. Adopting a conservative attitude amid robust disease ecologies preserves the locally immunized group. "In-group members are more likely to have been exposed to the same pathogens and parasites, resulting in similar antibodies and immunity," Terrizzi Jr et al. summarize, "moreover, they share norms and customs, which may help limit the transmission of disease" (2012, 106). It is precisely the sharing of norms and customs that prophylactically protects locally immunized groups from exposure to novel pathogens and parasites. Such prophylaxis seemingly works best when everyone has bought in. A lapse by one could lead to an infection for all. It was perhaps traditionally understood that such sharing resulted from enculturation, that is, one learns to be conservative, ethnocentric, and xenophobic. While that could be the case, there may yet be a more effective way of achieving this immunological goal. The reverse causation hypothesis proposes that culture *responds* to the predominant personality profile of the population in question. Religion's tribalism has a predominant personality profile. This profile is not taught. It is reared.

Childrearing

The human species is an altricial one.[13] Human infants require immediate attention and provisioning upon birth, and for several years thereafter. In other words, someone must undertake parenting, itself "a key potential adaptation toward reducing mortality rates" (Volk and Atkinson 2013, 189). How parents parent amounts to a childrearing strategy. There are multiple such strategies. Which one parents adopt will likely reflect a host of contributing factors. For instance, the parents' psychological dispositions—themselves a reflection of their own childhood experiences—will affect the nature of the parent-infant bond (Kakar 1979). Additionally, the cultural wisdom of the day will contribute to the childrearing strategy. Such wisdom generally reflects strategies that have proven successful in the particular ecology. "A parent who conforms to such customary prescriptions may be unaware of their past or present efficacy, but may view them as religiously or ethically ordained," observes R. LeVine, "this adaptive component concealed in child-rearing customs must be clarified to understand the constraints within which other cultural values operate" (1977, 17). In much the same way that premodern groups did not need to understand the parasitological effects of their purity and pollution codes, so too with childrearing practices. Parents need not be consciously aware of their facultative practices when rearing young. "Institutionalized patterns of child rearing," LeVine further notes, "need to be analyzed as means by which parents have responded adaptively to their experience of environmental hazards threatening the health or future welfare of their children" (1977, 26–7). Institutionalized patterns of childrearing tend not only to promote infant survival but also to inculcate in the developing child psychological dispositions that will be facultative for adult flourishing and reproductive success in the future. "Many of the cultural differences translate into differences in health and survival," argues M. F. Small. "Parenting in various ways, then, has a direct effect not just on personality, but on the bare essentials—growing up healthy and staying alive" (1998, 57).

Some contend that the collectivism/individualism taxonomy is the most significant when assessing cross-cultural variation. Small suggests another. She believes that one must take into consideration childrearing practices. "The general structure of any culture," Small writes, "can be understood at a fundamental level by following the treatment of children" (1998, 46), noting elsewhere, "watching how different societies handle their children has, in many cases, been the key to understanding the very foundations of culture" (1998, 69). The structure and dominant values of a culture, and a religion to be sure, ultimately depend upon the local childrearing practices. We can recall from the previous chapter that "many phenotypic differences result . . . from differences in the developmental expression of common genes," noted Murray et al., "gene expression is adaptively influenced by the ecological circumstances within which individual organisms develop" (2011, 327). There is no more important ecological circumstance for human ontogeny than parents (Zhang et al. 2006).

"The most adaptively significant feature of children's environments," J. Chisholm notes, "has always been . . . the quantity and quality of the parental investment they receive" (1996, 15).

The quantity and quality of parental investment a child receives directly reflects the parents' childrearing strategy. There are at least three sets of such strategies. The first set acknowledges four possible strategies, that is, authoritative, authoritarian, permissive, and neglectful (Sapolsky 2017). This set will not occupy too much of our attention here, though we will have the opportunity to draw some parallels with the set that will. The second set of childrearing strategies, equally one that will interest us insofar as it too shows interesting parallels, acknowledges two strategies, accepting and rejecting (Rohner 1975). The third set, and the one that will be of most interest to us, similarly acknowledges two strategies, the pedagogical and the pediatric. This last set is directly tied to infectious disease ecologies.[14]

The pedagogical style of childrearing focuses on the development of the child's cognitive capacities and personality, both emotional and behavioral. Parents employing this style tend to stimulate their infants and young children with such behaviors as "smiling, eye contact, face-to-face smile elicitation, chatting, cooing, and kissing" (LeVine 1977, 23). Through such behaviors, parents attempt to nurture in their children a sense of trust, competence, independence, and industriousness. The pedagogical style tends to produce adult personalities that are more individualist, openminded, and extraverted. Although such independence, confidence, and trust may appear imminently desirable, they are, all the same, traits quite possibly ill-suited for collectivist, and thus interdependent living. If collectivism is in fact an antipathogen psychology, then in robust disease ecologies, the pedagogical style of childrearing may be ill-advised. The style of childrearing most prevalent in infectious disease ecologies tends not to be pedagogical, but rather pediatric.

Pediatric childrearing practices differ rather significantly from the pedagogical ones. Where the latter seems intent on stimulating the emotional, intellectual, and social development of the infant, the former seems intent on simply keeping the infant alive. Emotional investment in infants is a privilege not enjoyed by those whose primary concern is physical safety and health. The pediatric style thus has its characteristic quantity and quality. Quantitatively, the pediatric style tends to involve a certain physical indulgence of the child.[15] For instance, the child is often within close proximity to a caretaker, often enjoys prolonged co-sleeping arrangements, and is breastfed well beyond the years at which weaning typically takes place in cultures adopting the pedagogical style.

If the infant cries, it is generally soothed by being offered the breast, though such offering does not seem accompanied by an emotional engagement. Qualitatively, the pediatric style lacks emotional involvement with and investment in the child (Kurtz 1992). There is "little organized concern about the infant's behavioral development and relatively little treatment of him as an emotionally responsive individual (as in eye contact, smile elicitation, or chatting)" (LeVine 1977, 23). Elsewhere LeVine notes, "there is no place for an organized concern about the development of the child's behavioral characteristics and social and emotional relationships, such concerns are postponed until later in his life" (1977, 25). Small (1998) similarly reports that Mayan mothers tend to keep babies in hammocks in dark recesses of the house and that they see their responsibility toward the child to be one of protection, not development. Similar observations have been made among the Gusii (Levine et al. 1994), the Ache (Small 1998), the Hindus (Ellis 2016), the Cameroonians (Morelli and Rothbaum 2007), and the Polynesians (Harpending et al. 1990), groups living in robust disease ecologies, to be sure. The pediatric style of childrearing is, in this regard, "an adaptation to a situation of chronic medical risk" (LeVine 1977, 25).[16] Chronic medical risk surely characterized the EEA.

The severity of the EEA would have favored parenting strategies that were primarily concerned with the physical health of the child. Concerns regarding psychological health were simply a luxury no one could afford. In fact, the pedagogical style of childrearing may have been selected against. "Organisms bearing a genetic code favoring intense saturating parental care in the context of preindustrial human society as well as in the context of most mammalian evolution," H. C. Harpending et al. propose, "would generally have lost in competition with organisms with more measured allocation of resources" (1990, 252). To this day, stressful environments influence the behavior of caregivers. N. Baumard and C. Chevallier note, for instance, that "maternal care is inversely associated with famine, warfare and high levels of pathogens" (2015, 3–4), adding elsewhere, "a negative attitude towards attachment and a lower emotional investment are associated, across cultures, with higher levels of ecological stress: relatively few resources, low life expectancy, high child malnutrition, high fertility rate and high teen birth rates" (2015, 3). "A lower emotional investment" primarily characterizes the pediatric style of childrearing, as does "a negative attitude towards attachment." Ecological stress thus has a direct implication for the attachment system.

Attachment theory addresses the proximity-seeking behaviors of human infants, children, and adults (Bowlby 1969, 1973, 1980). In moments of threat, distress, or fear of abandonment, humans tend to seek proximity to someone perceived to be stronger and wiser (Cassidy and Shaver 1999). The stronger, wiser other is the attachment figure. For vulnerable progeny, in particular, the attachment figure is a protective agent and as such serves as a "haven of safety." The attachment figure also serves as a "secure base." For the attached, once a sense of safety is restored, the attachment figure switches from the former to the latter. The secure base allows the attached to disengage attachment behaviors. Such disengagement facilitates other systems of behavior, for instance, exploratory behaviors. Exploratory behaviors are essential for foraging, hunting, and mating. When the attachment figure is seen as a secure base, the attached can explore the environment with confidence, knowing that the attachment figure is there for protection should the need arise. The attachment and exploratory systems are inversely related. While one is on, the other is off. Both are control systems (Kirkpatrick 2005).

Control systems turn on and off depending on a certain "set point." For instance, attachment behaviors turn on and off as the infant's level of distress rises and falls. The set point at which any one organism's attachment system turns off or on depends on the level of distress the organism feels. What is more, set points can vary over the course of a lifetime. What would have required immediate physical proximity in early childhood may only require visual recognition later on. Attachment needs can eventually find satisfaction through mere mentation. Sometimes it is simply enough to think about the attachment figure for attachment needs to be satisfied. The degree to which proximity is sought varies from individual to individual. The same can be said for the perception of threat. Some are more secure in their perceptions of threat and the availability of the attachment figure than are others. The inverse is of course true. This disparity in attachment behaviors depends in large part upon the quality and quantity of the relationship between the attached and the attachment figure throughout infancy and childhood.

Repeated experiences with the attachment figure(s) ultimately produce in the attached what has come to be called an internal working model, or IWM (Main et al. 1985; Bartholomew 1990). The IWM contains two dimensions, one for self and one for other. Each model can be either positive or negative. The self-model reflects the extent to which the individual believes himself to be worthy of love and attention. The other model reflects the extent to which the individual believes the attachment figure/other is available and dependable. IWMs generally inform the individual's expectations of how future relationships with others will unfold.[17] If one experienced an attachment figure that is always available and loving, one is likely to go through life believing that others are good and dependable and that one is worthy of their attention and solicitude. Those with such experiences and expectations are said to have a secure attachment style. Not all interactions with attachment figures are of such a nature. Not all attachments are secure.

Attachment theorists have identified four styles of attachment and their concomitant IWMs. These are secure, insecure-anxious, insecure-avoidant/dismissing, and insecure-avoidant/fearful.[18] Secure attachments are those with positive IWMs of self and other. Insecure-anxious attachments are those with a negative IWM of self and a positive IWM of other. Insecure-avoidant/dismissing attachments are characterized by a positive IWM of self and a negative IWM of other, while the fearful have negative IWMs of both self and other. Each configuration reflects the attached's perception of interaction with the attachment figure. Secure attachments reflect an experience with an attachment figure who is consistently available for help and protection. Insecure-avoidant attachments generally reflect an experience with an attachment figure who consistently rebuffs the attached's attempts at proximity. Insecure-anxious attachment styles result from experiences with attachment figures who are consistently inconsistent with their physical and emotional provisioning and availability (Noftle and Shaver 2006). For those so characterized, "their parents are described as having been emotionally unpredictable, sometimes warm and loving, at other times disapproving and withholding, often they were overprotective which resulted in the child's ongoing struggles with independence" (Magai et al. 2000, 302). Such emotional unpredictability coupled with overprotection are qualities associated with the pediatric style of childrearing. There is reason to think that the insecure-anxious attachment style would have been most prominent throughout the human animal's evolutionary past.

The EEA would have evoked pediatric childrearing practices. Such practices induce insecure-anxious attachments. Similar outcomes are found today in adult populations that experience great resource stress and robust infectious disease threat (Schmitt et al. 2004). This is adaptive. "The common individual differences in attachment that we observe today," writes Chisholm, "can be interpreted as facultative adaptations to parental behaviors that in the EEA were reliable indicators of what were probably two of the more recurrent (and not mutually exclusive) threats to juvenile survival and growth: parents' *inability* to invest in offspring, and parents' *unwillingness* (not necessarily conscious) to invest" (1996, 15; Belsky 1999). Weingarten and Chisholm similarly propose that "insecure attachments belong to a repertoire of adaptive attachment styles that reflect environments of evolutionary adaptedness that were often marked by great uncertainty, harshness, and deprivation" (2009, 767). Such facultative aspects of the insecure-anxious attachment style surely help explain why this is such a "highly conserved behavioral pattern" (Maunder and Hunter 2001, 559). "Research indicates that almost half of living human beings in every age group are insecure with respect to attachment," note T. Ein-Dor et al., "and the proportion is higher in more disadvantaged (e.g., poorer, less socially stable) populations" (2010, 124).[19] Physical provisioning and overprotection coupled with emotional unpredictability and withdrawal is the prescription for a negative self-IWM and a positive other-IWM. It is the prescription for insecure-anxious attachments.

Insecure-anxious attachments are facultative for situations in which parents may want to provision their children but face many challenges in doing so. It is reasonable to propose that in the EEA, "anxious, wary preoccupation with mother represents a facultative adaptation for extracting resources (i.e., felt security) from a mother who is irritable and preoccupied herself—with fear, hunger, or exhaustion" (Chisholm 1996, 17). Attachment anxiety "hyperactivates the attachment system in an attempt to gain the partner's attention, care, and love" (Ein-Dor et al. 2010, 125). Those with insecure-anxious attachments facultatively cling to the attachment figure with expectations that at least some provisioning and protection will be forthcoming. The insecure-anxiously attached pursue strategies for resource extraction. They equally pursue strategies for ensuring safety.

Attachment system hyperactivation results in "recurrent attempts to minimize distance from attachment figures" (Shaver and Mikulincer 2002, 141). Needing such minimization reflects the fact that the insecure-anxious tend to see the world as dangerous (Weber and Federico 2007). This makes good evolutionary sense. The EEA *was* dangerous. If attachment security is in doubt, at least one compensatory hypothesis predicts a heightened vigilance toward threat (MacBeth et al. 2008). M. Kavaliers and E. Choleris note that anxious attachments facilitate "sustained apprehension of the environment and elevated vigilance for ongoing and future threats" (2018, 4). J. Cassidy and L. J. Berlin similarly write, "the infant's perception (based on previous interactions) of probable parental unresponsiveness is . . . thought to necessitate a distorted perception of the environment as frightening" (1994, 985). Such heightened anxiety and distortion would have led to enhanced vigilance of the local environment for sources of danger, enabling thereby expeditious escape as well as alerting others to do so as well or, at least, to engage in collective efforts to thwart the threat (Frankenhuis 2010). Insecure-anxious attachments are thus adaptive when it comes to extracting resources from stressed-out attachment figures and when it comes to monitoring vigilantly the environment for macropredators. Lastly, insecure-anxious attachments are adaptive for environments in which the infectious disease ecology is most robust. Insecure-anxious attachments facilitate collectivism.

The first goal of the pediatric style of childrearing is to keep the child alive. The second goal is "to rear a compliant, obedient child who will easily fit into the extended family and be a productive member of the homestead" (Small 1998, 95; Kurtz 1992). Insecure-anxious attachments in childhood facilitate collectivism in adulthood. This is widely recognized. "Anxious attachment may be more compatible with a highly collectivist culture in which tight interdependence is regarded favorably" (Shaver et al. 2010, 104); "in cultures that socialize children to be highly reliant on others for comfort and support, the average adult score on the attachment anxiety dimension is likely to be relatively high" (Shaver et al. 2010, 97); "someone who scores ... high on attachment anxiety might score fairly high overall on a measure of group identification ... the adaptive advantages of insecure attachment patterns may be that they promote survival of individuals in a group rather than directly promotive reproduction" (Ein-Dor et al. 2010, 124); insecure-anxious attachments are adaptive at "the level of groups, tribes, and societies" (Ein-Dor et al. 2010, 135); "in collectivist societies, people are integrated from birth onward into strong, cohesive in-groups, often extended families (with uncles, aunts, and grandparents), protecting them in exchange for unquestioning loyalty" (Hofstede and McCrae 2004, 63); "preoccupied attachment cooccurred with high rates of collectivism" (Schmitt et al. 2004, 398). Regarding one of the other sets of childrearing strategies, Sapolsky notes that the authoritarian style of childrearing equally involves a certain disregard for the child's emotional needs and that this often results in an adult who "may be narrowly successful, obedient, conformist (often with an undercurrent of resentment that can explode), and not particularly happy" (2017, 203). As "the *reverse causation* hypothesis" (Hofstede and McCrae 2004, 75) would predict, the conformity associated with collectivism results from the personality profile most associated with insecure-anxious attachments.

Insecure-anxious attachments tend to correlate with some of the dimensions of the Big Five personality profile (McCrae and Allik 2002; McCrae and Terracciano 2005). The Big Five are openness (to experience), conscientiousness, agreeableness, extraversion, and neuroticism. Insecure-anxious attachments correlate with neuroticism and inversely correlate with extraversion, openness to experience/value, and conscientiousness.[20] Such attachments also tend to correlate especially with the depression and vulnerability aspects of neuroticism (Shaver and Brennan 1992; Noftel and Shaver 2006). The negative connotations we often associate with neuroticism today may have actually been adaptive in an ancestral past. "In ancestral environments, a level of neuroticism may have been necessary for avoidance of acute dangers," Nettle writes, "[it] enhances detection of threatening stimuli by speeding up the reaction to them, interpreting ambiguous stimuli as negative, and locking attention onto them," noting elsewhere, "very low neuroticism has fitness disadvantages in terms of lack of striving or hazard avoidance" (2006, 626). Curtis et al. similarly observe,

> the reason for the persistence of such an apparently maladaptive personality trait may be that it helped to reduce the risk of predation and accidents in dangerous ancestral environments. Given that there is covariance between neuroticism and disgust sensitivity scores and that parasites were one of the biggest dangers in ancestral environments, it is probable that disgust sensitivity is, in fact, a component of the neuroticism trait. (2011, 392)[21]

This appears to be the case. Disgust sensitivity is heightened in those with insecure-anxious attachment styles (Magai et al. 1995; Magai et al. 2000; Consedine and Magai 2003). It also correlates with concerns regarding purity and sanctity, concerns directly associated with religion (Koleva et al. 2014). "The correspondence between the ontogenetic onset of religiosity and infectious disease awareness," note Thornhill and Fincher, "suggests an important aspect of the developmental ecology of values" (2014b, 256). The previous chapter noted how disgust is evoked when in the presence of a free rider. Insecure-anxious attachments are also associated with concerns about fair tit-for-tat reciprocity within the ingroup (Koleva et al. 2014). Lastly, insecure-anxious neuroticism strongly correlates with what is called, uncertainty avoidance (Hofstede 2001; Hofstede and McCrae 2004).

A modicum of uncertainty regarding the future is endemic to human nature. No one knows what's coming next. For some, this may be better than knowing (Taylor 1984). For most, however, the uncertain future is a bit unsettling. The degree to which one is unsettled is directly correlated with one's level of neuroticism. Highly neurotic people and cultures have a low threshold for tolerance of the uncertain. In today's world, with all of the available technology capable of making oft-accurate predictions, the uncertainty of the future is mitigated. This was not the case in an ancestral past. The ancestral past faced an uncertain future (Weingarten and Chisholm 2009, 767). G. Hofstede argues that those cultures which are characterized by high levels of uncertainty avoidance display "tendencies toward prejudice, rigidity and dogmatism, intolerance of different opinions, traditionalism, superstition, racism, and ethnocentrism" (2001, 146). Hofstede and McCrae (2004) also note that such cultures show similar tendencies toward xenophobia. All of these are traits with which we associate religion's tribalism.

There is yet another dimension of uncertainty. One can be uncertain about oneself. This is especially the case for those with insecure-anxious attachment styles (Wu 2009). Identification with a strongly established group identity mitigates such personal uncertainty (Hart et al. 2005). "The greater the uncertainty, the greater the motivation to structure the self-concept in terms of prototypical properties of high entitativity groups," notes M. A. Hogg, "groups that are orthodox, distinctive, hierarchically structured, consensual, intolerant of internal dissent and diversity, and highly xenophobic and ethnocentric" (2004, 412; Hogg et al. 2007). High entitativity groups are tight groups. They are also often religious. Hofstede (2001) notes that one of the primary ways a culture handles high degrees of uncertainty is precisely through religion. Religion serves a compensatory function for the insecure-anxiously attached. "The compensation hypothesis," notes Kirkpatrick, "would predict that people with *insecure* childhood attachments might be those likely to turn to a relationship with God later, to provide the kind of haven of safety and secure base that were not perceived to be available in their childhood attachment relationships with parents or other (human) caregivers" (2005, 128; Kirkpatrick 1998). According to Kirkpatrick, God is often "an *ideal* attachment figure" (2005, 53), "an absolutely adequate attachment figure" (Kaufman 1981, 67). Here is precisely where it is important to recall that attachment needs can be satisfied through mere mentation. One only needs to perceive mentally the availability of God to compensate for one's attachment needs. Equally likely, though, is that an insecure-anxious individual may turn to religious authorities as substitute attachment figures. Throughout most of human history, a religious figure may have provided the necessary compensation and not a god. This is the case because those reared by the pediatric style most likely do not see the gods as being havens of safety and secure bases.

We noted above that there are multiple sets of childrearing strategies. The focus thus far has been on the pedagogical and pediatric because these are directly related to infectious disease ecologies. We also took brief note of Sapolsky's characterization of the authoritarian style of childrearing as this seems quite resonant with the pediatric style. It is time to draw attention to the other set of childrearing strategies, the accepting and rejecting (Rohner 1975).

The rejecting style resonates with the pediatric and authoritarian. "Rejection is a form of parental behavior that is characterized by the absence or withdrawal of warmth and affection" (Rohner 1975, 45). In keeping with the association of the pediatric style with insecure-anxious attachments, I. Bretherton notes that the "correlates of acceptance or rejection among societies read uncannily like the sequelae of secure and insecure attachment" (1985, 26). "Rejecting" parenting styles similarly promote insecure attachments. Significantly for us, childrearing practices and their concomitant attachment styles have direct implications for the perception of non-natural agents. Cultures in which rejection is prevalent tend to perceive the supernatural as malevolent *or* capricious (Lambert et al. 1959; Lambert 1992). The disjunction reflects the disjunction in rejection. Rejection admits of variation. One type of rejection is emotional withdrawal. The other type is physical and emotional abuse. When it comes to the latter, we can expect the documented correlation, that is, the supernatural will be perceived as malevolent. This is the supernatural associated primarily with insecure-avoidant/ fearful attachment styles. The *inconsistency* associated with the pediatric style and the attendant insecure-anxious attachments tend to induce perceptions of the supernatural, not as wholly malevolent, but rather as capricious. "Gods are often ambivalent or capricious in their dealings with human beings" (Jong and Halberstadt 2016, 43). The gods' behaviors, in this regard, correspond with the behaviors of pediatric parents. The supernatural world often associated with the first religion, that is, animism and the concomitant shamanism, was precisely a world of such unpredictable supernatural agents. The "mild rejection" of the pediatric style promotes compensatory attachments to a religious figure, perhaps a shaman, who engages the capricious spirits on behalf of the insecure-anxiously attached.

Cultures that are high on uncertainty avoidance, with personality profiles attending the insecure-anxiously attached, are also quite committed to purity and pollution codes. Hofstede notes that in cultures with a high uncertainty avoidance profile "among the first things a child learns are the distinctions between clean and dirty and between safe and dangerous" (2001, 161). He also notes that such concerns with what is pure and what is polluted pertain equally to other people as well as their ideas. Children come to learn about taboos, "a characteristic of traditional, primitive societies" (Hofstede 2001, 162). Saroglou and Anciaux also remind us that "rituals of purification in many religious traditions suggest a high concern in religion with cleanliness and purity, and many studies confirm that the religious personality is marked by (obsessive) traits of orderliness-cleanliness" (2004, 261). Additionally, it would appear that insecure-anxious attachments are associated with obsessive-compulsive disorder (Doron et al. 2012). Cultures high on uncertainty avoidance often include "tight rules on what is dirty and taboo" and that "children learn that the world is hostile" (Hofstede 2001, 169). Finally, those same cultures also "manifest intolerance toward other religions" (Hofstede 2001, 176).

Ecologies burdened with resource scarcity, predators, and infectious disease tend to evoke a pediatric style of childrearing. Such a style tends to induce insecure-anxious attachments. These attachments are often linked to neuroticism, anxiety, and depression. Such characteristics are today generally considered psychologically untoward. They were adaptive for life in the Pleistocene. "Traits or behaviors that are adaptive from the perspective of natural selection (i.e., promoting survival and reproduction) may not be adaptive from the perspective of developmental psychology (i.e., promoting subjective well-being, emotional stability, and social competence)," notes L. M. Diamond, "although 'strategies' such as attachment anxiety or avoidance may have a range of detrimental psychosocial 'side effects' in benign environments, they should successfully promote infant survival and protection *in stressful environments*" (2015, 111; Zhang et al. 2006). K. Valli and A. Revonsuo similarly note, "From an evolutionary point of view, it is more adaptive to suffer psychologically and survive than to feel great but perish quickly" (2006, 465). Childrearing strategies that are prevalent in robust disease ecologies facultatively nurture insecure-anxious attachment styles that promote adult concerns with inclusion in and maintenance of the prophylactic collective. The prophylactic collective is the religious tribe. Religion's tribalism, with its ubiquitous and persistent purity and pollution codes, was ultimately in the service of maintaining the geography of immunocompetence, that is, a sound body amid robust disease ecologies. Religion's tribalism is in this regard a preeminent manifestation of the behavioral immune system. Maintaining a sound body is one prerequisite for a healthy economy and family. Another prerequisite is a sound mind. Maintaining a sound mind often requires accepting religion's vital lies and illusions of control.

4

Religion's Vital Lies and Illusions of Control

The Psychological Immune System

We saw in Chapter 2 that many authors suggest that the selection pressure for economic and reproductive cooperation is what led to the emergence and evolution of religion. As possible and plausible a suggestion as this is, we saw in the last chapter that a healthy economy and family ultimately require a healthy community. Thus, we considered the various ways in which religion reflects the operation of the behavioral immune system, that part of the integrated immune system dedicated to motivating prophylactic behaviors. Foremost among such behaviors are those associated with tribalism. Religion's tribalism is an iteration of collectivism, itself an antipathogen psychology. Because local groups develop a certain immunity to their local disease ecologies, the outgroup other always poses the risk of a novel outbreak. Such is the reality of the geography of immunocompetence. Religious traditions maintain the health of the tribe by promoting collectivist values and behaviors. This was adaptive.

Healthy economies and families require healthy bodies. They equally require healthy minds. Having now addressed religion's role in facilitating the former, it is time to direct attention to the latter. In much the same way that the behavioral immune system prophylactically protects healthy bodies, the psychological immune system prophylactically protects healthy minds. As we saw toward the end of the previous chapter, a healthy mind may not be the mind of the insecure-anxiously attached. Insecure-anxious attachments may be facultative for physical survival. They may not be so conducive to psychological health. The insecure-anxiously attached presented one of the selection pressures for the psychological immune system. Although the comparison is with the physiological immune system—the third and final arm of the integrated immune system and the topic for the next chapter—R. Trivers notes, "we have a 'psychological immune system' to protect our mental health just as the actual immune system protects our physical health"

(2011, 68). T. D. Wilson similarly writes, "Just as we possess a potent physical immune system that protects us from threats to our physical well-being, so do we possess a potent psychological immune system that protects us from threats to our psychological well-being" (2002, 38). Perhaps as it is with the behavioral immune system, so too is it with the psychological one: there is no better manifestation of it than religion.

There are many threats to psychological well-being. This chapter addresses one in particular. It addresses chronic stress. Chronic stress is responsible for a range of deleterious effects. The two most serious effects are immunosuppression and depression. Those who are immunosuppressed are rendered most susceptible to the contraction of disease. Nothing good can come from immunosuppression. The same cannot be said for depression. There are some adaptive advantages to the occasional, depressive mood. Major depression, however, is wholly maladaptive. It contributes directly to subfecundity. Subfecundity is the failure to reach optimal reproductive success. If there is any pressure in most need of natural selection's ingenuity, it would certainly be the one that results in subfecundity.

Lack of control is the primary, psychological stressor for the human animal. The previous chapter indicated uncertainty avoidance is a principal motivator for many traditional religions. Lacking control is directly related to the inability to predict, both of which are inversely proportional to uncertainty avoidance. The ability to control and thus predict are two primary factors directly related to positive mood. Of all the events over which the human animal may wish to exert control and thus be able to predict, but cannot in fact do so, is death. S. Solomon et al. note, "Death can occur at any time for unpredictable and uncontrollable reasons" (2010, 101). This is quite possibly the most stressful realization for a self-aware animal. If one cannot manage the stress associated with the awareness of death, one might end up in a certain behavioral paralysis, the maladaptive nature of which should be obvious. Death anxiety must be managed in order for the human animal to be able to get on with the business of living and reproducing. Terror management theory (TMT) proposes that our strategy for managing existential terror ultimately entails constructing a worldview, or culture, that can provide our lives with a sense of meaning and purpose. Insofar as these worldviews are symbolic constructs intended to mask the naked reality of our mortality, they are, in the words of E. Becker, vital lies. Vital lies are, to be sure, "*brainsoothing*" (McGuire and Tiger 2009, 125). The most effective of these vital lies is religion. The psychological immune system deploys religion's vital lies to soothe our brains, to protect mental health.

Disgust was first introduced in Chapter 2. It attends perceptions of economic cheating and suboptimal sex. Disgust was associated in the previous chapter with the promotion of prophylactic behaviors when in the presence of potentially infectious matter and agents. In all such instances, it was the other that was the object of our disgust. This chapter considers those moments when we ourselves are the objects of disgust. We occasionally find our bodies and their exuviae disgusting. This is animal-nature disgust. Animal-nature disgust attends reminders that we are just another animal destined for the grave. It accompanies the activation of the psychological immune system.

A primary function of religion is to manage stress (McGuire and Tiger 2009). It does this in two primary ways. First, religion promotes vital lies. The most momentous of such lies is the one pertaining to our survival of death. Although clearly lacking empirical evidence and rational warrant, most religions promote narratives concerning well-earned lives beyond the grave. "With remarkable, even astonishing, boldness and invention religious beliefs reduce ambiguity and uncertainty about matters of life, death, the soul, and eternity," note M. McGuire and L. Tiger, "they provide a menu for the afterlife as the antidote to the cold prospect of complete postlife nothingness. This is apparently unendurable to the majority of human beings" (2009, 133). Second, religion fosters illusions of control (Langer 1975). Religion's ritualized behaviors promote a sense that the practitioner wields greater control over a situation than is in fact the case. This often involves appeals to non-natural agents. Such appeals reflect the adaptive illusion of qualified, internal control (IoQC). Like vital lies, illusions of control are equally brainsoothing.

Others are often contagious. Their free-riding behavior is contagious. Their infections are contagious. This chapter considers the extent to which the others' ideas are contagious. The psychologically contagious other can infect our vital lies, resulting in "cognitive infections" (Pinker 2021, 321). Thus, and as it is with all things contagious, the other's vital lies can evoke disgust. D. S. Wilson identifies what he calls, "mental contamination": "We can be influenced in unwanted ways without being aware that we are being influenced.... Our minds can unknowingly become 'polluted' with information we would rather not have influence us" (2002, 187). P. J. Richerson and R. Boyd offer this apt analogy: "Our culture is a lot like our lungs. They both work for their evolved functions, but they also make us susceptible to infection by pathogens. You would be a lot less likely to catch either a serious respiratory disease or a selfish cultural variant if you kept away from other people as much as possible" (2005, 188). In much the same way that the other may harbor biological pathogens capable of disturbing our physiological homeostasis and as such disgusts us, so too the other may harbor propositional pathogens that could equally disturb our psychological homeostasis and as such disgusts us. "The emotion of disgust emerged in humans to protect us from the problem of our death both physically and psychologically," writes R. Herz, "and this is why it motivates us to recoil from scabby sores, piggish eating, and people who threaten our way of life" (2012, 131). A strong commitment to a set of religious propositions and their accompanying ritualized behaviors amounts to "cognitive immunity." "Belief can also be defined as a state of cognitive immunity," writes L. P. Villarreal, "in which meaning is stably held and resists other sensory inputs or identifiers" (2008, 58), noting elsewhere, "strong religious belief is a stable state of cognitive immunity" (2008, 62). Religion's vital lies and adaptive illusions of control are the psychological immune system's mechanisms for promoting cognitive immunity and psychological homeostasis. These lies and illusions maintain a sound mind, the second prerequisite for healthy economies and families.

Stress

There are at least three primary threats to mental health. The first threat is organic. Some individuals are simply born with congenital brain defects. Such defects usually render the victim—if such be the correct word—unfit for economic and reproductive activity. The second threat is environmental insult. Environmental insults result from physical injuries to the head and brain. They, too, can render the victim unfit for economic and reproductive activity. As significant as these two threats are, they are not the focus here. Religious beliefs and practices simply cannot remedy such physical afflictions. If there is a lesion in your temporal lobe, no amount of prayer can fix it. It is thus the third threat to mental health that is within the remit of religion. The third threat is a psychological threat. Foremost among such threats is stress. Religion manages stress. "To the extent that religiosity is good for health, once you control for social support and decreased risk factors, why is it healthful?" asks R. Sapolsky, "For lots of reasons that have everything to do with stress, and with the type of deity(ies) you believe in" (2004, 410). M. Winkelman similarly notes that one of religion's functions is the "management of health, particularly stress" (2011, 56). S. K. Sanderson is a bit more specific, "the role of religion in promoting physical health seems to be that it alleviates 'existential stress'" (2018, 153).

Stress involves three elements. First is the stressor. A stressor is "anything that disrupts homeostatic balance" (Sapolsky 2017, 125). Next is the brain's perception of stress. The perception assesses the degree to which the stimulus is antagonistic to an organism's goals (Boyer et al. 2015; Nesse and Young 2000). There are two degrees of antagonism. The antagonism is either a challenge or a threat (Diamond 2015). The stressor is a challenge when the stressed organism perceives that its resources are sufficient to meet and overcome it. Such instances can actually be pleasurable (Sapolsky 2004). The stressor is a threat when the organism perceives that its resources are insufficient to meet and overcome it. There are two types of threats. A threat can issue either from a physical or psychosocial source. The former is often "an external challenge to homeostasis." The latter is an "anticipation, *justified or not*, that a challenge to homeostasis looms" (Sapolsky 2005, 648, emphasis added). The third element of stress is the response. There are two responses. One can either fight the stressor or flee the stressor. This is, of course, the physiological fight-or-flight response (Viswanathan et al. 2005).

The fight-or-flight response occurs when the sympathetic nervous system—itself part of the autonomic nervous system—sends a signal in the form of a neurotransmitter called acetylcholine to the adrenal medulla. The acetylcholine combines with the adrenal medulla's chromaffin cells, affecting thereby the release of catecholamine hormones. One such hormone is epinephrine, also known as adrenaline. Epinephrine affects the level of glucose in the bloodstream. It does this by drawing glucose out of liver cells and skeletal muscle, providing thereby extra sources of energy to the stressed animal. It also causes the release of fatty acids from fat cells, once again providing another source of energy. The adrenal medulla also releases norepinephrine. An increase in norepinephrine raises blood pressure, increasing thereby heart rate and blood flow to the muscles. Norepinephrine also acts as a neurotransmitter. It causes an increase in sensory alertness. Together, epinephrine and norepinephrine direct blood flow away from such organs as the skin, kidneys, and gut and toward the brain, heart, and skeletal muscles, preparing thereby the body for either an agonistic fight or a frantic flight. This process is often referred to as the sympathetic-adrenal-medullary axis, or SAM (Glaser and Kiecolt-Glaser 2005).

The adrenal medulla emits catecholamine hormones upon receiving signals from the sympathetic nervous system. The adrenal cortex emits steroid hormones. This happens when the hypothalamus receives a stress signal. The hypothalamus, in turn, stimulates the pituitary gland. It does this by means of corticotropin-releasing hormone (CRH). CRH causes the pituitary gland to secrete adrenocorticotropic hormone (ACTH). ACTH causes the adrenal cortex to synthesize and secrete corticosteroids. One set of corticosteroids is the glucocorticoids (Sapolsky 2017). Of the glucocorticoids, cortisol is perhaps the most widely known. Cortisol is "the principal human glucocorticoid regulating blood pressure, glucose metabolism, and immune competence" (Ellis et al. 2006, 179). Whereas the catecholamine hormones affect already existing glucose, the steroids synthesize glucose. Steroids thus add to the volume of energy available to the stressed organism. This process is often referred to as the hypothalamic-pituitary-adrenal axis, or HPA (Glaser and Kiecolt-Glaser 2005; Nesse and Young 2000).[1]

The distinction between a challenge and a threat depends entirely upon perception. Misperception is always a possibility. An organism may occasionally, if not routinely, misperceive the severity of a stressor. As it is with all cognitive errors, the misperception can go both ways. One can misperceive a threat as a challenge, or a challenge as a threat. Such perceptions and misperceptions reflect the calibration of the stress response. The calibration takes place in childhood. "Aspects of early experience, particularly parent-child experiences, appear to play a central role in the calibration of stress responses," note B. J. Ellis et al., "ongoing exposure to familial and ecological stressors can cause changes in the set points of the CRH [corticotrophin-releasing hormone] and LC-NE [locus coeruleus-norepinephrine] systems, resulting either in hyper- or hypo-reactivity of these neuroendocrine pathways" (2006, 180). The calibration of the stress response in the environment of evolutionary adaptedness (EEA) would have been more on the hyper-reactivity end of the spectrum than otherwise. Those who are insecure-anxiously attached do have a heightened vigilance toward threat. Heightened vigilance and hyper-reactivity are two sides of the same coin. According to R. G. Maunder et al., "attachment anxiety is associated with greater self-reports of stress or distress" (2006, 289).

The ancestral world was clearly replete with selection pressures, that is, stressors. In moments of *immediate* threat, a stress response would have been adaptive. Should a predator make its presence known, it is good to have an immediate boost of energy along with heightened sensory alertness to handle the situation. Such threats tend to come and go rather quickly for most species of animal. A predator that is out of sight is a predator that is out of mind. Predators that are out of mind do not induce a stress response. Such is not the case for the psychosocial stressor.

Most physical stressors evoke an acute-stress response. The *looming*, psychosocial ones don't. They tend to evoke a chronic stress response. It is the duration of response that makes all the difference. "An important distinguishing characteristic of stress is its duration," note K. Viswanathan et al., "we define acute stress as stress that lasts for a period of minutes to hours, and chronic stress as stress that persists for several hours a day for weeks, months or years" (2005, 1059). Acute stress is adaptive. Chronic stress is not. Most species of animal can only experience acute stress. Chronic stress is a "recent mammalian innovation" (Sapolsky 2017, 126). Truly, zebras don't get ulcers (Sapolsky 2004).

Most species of animal are capable of only an acute-stress response. They do not possess the cognitive capacities requisite for long-term anticipation. The recent mammalian innovation of which Sapolsky writes is the ability to imagine and thus anticipate a threat looming in the distant future. "The stress response is about preparing your body for an explosive burst of energy consumption *right now*," Sapolsky notes, "psychological stress is about doing all the same things to your body for no physical reason whatsoever" (2004, 255). Elsewhere, he adds, "An anticipatory stress response is adaptive if there really is a physical challenge coming. However, if you're constantly but incorrectly convinced that you're about to be thrown out of balance, you're being an anxious, neurotic, paranoid, or hostile primate who is *psychologically* stressed.... The stress response did not evolve for dealing with this" (2017, 126). The stress response could not anticipate the evolution of an animal with the capacity to project itself into the distant future and the threats associated therewith. Future threats cannot be resolved in the here and now and as such provoke a chronic stress response. Chronic activation of the stress response has several deleterious consequences.

Chronic stress is deleterious for the physiological immune system. Sustained, heightened levels of glucocorticoids in the bloodstream, for instance, cortisol, are immunosuppressive. The chronically stressed animal is thus more vulnerable to infectious diseases (Glaser and Kiecolt-Glaser 2005; Fabrega Jr. 1997). Chronic stress similarly makes preexisting conditions even worse (Sapolsky 2004).[2] It reduces by 40–70 percent any measurable immune system component, for instance, natural killer cells, lymphocytes, and antibodies (Cohen and Herbert 1996; Sapolsky 2004; Segerstrom and Miller 2004; Glaser 2005; Dhabhar 2008; Bowers et al. 2008). According to Sapolsky, heightened levels of glucocorticoids

> can cause the shrinking of the thymus.... Glucocorticoids halt the formation of new lymphocytes in the thymus, and most of the thymic tissue is made up of these new cells, ready to be secreted into the bloodstream. Because glucocorticoids inhibit the release of messengers like interleukins and interferons, they also make circulating lymphocytes less responsive to an infectious alarm. Glucocorticoids, moreover, cause lymphocytes to be yanked out of the circulation and stuck back in storage in immune tissues. Most of these glucocorticoid effects are against T cells, rather than B cells, meaning that cell-mediated immunity is more disrupted

than antibody-mediated immunity. And most impressively, glucocorticoids can actually kill lymphocytes. (2004, 151–2)

We will have the opportunity to return to the intricacies of the physiological immune system in the next chapter. For now, and in addition to the immunosuppressive effects of sustained glucocorticoid levels in the bloodstream, such conditions also compromise the efficacy of vaccines, hinder proper wound healing, pose a greater risk of developing cancer, and raises the risk of developing an autoimmune disorder (Segerstrom and Miller 2004; Glaser and Kiecolt-Glaser 2005; Dhabhar 2009; Dhabhar 2014). Lastly, "stress-induced immune dysregulation can cause mortality" (Glaser and Kiecolt-Glaser 2005, 249). The effects of chronic stress are calamitous.

Morbidity due to a chronically suppressed immune system can end in mortality for the stressed organism. One would be forgiven for thinking that such an outcome is the direst consequence of chronic stress. But it isn't. Or, at least it isn't from a strictly biological perspective. Worse than suppressing the immune system is chronic stress's contribution to major depression (Koenig et al. 2001; Sapolsky 2017). "Major depression," Sapolsky observes, "is utterly intertwined with prolonged stress" (Sapolsky 2004, 221). Chronic stress and depression have direct implications for inclusive fitness. Inclusive fitness is the appropriate metric by which to judge the truly deleterious effects of chronic stress (Sanderson 2018).

Short-lived, depressive episodes have their adaptive moments.[3] Chronic stress and major depression do not. They are maladaptive in the most biological sense of the word. Stress and depression are the leading causes of coital failure and its attendant subfecundity. There are a few reasons for this. First, sexual intercourse is one of the primary means of transmitting and contracting disease. For this reason, "sexual drive and receptivity will fall when the organism is stressed, starved, or sick," C. Loehle notes, "because disease susceptibility is higher under these conditions" (1995, 330; Lourenco et al. 2011). R. Balon similarly observes, "Most experts and clinicians would agree that decreased libido is probably the most frequent dysfunction associated with depression" (2011, 43; Williams and Reynolds 2006). Stress and depression can also lead to menstrual cycle irregularity, depleted testosterone levels, and lowered sperm count (Sapolsky 2004, 2017). The severity of these problems still do not constitute the primary problem associated with stress and depression. They do not *prevent* sexual intercourse. Something that prevents sexual intercourse is truly a problem for inclusive fitness. Can stress and depression actually prevent sexual intercourse?

Yes. "Stress will knock out erections quite readily," Sapolsky writes, "the problems with erections are more disruptive than problems with testosterone secretion.... . A little testosterone and a couple of sperm wandering around and most males can muddle through. But no erection, and forget about it" (2004, 126).

Stress and depression contribute directly to erectile dysfunction. Some estimate that psychic stress accounts for about 90 percent of all cases of impotence and thus coital inability (McFalls 1979). This is the case because of the heightened activity of the sympathetic nervous system during stress. For the male primate to achieve and maintain an erection, he must engorge his penis through diverting blood flow to the organ (Sapolsky 2004). This can only be done if he is relaxed, that is, if his parasympathetic nervous system is dominant. Because only an erect penis can ejaculate, a stressed, male animal is the primary contributor to subfecundity. "There is no doubt that psychic stress causes enough subfecundity to be of demographic significance," observes J. A. McFalls, "the fact that it is responsible for up to 90 percent of impotence, the single most important form of coital inability, would be basis enough for this judgment without even considering its many other links to coital inability and to conceptive failure and pregnancy loss as well" (1979, 91). The chronically stressed animal cannot reproduce with enough success to make the psychological state reproductively neutral. This makes chronic stress and depression a target for natural selection. In a world where "children grew up, and adults lived out their lives, in the constant awareness, and sooner or later the personal experience, of woeful illness, painful injury, physical handicaps, debilitation, and death," and where "there were no antibiotics, tetanus shots, or anesthetics, no plaster casts, corrective lenses, or prosthetic devices, no sterile surgery or false teeth" (Nesse and Williams 1996, 141), chronic stress and depression were ubiquitous problems throughout most of human history. "The ancestral world was to a substantial degree a traumatic world" (Bulbulia 2005, 89). Although it may be hard for some of us to imagine just how traumatic and thus stressful the ancestral world was (Nesse and Williams 1996; Nesse and Young 2000; Bulbulia 2005, 2006; Turner et al. 2018), this can only be because we have begun to assert a modicum of control over many of our problems. A modicum of control can make all of the difference.

The core problem that leads to depression is the stress-inducing perception that one lacks control and thus the ability to predict (Langer 1975; Seligman 1975; Abramson et al. 1989; Wilson 2002; Sapolsky 2004, 2005; Gilbert 2006; Badcock and Allen 2007; Lourenco et al. 2011). Depression is "a pathological sense of lack of control" (Sapolsky 2017, 197). "Loss of control and predictability" is "the core of psychological stress" (Sapolsky 2017, 127; Ellis and Del Giudice

2019).[4] C. P. Reynaert et al. similarly note, "If we reconsider the depressive state in the light of 'control,' depression often corresponds to a situation in which the individual has lost his or her sense of being in control of events . . . reflected by the concepts of hopelessness, helplessness, and powerlessness" (1995, 294). As it is with all traits, some individuals are more vulnerable to experiencing depression than others (Sapolsky 2004). Who might they be? Gilbert suggests that "our brains appear wired to tone down positive affect [i.e., depression] in contexts of *poor attachment and affiliation*" (2006, 294, emphasis added), noting elsewhere, "early experiences of parenting, social support and personal meaning of events influence resilience to adversity" (2006, 289). The insecure-anxious attachment style is particularly predisposed to both stress and depression. "In cognitive theories of depression," E. E. Noftle and P. R. Shaver note, "a negative self-image is a central aspect of depression" (2006, 200). A negative self-image is the negative self-IWM of the insecure-anxious attachment style. Significantly for what follows, those with insecure-anxious attachments have particular difficulties managing existential stress. Mikulincer et al. note, "ambivalent subjects exhibited stronger fear of death than did secure subjects at both conscious and below-conscious levels of awareness" (1990, 278; Pyszczynski et al. 2003).

The human animal faced a slew of selection pressures in the EEA. These pressures led to the emergence of various modules in the human mind/brain. They also led to the emergence of the primary emotions. This, at least, is the story evolutionary psychology and cognitive science tell. All of the pressures considered up to this point have been external to the pressed organism. Some are now willing to argue that internal, psychological pressures may equally lead to a selection event. "The contents of human consciousness (rather than strictly external environmental forces), exerted selective pressure on the way the human mind evolved" (Pyszczynski et al. 2004, 453). One such content appears to be the awareness of death. T. Pyszczynski et al. write, "the recognition that we will all die some day, an idea that appears to correspond very well with the nature of reality, exerted selective pressures" (2004, 453). A. Varki similarly proposes that an unqualified awareness of death is terribly anxiogenic and thus would "be a dead-end evolutionary barrier, curbing activities and cognitive functions necessary for survival and reproductive fitness" (2009, 684). Such existential terror and the accompanying stress seem to be uniquely within the purview of the human animal today. Sapolsky notes that "it is not a general mammalian trait to become anxious about . . . the inevitability of death" (2004, 7). This may not have always been the case. Varki suggests that there may have been more than one species in history to have acquired the cognitive capacity and complexity requisite for existential terror. The reason there is seemingly only one such species remaining, he further proposes, is that these other species were incapable of deceiving themselves. "Many warm-blooded species may have previously achieved complete self-awareness and inter-subjectivity, but then failed to survive because of the extremely negative immediate consequences," Varki writes, "perhaps we should be looking for the mechanisms (or loss of mechanisms) that allow us to delude ourselves and others about reality" (2009, 684). Perhaps we should be looking for the mechanisms that enable religion's "vital lie" (Becker 1973, 51; Trivers 2011).

Religion's Vital Lies

Nomadic hunting-and-gathering was the subsistence technique throughout most of human history. This all changed some 12,000 years ago. After millennia spent as hunter-gatherers (HGs), our evolutionary forebears quickly became farmers. They settled down. What accounts for this transition? One might similarly be forgiven for suggesting that farming provided for a better quality of life. Such, however, does not appear to be the case, at least not at first. Farming was initially a more difficult form of subsistence technology. If comparisons can be drawn between today's HGs and those of a Pleistocene past, then it would indeed seem that farming was more burdensome. According to Sapolsky, "HGs typically work fewer hours for their daily bread than do traditional farmers and are longer-lived and healthier" (2017, 318). Why would our ancestors adopt subsistence technologies that led to an increase in hardships? What would have been the benefit that would offset such a cost? Some suggest that the first farmers were willing to put up with this increase in physical burden because agriculture was the by-product of a greater need to manage existential stress. This raises the provocative possibility that "early forms of terror management altered the course of human history" (Solomon et al. 2015, 63). In other words, the psychological immune system altered the course of human history. Religion altered the course of human history.

Located in southeastern Turkey, Gobekli Tepe (*c.* 10,000 BCE) is often regarded as the first coordinated, architectural achievement in material history. Predating both agriculture and the invention of the wheel, the site consists of seven, concentrically placed stone circles. Each circle contains limestone pillars—anywhere between 30 and 100 feet tall as well as between 10 and

20 tons—that are adorned with images of animals and insects. Archaeologists surmise that it would have taken perhaps 500 workers to produce and erect these pillars, quite an investment of material and human resources. It appears that there are no indications of human settlement or cultivation at the site. Rather, what are found are bodily remains—some of which appeared daubed with red ochre, itself a Paleolithic indication of symbolic behavior—and vulture wings. What is more, some of the bodily remains appear decapitated. According to K. Schmidt, a leading excavator at Gobekli Tepe, the site appears to present the remnants of a mortuary cult.

Close by Gobekli Tepe is Catalhoyuk, another evocative, archaeological site. Dating back approximately 9,000 years, Catalhoyuk equally presents evidence of a mortuary cult. Here too are found remnants of skull-less bodies and images of vultures. The two sites combined suggest that concerns with *systematically* addressing death and the dead *predate* the onset of agriculture. The sedentary living associated with agriculture may reflect the repercussions of the need, the desire to remain in proximity to a temple-like structure. Existential concerns, not subsistence ones, provided the original impetus for human settlement. S. Solomon et al. write, "living in and around monuments constructed for ritual and religious purposes may have encouraged people to learn to farm, which would not have occurred as readily if they continued to maintain a more nomadic lifestyle" (2015, 78). A. Norenzayan similarly notes, "If the builders and early worshippers of Gobekli Tepe were indeed hunter-gatherers, then we face the intriguing possibility that early forms of organized religious activity predated the agricultural revolution and the massive cultural transformations it ushered. . . . Gobekli Tepe suggests the idea that early stirrings to worship Big Gods motivated people to take up early forms of farming" (2013, 120). If this is correct, then it would overturn a long-standing hypothesis of how the human animal came to adopt a subsistence pattern different from hunting-and-gathering. "Scientists had previously assumed the march of human progress was based on procuring food: we evolved from hunter-gatherers into farmers, domesticating plants and animals along the way and then building towns and cities around our collective farms," Solomon et al. note, "the discovery of Gobekli Tepe cast [sic] doubt on this assumption, suggesting that the problem of death motivated architectural advances that had nothing to do with practical concerns" (2015, 77). The psychological dis-ease induced by the existential helminth, that is, "the worm at the core" (James 1961 [1902], 123), drove the human animal to switch from hunting-and-gathering to domesticated agriculture and eventually animal husbandry. As Schmidt puts it, "First came the temple, then came the city" (quoted in Solomon et al. 2015, 77).[5] We may thus surmise that insecure-anxious hunter-gatherers, fearing death, built the first temple.

Sapolsky (2004) argues that the two major chronic stressors are lack of control and the inability to predict. This may need emendation. The human animal's primary stressor is something over which we yield little-to-no control. It is, simultaneously, something we can actually predict with great accuracy. If we are being honest with ourselves, something against which Varki might counsel, we can predict with unparalleled confidence that we will all die. True, we may not be able to predict the precise hour of our deaths, but we know that that hour awaits us. This is what McGuire and Tiger call an "unexpected uncertainty." They write, "Unexpected uncertainty is about events when the outcome is known but its date is unknown—for example, the date and location of one's death" (2009, 134). Perhaps as early as three years of age (Solomon et al. 2015), we are "initiated into the great secret of our species: we will die and we know it" (Sapolsky 2004, 239). Anticipation of mortality, that is, unexpected uncertainty, is the primary, *chronic* stressor. "We activate a stress response," Sapolsky notes, "when thinking about mortality" (2017, 11). "These unsettling realizations conspired to render humans prone to debilitating terror that is not conducive to effective instrumental behavior," Solomon et al. write, "quivering masses of biological protoplasm bathing in their own dread-induced urine do not make efficient hunters or mates" (2010, 101). A sick mind is indeed incapable of maintaining healthy economies and families. Existential terror is a vital problem. It must be managed.

Terror management theory (TMT) proposes that death anxiety accounts for much of what motivates human behavior and the construction of culture. The terror of which the theory speaks is the terror of annihilation.[6] Annihilation is the wholesale end to an organism's existence. Unadorned awareness of future annihilation can be catastrophic, psychologically speaking, leading ultimately to behavioral paralysis. For any open system seeking to thwart the onset of entropy, behavioral paralysis is a fast track to termination. An inability to manage the stress attending existential awareness is for this reason maladaptive. Existential stress is a selection pressure.

Human animals must lie to themselves. They must do this in order to manage the chronic stress accompanying death awareness. Lies are often brainsoothing (McGuire and Tiger 2009). TMT proposes two primary means by which such management, such soothing occurs. First, and though not itself necessarily a lie, there is the need to maintain self-esteem. Employing language resonant with our larger discussion, Solomon et al. suggest that "self-esteem is a powerful *vaccine* against fear . . . our symbolic protection against death" (2015, 58, emphasis added). The vaccine that is self-esteem makes the individual feel significant (Pyszczynski et al. 2004). This significance is meant to offset the inevitable insignificance attending the realization that we exist but for only a few decades on a tiny planet in a backwater of a galaxy that is but one among billions. It would appear that our lives really do not matter in the long term (Stewart-Williams 2010). We would prefer that it be otherwise. The overwhelming majority of us want the purpose-driven life (Warren 2013). Finding purpose requires that we adopt, abide, and prop up a cultural worldview. Worldview construction and maintenance is the second means by which the human animal protests against the meaninglessness of events (Nilsson 1954). Here is where the vital lie comes into play.

TMT suggests that we create and perpetuate culture in order to invest our lives with meaning. Cultures, or worldviews, are sets of symbols concocted to allow insignificant creatures to feel significant. They outline roles to play in the larger, cultural drama. One feels valuable when one performs well according to a cultural script. Wholly constructed worldviews provide opportunities to feel good about oneself, that is, for enjoying high self-esteem. Worldviews can do this because they tend to "explain the nature of reality to ourselves—give us a sense of meaning, an account for the origin of the universe, a blueprint for valued conduct on earth, and the promise of immortality" (Solomon et al. 2015, 8). Here is the vital lie. Any worldview other than philosophical naturalism (Forrest 2000)—and its rather bleak repercussions for meaning and purpose—is most likely wholly made up, that is, wholly fictional. Worldviews are coherent sets of lies. This is the case because of the second law of thermodynamics. Meaning and purpose appear predicated on connections with a future moment (Sheffler 2016). The second law shows that there will come a time when there is no more future. There can be no ultimate meaning and purpose in such a universe as ours (Rosenberg 2011, 2018; Stewart-Williams 2010). TMT suggests that it is this reality that must be covered over. Our cultures do so cover.

Humans concoct a cultural veneer with which to cover over the brute facts of reality. We similarly entertain fantasies. Fantasy enables temporary escape. It would appear that there is one rather prominent theme in many fantasies throughout the world (Ogilvie 2003). "Flight fantasies are an archetypal example of humankind's imaginative construction of supernatural conceptions of reality in response to the awareness of, and unwillingness to accept, death" (Solomon et al. 2010, 99). From deities who ascend to flying superheroes with capes, the human animal is particularly fascinated with that which defies gravity and earth-boundedness (Cohen et al. 2011). The earth is, after all, the place of graves, the skies the heavens. TMT argues that humans use their self-esteem, worldviews, and fantasies as buffers against existential anxiety, to manage the chronic stress attending death awareness. "All systematizations of culture," E. Becker writes, "have in the end the same goal: to raise men above nature, to assure them that in some ways their lives count in the universe more than merely physical things count" (1975, 4). Not all systematizations of culture are equally effective.

TMT claims that human beings typically strive for immortality.[7] There are two types of immortality, symbolic and literal. Symbolic immortality pertains to the idea that we find some consolation in the face of death if we believe that what we have accomplished during our lifetimes will somehow be remembered by those who survive us. This is what drives us to write the great American novel, to discover the much-needed vaccine, to discover the theory of everything. TMT proposes that striving for symbolic immortality is the engine of progress, if there should be such. Symbolic immortality is enough for some to get them through the day, through life. Recent surveys document that it is not enough for most.

"Almost three quarters of Americans in the twenty-first century are confident that they possess an indestructible soul of some sort" (Solomon et al. 2015, 90). The same perhaps could be said for the world's population at large. The overwhelming majority of people do not want symbolic immortality. They covet literal immortality. People who long for literal immortality believe that there is some crucial aspect of themselves—perhaps the most crucial—that survives the death of the physical body. "Belief in a literal afterlife," T. Newton and D. N. McIntosh note, "enables people to feel significant and eternal, contributing to a subjective sense of meaning in life and potentially effectively warding off existential terror" (2013, 265). A. Damasio adds, "Immortality would eliminate the most powerful engine of feeling-driven homeostasis: the discovery that death is inevitable and the anguish that the discovery generates" (2018, 199). Chapter 2 showed how mind-body dualism is cognitively seductive. It is affectively seductive as well. Embracing "intellectual dishonesty" (Haack 2003, 306), most people simply do not want to die and as such adopt worldviews that pander to such desire. The project most suited to promoting the lie that is literal immortality has been, and remains, religion.

Religion tends to promote a set of false propositional claims (*pace* Oviedo 2016). The false propositional claims are vital lies (Becker 1973; Bulbulia 2006; Flanagan and Barack 2010; Stewart-Williams 2010). Vital lies are often adaptive. "The central point," K. E. Vail III et al. argue, "is that religion cannot be understood without acknowledging the role that it plays in helping people cope with death and deny the possibility that it entails the absolute end of life" (2010, 91). I. Yalom similarly notes, "Death anxiety is the mother of all religions, which, in one way or another, attempt to temper the anguish of our finitude" (2009, 5). Perhaps the progenitor of terror management theory itself, Otto Rank notes that "the soul was created in the big bang of an irresistible psychological force—our will to live forever—colliding with the immutable biological fact of death" (quoted in Solomon et al. 2015, 88). Once again employing language particularly relevant to this project, Vail III et al. write, "there may be no *antidote* to the human fear of death quite like religion" (2010, 85). J. Jong and J. Halberstadt conducted a systematic appraisal of thanatocentric theories of religion.[8] They concluded, "fear of death ... motivates religious belief in particular, by virtue of its association with literal immortality" (2016, 173). Even self-professed atheists make more rapid connections between words such as "real" and "God" when reminded of their death, a rapidity "which psychologists use as a measure of 'implicit' or unconscious religiosity" (Solomon et al. 2015, 88). If existential despair is a selection pressure, and if religion is uniquely positioned to mitigate such despair and the attending stress (Newton and McIntosh 2013), then perhaps religion is an adaptation after all. "Many evolutionary theorists view art and religion as superfluous by-products of other cognitive adaptations that have no adaptive significance or enduring value. This view is simply wrong," Solomon et al. assert, "these products ... were essential for early humans to cope with a uniquely human problem: the awareness of death" (2015, 80). M. Winkelman similarly observes, "Religion is well-noted for its ability to assist in coping, providing a collective process for engaging with our existential needs for security and our inevitable anxieties such as fear of death.... This poses a challenge to the view that religion is merely an evolutionary byproduct" (2010, 271). This surely puts a new spin on the notion of *Homo religiosus* (Eliade 1958).

There is a possibility that other species gained existential insight. There is a possibility that they, too, knew (*sapiens*). There is equally a possibility that they were unable to take the next vital step. They couldn't deny what they knew (Trivers 2011). They couldn't think otherwise. "Brains that think otherwise—brains that deny they are brains and believe instead that they are eternal souls," argues Stewart-Williams, "are brains that hold false beliefs about themselves" (2010, 150). Homo sapiens survived because they came to perceive themselves as *Homo religiosus*. They held false beliefs about themselves. The motivation for such beliefs and perceptions has an affective component.

Religion is in the business of facilitating economic and reproductive cooperation. It also promotes an effective public health policy. One often feels disgusted when confronted with those who threaten economic, reproductive, and public health cooperation. Disgust has yet another dimension. It attends the vital lie. D. G. White asserts, "transcending the human condition . . . seems to constitute the motor of every religious system" (2003, 99).[9] The human condition is the embodied condition. Existential terror may motivate us to abide the vital lie. Disgust motivates us to transcend the embodied condition.

The primary emotion of disgust was first selected as an infectious disease prophylaxis. It was eventually elaborated into an emotional reaction to our awareness of our embodiment, our animality (Haidt et al. 1994). The trouble with animals is that they die. No one denies that. It is for this reason that humans pretend to be something more (Stewart-Williams 2010). After all, if we are wholly animal, then we too shall die. Pretending to be immortal is one thing. Being reminded that we are mortal is another. That which so reminds disgusts us. This is animal-nature disgust. "Disgust is fundamentally about our awareness of our own death and our terror of it," argues R. Herz. "The emotion of disgust arose from our need to protect ourselves from triggers that remind us of this truth—such as our animalistic nature—and puts us in its harmful way—such as disease. Disease is a primary motivator of disgust, but it is not the psychological construct that controls it; our fear of death is" (2012, 130). Goldenberg et al. similarly note, "Disgust can be understood as the emotional protest against any reminder of our creatureliness, an affective assertion that says 'I am fundamentally better than that'" (2001, 429). For those who aspire to be more than what they are, that is, more than an animal destined for the grave, anything that contests such aspiration elicits disgust. The human animal appears uniquely incapable of simply being what it is because being what it is requires accepting the fact that animality is a terminal condition (Becker 1973). Life is a terminal condition. "The inevitability of aging and dying casts the longest shadow on human life" (Nesse and Williams 1996, 108). Terror management theorists draw attention to a particularly troubling aspect of animal-nature disgust. Humans are capable of finding sexual intercourse disgusting. This is a problem.

Sexual intercourse is of utmost importance to any animal's inclusive fitness. It can, all the same, be a source of great disgust, anxiety, and occasionally psychopathology for the human animal (de Jong and Peters 2009). Terror management researchers have persuasively demonstrated that sex is problematic in that it reminds us of our fundamental animality (Goldenberg et al. 1999, 2000, 2002). These reminders appear particularly troubling for those who score high on the neuroticism scale. Due to the "creaturely aspects of sex," "people scoring high in neuroticism," write C. R. Cox et al., "find physical sex troubling because it activates death-related thoughts" (2007, 497). S. P. Koleva et al. (2014) also note that those with insecure-anxious attachments are especially apt to find sex disgusting. If neuroticism is associated with the insecure-anxious attachment styles most prominent in the EEA, then mitigating efforts would have been all the more pressing. Humans must mitigate their animal-nature disgust concerning sexuality. Such mitigation takes place through notions of romantic love and soul mates. "Romantic love, like religion, is a vitally important human motive because it elevates us beyond our animal nature to an abstract spiritual plane of existence," Goldenberg et al. write, "we become soul mates with our beloved" (2000, 206–7). B. Hayden similarly notes that "many traditional religions recognize human intercourse as a sacred act that makes an important connection between the world we live in and sacred forces" (2003, 71). Even the sex manual, so-called, of India, Vatsyayana's *Kama Sutra*, is ultimately about subjecting the "bestial act" of sexual intercourse to a method. The *Kama Sutra* distinguishes pure animal sexuality from human sexuality, indirectly indicating that to submit to the uncontrolled former is to forfeit the methodical latter (Doniger and Kakar 2002).

The human animal lies to itself. It does this in order to mitigate the stress that attends the awareness of death. Among the many lies it might tell, religion's vital lies appear uniquely prepared to alleviate death anxiety. They do so by investing life with transcendent meaning and purpose, as well as encouraging fantasies about a better life beyond the grave. Religion's alleviative efforts are not exhausted by such fantastic beliefs and perceptions. Death anxiety is not the only debilitating stressor. Recall, the absence of control is another. The two things that appear to be the most uncontrollable, and thus unpredictable, are precisely disease and death. Self-aware, religious proclamations regarding God's power and sovereignty notwithstanding, perhaps another crucial benefit of religion rests with empowering the self. Religion often fosters an illusion that one has more control over an adverse situation than one in fact does. A. C. Kay et al. write, "Some of the enduring psychological power of religious conviction may derive from its capacity to promote both external and personal control, which together provide a powerful shield from the anxiety aroused by randomness, confusion, or uncertainty" (2010, 37). Religion can achieve this through its many ritualized behaviors (Boyer and Lienard 2006; Lienard and Boyer 2006). C. H. Legare and A. L. Souza note, "perceptions of the efficacy of ritualistic behavior are influenced by the desire to regain a sense of control" (2014, 157). Religion's vital lies thus includes not only a set of false propositional claims about meaning, purpose, and everlasting lives. They also include a set of behaviors oriented toward promoting adaptive illusions of control.

Gods and Devils, Worship And Exorcism

Chapter 2 presented a definition of religion. We considered that religion may be collectively sanctioned perceptions of socioeconomic intercourse with causally efficacious, non-natural agents. It is time to add some nuance. This is the case because the pantheon of non-natural agents, like natural ones, is not all of a piece. Friends and foes populate the natural and supernatural worlds alike. The intercourse between religious practitioners and gods is socioeconomic in nature. This is not the case with intercourse between practitioners and devils. The former counsels affiliative behaviors. The latter counsels disaffiliative ones. Herein rests the distinction between worship and exorcism.

Cognitive science of religion has, to date, focused its attention on the theory of mind and the intentional stance. Such focused attention has been purchased at the expense of the design stance. While the intentional stance can inform our perceptions of non-natural agents, it does not exhaust such perceptions. Some perceptions of non-natural agency are predicated on the design stance. The design stance operates under "the assumption that it (i.e., an object) has a certain design, predicts that it will behave *as it is designed to behave* under various circumstances" (Dennett 1989, 16–17). The intentional stance allows for a degree of uncertainty regarding the desired outcomes. The design stance expects certainty. This distinction between the intentional and design stances maps onto S. Atran's hypothesis that gods and devils are ultimately modeled on protectors and predators, that is, humans and animals. The intentional stance informs the affiliative behaviors and intentions of worship. The design stance often informs the disaffiliative behaviors and intentions of exorcism.[10] Socioeconomic intercourse and the design stance are incompatible. M. Milner, Jr. identifies the distinction: "The key point is that all human beings face contingency and moments of powerlessness, and they seek *techniques and alliances* that will make them less vulnerable" (Milner Jr. 1994, 165, emphasis added). The distinction between techniques and alliances reflects the distinction between the design and intentional stances. R. Horton identifies a similar distinction: "every man-to-god relationship can be assigned a place on the communion/manipulation dimension of variability" (1993, 41). Communions are alliances predicated on the intentional stance. Manipulations are techniques predicated on the design stance. Communions and manipulations are the practitioner's attempts to assert control.

The aim of deploying the intentional stance in worship is not simply to acknowledge the other's intentions for their own sake. Worship is social manipulation or, perhaps more acceptably stated, negotiation. "One can negotiate with intentional beings," note M. J. Young and M. W. Morris, "based on an understanding of their perceptions, goals, emotions, and actions" (2004, 222). Worship entails affiliating with an anthropomorphic, non-natural agent through the presentation of gifts and adoration. These are the means by which human agents not only ingratiate themselves to powerful, natural others, but similarly manipulate each other with manners. The devotee perceives that the deity will be flattered with such ministrations and will, *hopefully*, respond in kind. The sought response is often a protective alliance. Young and Morris point out, "The prototypical risk coping strategy within the intentional stance framework is petitioning divine intervention through prayer . . . making promises to the deity about changing one's own behavior for more immediate favorable outcomes" (2004, 223). Petitioning divine intervention through prayer is socioeconomic intercourse with causally efficacious, non-natural agents. As it is with any natural agent, so too is it with the non-natural one. "We can be sure in advance that no intentional interpretation of an individual will work to perfection" (Dennett 1989, 29). There is always the possibility that the other may have other intentions in mind.[11] "Much of what happens in worship is modeled after relations between people of unequal status," notes Milner Jr.. "Acceptance is rarely a forgone conclusion; one can be rejected" (1994, 172–3).[12]

The social contingency implicated in worship's intentional stance is mostly absent in exorcism. The social manipulations and alliances of worship (and some types of exorcism) are calibrated to persuade. The mechanical manipulations and techniques of many forms of exorcism are calibrated to manipulate, to compel (Cohen 2007). The non-natural agent engaged during exorcism is often modeled on an animal, not a human. Dennett notes, "Not just artifacts but also many biological objects (plants and *animals*, kidneys and hearts, stamens and pistils) behave in ways that can be predicted from the design stance" (1989, 17, emphasis added). Although animals may be seen as agents through the intentional stance (Barrett 2005), they can also be seen as designed objects. This is a ramification of folk biology. Attributing essences to species is in effect to attribute design. The same human animal that has the capacity to attribute agency to non-agential realities has the capacity to reduce agency. Employing a design stance, humans reduce the agency of nonhuman animals. One does not socially plead with animals to affect one type of behavior rather than another. One similarly does not socially plead with devils. This is seen primarily in the use of artifacts/tools in apotropaic rituals (Gibson 1986; Burkert 1996; Dwyer 2003). For instance, during Hindu *puja*, the priest will often wave a plate with a burning piece of camphor on it as well as make cacophonous noise with bells—especially during *arati*—to drive away the evil eye. The evil eye is a predator's eye (Ellis 2015). Similarly, smudge sticks are often used to clear rooms of evil spirits. The fire, smoke, and noise are not intended to persuade the unwanted agent to withdraw. They are in the service of *compelling* such withdrawal.

The apotropaic behaviors engaged during ritual are the same that the human animals' ancestors would have used in a distant past to drive away predators (Mayr 2001, 245; Rosenberg 2011, 127). To this day, hikers use "bear bells" on backpacks to scare away any objects looming in the distance, be they bears or boulders. In all such instances, it is/was understood that the mechanical manipulation of objects, that is, the technique will affect the desired result. J. Goodwin et al. observe in this regard, "Sacred objects used in exorcisms include holy water, crucifixes, candles, incense, holy scrolls or tablets, oil for anointing, holy swords, prayer books, and relics of the deity. These objects are believed to overpower and weaken the demon" (1990, 95). The use of objects and commands, not prayerful petitions, to overpower and weaken ultimately serves to compel rather than persuade. Addressing several traditions of exorcism, Goodwin et al. identify the compulsory technique: for Jewish exorcism, they write, "Finally, the spirit is *ordered to leave* through a particular place on the body"; for Christian exorcism, "Once the name and information is obtained, the evil spirit is *commanded* with authority to leave"; for Daoist exorcism, "the priest continually proclaims his deity's superior power, finally *using a ritual sword to threaten* the spirit . . . *commanding* it to free the possessed"; for Navajo exorcism, "the patient is given a concoction to drink to make him *vomit out* the enemy" (1990, 96, emphases added). These emphases on forcing, commanding, and compelling reflect the influence of the design stance. The implicit emphasis is on manipulating the non-natural agent not through socioeconomic persuasion but ultimately by mechanical compulsion. Like an engine rather than an agent, designed objects follow a set of inviolable processes. If one knows the process, one knows how to exact the outcome. My definition of religion thus needs emendation. Religion is either collectively sanctioned perceptions of socioeconomic intercourse with non-natural agents, or similarly sanctioned perceptions of mechanical manipulation of non-natural agents. Sapolsky was right. It depends on the type of non-natural agent in question.

Predatory devils are often driven away; protector gods are persuaded to stay.[13] Sometimes the non-natural agent can possess qualities of both devils and gods, in which case, there is a spectrum of non-natural agency. At one end we find the design stance and exorcism. At the other we find the intentional stance and worship. At its purest, the design stance informs magic and wholly insentient, *esoteric* processes. The magician perceives himself to be fully in control. Nothing is left to chance. The intentional stance, at its purest, informs Calvinism's theology of predestination, a theology in which the practitioner is wholly at the mercy of the powerful other. Most religious practitioners are neither magicians nor strict Calvinists. Religious practitioners, by definition, perceive themselves to be in communication with a non-natural agent, not a non-natural process. Similarly, most religious practitioners wish to exercise a modicum of control through their petitions to their non-natural agent. Calvin's god cannot be petitioned. One of the primary, psychological functions of religion is precisely to preserve some sense that one can exert a modicum of control over the deity and its responses, and this especially when all other outlets of control have been exhausted. Without an appeal to the gods in such times, one may just slip into a depression, the core etiology of which appears to be a pathological sense of lack of control. "The desire to combat uncertainty and maintain control," observe J. A. Whitson and A. D. Galinsky, "has long been considered a primary and fundamental motivating force in human life and one of the most important variables governing psychological well-being and physical health" (2008, 115; Laurin et al. 2008). "Healthy living" depends upon a modicum of "optimism, subjective well-being, resilience, meaning, hope, and spirituality/religiousness" (Salsman et al. 2005, 522).

There are two forms of perception of control, internal and external. The perception of internal control reflects the agent's belief that she can affect a desired outcome using her own resources. For instance, the student who studies for the next exam believes that her efforts will achieve the desire result, a passing grade. As previously noted, such stress would be perceived as a challenge. The perception of external control, on the other hand, reflects the agent's belief that his resources are insufficient to affect the desired outcome and so turns to another agent who appears capable of achieving the desired result. For instance, a homeowner may have difficulties with a pesky neighbor and realizes that he cannot affect his desired outcome and so turns to the police. In this instance, the stressor would be perceived, temporarily, as a threat. There are, of course, many times when the desired outcome appears to exceed what any agent can achieve either alone or with another's help. Such moments are truly aversive and stressful. In keeping with TMT, E. J. Langer notes, "perceived absence of the ability to control is *debilitating*" (1975, 326, emphasis added). Once again, a lie, or better yet, an illusion comes to the rescue.

In the face of life's antagonistic vicissitudes and contingencies, one may believe that one has control beyond objective probabilities. When the perception of control exceeds what is in fact objectively probable, it becomes an illusion (Langer 1975). L. B. Alloy and C. M. Clements write, "the *illusion of control* refers to a phenomenon whereby persons judge that they have control over outcomes that are, in fact, uncontrollable" (1992, 234). Illusions, by definition, cannot exert any actual control. Fortunately, that doesn't matter. The illusion provides the desired psychological benefits. "The *exercise* of control is not critical," Sapolsky notes, "rather, it is the *belief* that you have it" (2004, 261). G. Keinan refers to this phenomenon as the "motivation-control explanation, which posits that stress undermines individuals' sense of control and that resorting to superstitious behavior may provide a means of regaining control" (2002, 106). D. Eilam et al. similarly note, "The same purpose of gaining controllability and reducing unpredictability applies to superstitious behavior" (2011, 1003). While Langer and others refer monolithically to the "illusion of control," this is a mistake. There are in fact multiple illusions of control. In just the same way that there are realistic perceptions of internal and external control, so too are there are unrealistic perceptions of internal and external control. "Although researchers often refer to a global 'paranormal belief,'" note C. Watt et al., "this may be an oversimplification with references to the sense of control. . . . Some paranormal beliefs (e.g., belief in psi and witchcraft) suggest belief in one's ability to exert an influence over the world, whereas other beliefs (e.g., superstitious and traditional religious beliefs) seem more fatalistic and associated with a higher controlling force" (2007, 336). Although the fatalism about which Watt et al. write may constitute the theological core of Calvinism, most religious traditions, once again, do not embrace such an illusion of *exhaustive*, external control.[14] M. Zuckerman et al. note, "religiosity can also provide a sense of personal control by empowering believers directly through their personal relations with God" (2013, 342).

The illusion of internal control (IoIC) pertains to one's magical abilities. The illusion of external control (IoEC) pertains to the belief that there is a non-natural agent available to help in a time of need. This is the adaptive illusion at the heart of religion (Davies and Kirby 1985). "Religious beliefs and practices," notes H. G. Koenig, "can comfort those who are fearful or anxious and return a sense of control" (2008, 76). Religious practitioners perceive that they can swing their current situations in their favor by appealing, socio-economically, to a powerful, non-natural other. As it is with any socioeconomic petition of another, the return on investment is never guaranteed. Worship will always be a risky investment. It is precisely because it involves such risk that worship admits of socially manipulative elements. The devotee tries to affect the desired outcome by means of social persuasion. Although complete internal control is compromised—religion is not magic—the devotee all the same maintains a sense that his or her social appeals will affect the god's responses. Religion facilitates precisely in this way an illusion of *qualified*, internal control (IoQIC). Significantly for our larger discussion, the illusion is immunoenhancing. Reynaert et al. write, "The reason some patients are depressed and less immunocompetent, whereas others who are also depressed show no alterations in immunity, may lie in the degree of subjective control, i.e., in perceived control. Among depressed patients, those who develop a conviction that they have lost control are also those who have the most significantly decreased cellular immunity" (1995, 299).

The design stance and the intentional stance both afford perceptions of control. Often such perceptions are entirely realistic. However, in moments of chaos and confusion these perceptions may become illusions. These illusions are compensatory insofar as they encourage a belief in one's power to affect change either by appealing to paranormal abilities or socially available, non-natural agents (Zuckerman et al. 2013). Because these illusions restore a sense of potency, they are truly anxiolytic with respect to chronic stress and depression (Alvarado et al. 1995; Smith et al. 2003; Edmondson et al. 2008; Sanderson 2018). "Some perception-of-control styles, such as the illusion of control," note L. B. Alloy and C. M. Clements, "may decrease vulnerability to depression by reducing the likelihood of becoming discouraged or hopeless in the face of negative life events" (1992, 235). Objectively unwarranted confidence in one's potency can be psychologically adaptive. Perhaps it is better to indulge illusions of patterns and control in the face of life's harsh realities, especially the harsh reality of personal death. "Illusory pattern perception may not be entirely maladaptive," note Whitson and Galinsky, "if pattern perception helps an individual regain a sense of control, the very act of perceiving a pattern, even an illusory one, may be enough to soothe this aversive state, decreasing depression and learned helplessness, creating confidence, and increasing agency" (2008, 117). In the hostile EEA, illusory perceptions of patterns and control would have been a source of great hope, itself a natural anti-depressant. "Misconstruing the traumatic world as not hopelessly bad may reduce stress, fear, and malaise," J. Bulbulia suggests, "here salubrious religious illusions shield agents from the slings and arrows of existence by altering damaging (though accurate) assessments of the world" (2005, 89). Religious beliefs and rituals artificially inflate perceptions of control, and thus optimism and hope (Alloy and Clements 1992; Rammohan et al. 2002; Eilam et al. 2011). M. Zuckerman et al. succinctly conclude, "Religiosity provides compensatory control when an individual's personal control beliefs are undermined" (2013, 342). Religion is a manifestation of the psychological immune system.

Religion's vital lies and illusions of control indirectly contributed to the survival of the human animal. They did this by decreasing susceptibility to chronic stress and depression, increasing optimism and hope (itself immunoenhancing), all of which would forestall the contraction of disease, sexual dysfunction, and subfecundity. "Persons who tend to succumb to an illusion of control may be at decreased risk for depression after life stress," Alloy and Clements observe, "optimistic illusions, positive affect, and subjective and physical well-being may operate as a mutually interdependent, self-perpetuating adaptive system" (1992, 243). While the literature pertaining to terror management theory and positive illusions is robust, it has yet to draw the direct connection between simply feeling good about oneself and one's situation and interests in sexual intercourse. It is this link that ultimately accounts for the adaptiveness of religious lies and illusions of control. Religion indirectly served, and perhaps still serves as a certain aphrodisiac. Despite life's stressful vicissitudes and contingencies, the optimism and hope that religion's vital lies and illusions of control confer may just constitute the first steps back to the conjugal bed.

Religious worldviews are unique. They uniquely offer the hope for literal immortality, the longest-lasting vaccine against death anxiety. The problem, however, is that there is simply no good, empirical evidence or rational warrant for such a belief. No one has ever come back from the dead, despite Iron Age tales to the contrary.[15] How then might one maintain confidence in one's religion and thereby enjoy the anxiolytic effects of the vital lies and illusions of control? In the absence of empirical evidence and rational argument, the only thing left is consensus. Vital lies rely upon collective sanction. The nagging trouble for the literal immortality projects that we associate with religion is that we do not, in fact, have a collective sanction. No religion enjoys unanimous consent (Kitcher 2015). The religious other disagrees with us. The other is, yet again, a problem.

The Disgusting Other, Redux

The trouble with using symbolic constructions to mitigate death anxiety is that no symbol can ever truly convince us of its truth (Pyszczynski et al. 2003). A symbol cannot overcome the direct, material reality of embodiment. Insofar as it is a lie, and lies are not predicated on anything other than unsubstantiated claims, the only way to gain confidence in one's symbolic construction is to have other people agree with you. Goldenberg et al. note in this regard, "Because all worldviews are, to some extent, arbitrary humanly created social constructions, their perceived validity is tenuous and requires continuous validation from others" (2000, 201). And therein lies the rub. We need others to agree with us when we make claims regarding the truth value of our "necessary lie" (Solomon et al. 2015, 123). Disagreement, after all, sows doubt. Should one begin to doubt one's worldview, the terror and stress of meaninglessness, purposelessness, and death come rushing back in. Accordingly, one tends to keep company with those who in fact do share the same necessary lie. This is one of the psychological benefits of belonging to a religious tribe. Religious tribes promote consensus, that is, confidence in their immortality projects. Such confidence amounts to cognitive immunity. Unlike a biological vaccination that can truly ward off infectious agents, however, cognitive immunity is never failsafe. The possibility always remains that we will run into a persuasive, disagreeing other. What are we to do in such a situation?

There are two types of disagreement. The first type of disagreement is due to innocent ignorance. The other person simply has not been fortunate enough to have been informed of the one way, the one truth, and the one lie. Such an other is a viable candidate for proselytization and ultimately conversion. Once again using language particularly relevant to our larger discussion, Solomon et al. write, "studies show that proselytizing is prophylactic: if I learn that you have adopted my beliefs, I feel more confident of their validity and consequently don't worry so much about my own death" (2015, 134). The seemingly selfless missionary, who simply wants to share the good news that is his lie, is, in this regard, an existential narcissist. Of course, even missionaries can fail at their mission. Here is the second type of disagreement. Occasionally one comes across the willful ignorance, so-called, of the learned opponent. When one broaches the learned opponent, one is confronted with an opposition that is unwilling to cave. This opponent is as convinced of her lie as we are of ours. This is a problem.

One has a few options for managing the learned opponent. One option is to give up one's lie and adopt the other's. Sunk cost bias tends to dissuade us from this option (Kahneman 2011). If we've seriously invested time and energy into constructing and abiding our vital lie, and this perhaps all of our lives as Chapter 2 would have us believe, then we are most likely to double-down on our lie rather than simply give it up. An alternative strategy for dealing with the learned opponent is to dehumanize him. The dehumanized other is the disgusting other.

We saw in the previous chapter that people who behave differently from us offend our behavioral immune system and as such we find them disgusting. The same applies for our psychological immune system. Those ideas that conflict with our own disgust us. Yet again, this is not mere hyperbole. S. Harris et al. (2008) showed that the same regions of the brain that are responsible for responding to odors and tastes are similarly active when judging propositional claims. They write, "When compared with both belief and uncertainty, disbelief was associated in our study with bilateral activation of the anterior insula, a primary region for the sensation of taste.... This region, together with left frontal operculum (also active in the contrast disbelief—belief), appears to mediate negatively valanced feelings such as disgust" (2007, 145). Sapolsky similarly notes, "Being disgusted by another group's abstract beliefs isn't naturally the role of the insula, which evolved to care about disgusting tastes and smells. Us/Them markers provide the stepping stone" (2017, 398). R. S. Ritter and J. L. Preston (2011) performed a series of experiments that demonstrated a link between exposure to untoward ideas and a literal disgust response. For instance, they had Christian subjects write down passages either from the Qur'an or Richard Dawkins's *The God Delusion*. After performing this task, the subjects tended to rate a drink to be more disgusting than the control group. This effect did not occur, however, if the subjects were instructed to wash their hands after writing down the offending passages. Ritter and Preston also found that having test subjects entertain ideas that they found morally wrong, for example, incest, "activates areas of the brain associated with more primitive forms of disgust" (2011, 1225). They conclude, "moral impurities may *elicit* gustatory disgust" (2011, 1226), noting in particular, "contact with rejected religious beliefs elicits disgust" (2011, 1229). S. Blackmore makes a similar observation, "Disbelievers in life after death and researchers who pursue brain-based explanations are treated as *nasty* people who, if only they were nicer, would come to The Truth.... No one wants to share the beliefs of a *nasty* person" (1999, 181, emphases added). Dirty atheists, indeed.

Experiencing disgust is one reaction to an other who is recalcitrant in his beliefs. There is another, violence. If you are unwilling to accept my vision of reality, and such resistance causes me to doubt my immortality project, thereby eliciting my death anxiety, then I may just have to do away with you. Terror management theorists have shown that people will resort to violence when they cannot otherwise manage the threat issuing from the learned opponent. One's immortality may ultimately depend upon another's mortality. Otto Rank may not have been too far off the mark when he quipped, "The death fear of the ego is lessened by the killing, the sacrifice of the other" (quoted in Becker 1975, 108).[16] Empirical evidence bears this out.

It is unethical to ask test subjects to engage in physical attacks. No internal review board would ever sign off on such an experiment. Fortunately, a newspaper article crossed the desks of the terror management theorists that reported an incident in a diner in which an ex-convict served two police officers. Still bitter about having had to serve time, the ex-convict doused the police officers' meals with hot sauce. The theorists realized that that may be a way to test the willingness to hurt physically a learned opponent. Following their experimental protocol, the first step in assessing the hypothesis involved test subjects being subtly reminded of their deaths. This is what TMT refers to as a mortality salience induction. Then in the second step, they had the test subjects read an article that directly challenged and/or insulted their religion or worldview. In the final step, the experimental step, they had the test subjects administer hot sauce to the supposed author of the insulting piece under the auspices of assessing taste. The control group had not been induced with mortality salience nor had their worldview disputed. The control group administered just enough hot sauce for the other to have a sip. The experimental group administered an entire cup. The results supported the hypothesis. When people are reminded of their deaths and are faced with an intentional insult regarding their worldview, they will attack the source of the insult physically (McGregor et al. 1998). Solomon et al. conclude, "This was the first direct evidence that fear of death magnifies the desire to physically harm those who challenge and insult our beliefs" (Solomon et al. 2015, 145). They go on to contend that such aggression in defense of one's vital lie accounts for the majority of international conflicts. "The strange beliefs, values, customs, and even physical appearance of the others seem to affirm their wrong-mindedness and malevolent intent. Material disputes quickly escalate into cosmic battles of Good (us) versus Evil (them)," Solomon et al. argue, "rather than battling over trade routes or water rights, the individuals who do the actual killing and dying fight for the glory of Rome, to chase the infidels from the Holy Land, to rid the world of Jewish vermin, or to stop the malignant spread of Communism, capitalism, or Islam" (2015, 147). J. H. Turner et al. concur, "Religious conflicts tend to be particularly intense and violent because they are over more than material resources. They are also over beliefs and rituals by which people verify themselves as moral persons, and such moralization of people's worldviews is less subject to compromise" (2018, 223).

The psychological immune system protects us from existential stress. It can also lead to the violent eradication of that which would disturb our psychological homeostasis. In much the same way that the physiological immune system will destroy an unwanted pathogen or parasite (more on that in the next chapter), so too the psychological immune system appears prepared to destroy the source of cognitive pathogens. Physiological and cognitive immunity can both resort to curative violence.

We have now seen how religion manages to facilitate economic and reproductive cooperation. We noted that healthy economies and families require sound bodies and sound minds. Religion facilitates sound bodies by instituting purity and pollution codes intended to promote hygiene practices. These codes also serve to establish local hygiene tribes that are suspicious of parasitologically strange others. Religious tribalism is in the business of maintaining the geographies of immunocompetence. This chapter addressed how religion facilitates and maintains sound minds. It does this primarily by managing chronic stress. Managing chronic stress is essential if the human animal wishes not to fall victim to immunosuppression and subfecundity. Religion forestalls such psychological disease, especially the disease the human animal faces when contemplating its death, by telling fantastic lies about the afterlife and fostering illusions of control. Such lies and illusions are the stuff of the psychological immune system. Thus have we addressed up to this point the prophylactics of religion.

Religion cannot, of course, preclude in perpetuity the contraction of disease. Everyone eventually gets sick. It is therefore time to direct our attention to the strategies religion deploys to heal a sick individual and community. It is time to direct our focus toward the physiological immune system. Might religion facilitate the proper functioning of this, the third arm of the integrated immune system? There is reason to think so.

5

Religion's Curative Violence
The Physiological Immune System

Religion is a manifestation of both the behavioral and psychological immune systems. It facilitates prophylactic tribalism as well as prophylactic vital lies and illusions of control. All such prophylaxes contribute directly to health and inclusive fitness, the very reason animals behave in the first place. Of course, no prophylaxis is foolproof. Everyone eventually gets sick. Insofar as religion can protect prophylactically a locally adapted group from novel infections, and reduce prophylactically the existential stress directly linked to subfecundity, morbidity, and mortality, can it equally heal those who are sick? In other words, what role does religion play with regard to biologically based disease? Can religion facilitate the third arm of the integrated immune system, that is, the physiological immune system? This chapter pursues answers to these questions.

Many authors in the biology of religion propose that religion's primary function is to foster economic and reproductive cooperation. It does this through the deployment of costly and hard-to-fake signs of commitment. Such signs were meant to appear irrational. This is the case because the human animal is naturally a rational actor. Rational actors are selfish actors. Selfish actors make trouble for religious tribes. As we saw, they are often free riders. Free riders enjoy the benefits of collective action but pay none of the costs. Selfish actors are also often promiscuous riders. Promiscuous riders enjoy the reproductive success that comes from having multiple partners without having to invest resources in all of the progeny. To avoid the infiltration of the free and promiscuous riders, religions afford opportunities for the practitioner to demonstrate his willingness to cooperate. The demonstration is often either some form of bodily mutilation or the acquisition of biologically useless information. Truly, the costly-signaling theory of religion is both plausible and persuasive. It runs into a problem, however. "The costly signaling theory of religion does not explain why shamanistic religion should focus on healing" (Sosis and Alcorta 2003,

270). As the first religion (Winkelman 2010), and the one that quite possibly sets the blueprint for all future religions (McClenon 2006), shamanism's focus on healing requires an explanation that goes beyond costly-signaling theory's interests in forging cooperative economic and reproductive bonds.

Any final, biological explanation of religion will necessarily include costly-signaling theory. It will equally include ritual healing theory (McClenon 1997, 2002, 2006). The management of stress associated with each makes these theories appear analytically distinct. The induced stress associated with costly and hard-to-fake signs of commitment seems incompatible with the reduction of stress routinely associated with healing. "*Moral* religiosity will frequently ramp stress levels up to new thresholds, for often a stressful response to the gods functions precisely as the hard-to-fake signal that an audience seeks to evaluate," writes J. Bulbulia, "if rituals are stressful or anxiety provoking, the function of *moral* religiosity and *healing* religiosity will at least occasionally diverge" (2006, 108, emphases added). Healing religiosity apparently ought not to involve stressful and anxiety-provoking rituals. And yet, Bulbulia's proposed divergence runs afoul of the ethnographic and historic records. A stress-inducing ritual, for instance, a blood sacrifice, is precisely what the doctor, or better yet, the shaman often orders when a tribal member contracts an infection. Religion's curative violence thus presents a seemingly insoluble mystery. P. McNamara confesses, "ritual sacrifice remains a mystery to me—yet it is clearly fundamental to religion" (2009, 223). R. N. McCauley and G. Graham similarly note that "no plausible mechanism connects the sacrifice of a goat with recovery from illness" (2020, 142). Bulbulia likewise observes, "sacrificing livestock before statues and worshipping the sky are practices that seem *contrary* to effective health maintenance" (2006, 88). Something as clearly fundamental to ritual healing as blood sacrifice cannot remain a mystery.[1]

There are many explanations for religion's curative violence already on offer. None of them are satisfactory. They invoke non-natural entities as the reason for the practice and the efficacy of the results. The practitioners of blood sacrifice routinely claim that the blood offering appeases the angered deities or ancestors. The deities or ancestors are usually angry because of some moral transgression. They send disease to punish the guilty. This will not do. What we need is a natural explanation. This chapter provides one. It identifies the plausible mechanism. It answers M. Bloch's "simple but centrally relevant question: why does killing cattle cure people?" (1992, 31)

The discussion that follows unfolds over four sections. The first section addresses the third arm of the integrated immune system, the physiological immune system. The discussion then turns to shamanism, the tradition that initiated blood sacrifices. Shamanism appears to be the first religio-medical tradition humans adopted in their unending battle against infectious disease. To be sure, it is widely noted that "healing is the primary shamanic activity" (McClenon 2002, 158). The healing involved is characteristically associated with social, psychological, and psychosomatic disorders. Psychosomatic disorders are physical disorders the etiology of which is wholly psychological. There would seem to be, in this regard, "no conclusive evidence that shamanic treatment was effective against a biologically based disease" (McClenon 2002, 63). Perhaps falling just shy of being conclusive, there is reason to believe that blood sacrifice plays an effective role in the mitigation of biologically based diseases.

The discussion returns in the third section to a consideration of psychological distress. We will do this because most authors recognize that the shaman, as an indigenous psychotherapist, heals the psychologically troubled. This is often accomplished through the induction of altered states of consciousness. What often seems to be missing from most accounts of the psychologically troubled is an account of the etiology. In other words, why might so many be in need of the shaman's therapeutic assistance? As we will see, shamans and their patients often suffer precisely from attachment anxieties. Such anxieties may account for many of the shaman's ecstatic behaviors and fantastic claims. This is the case because attachment anxieties have been associated with schizotypy. The shaman is quite possibly schizotypal, if not in fact schizophrenic (Polemini and Reiss 2002; Crespi and Summers 2014).

The final section of the present chapter considers how shamans come to the aid of the biologically diseased. This will require returning to religion's management of stress. We saw in Chapters 2 and 3 how religion manages stress by occasionally inducing it. The induction of stress serves as a hard-to-fake sign of commitment as well as health. The previous chapter addressed how religion manages chronic stress by reducing it. Reducing chronic stress is immunoenhancing. What we will see here is that a ritually induced, acute-stress response can equally be immunoenhancing. Killing cattle actually cures people.

The Physiological Immune System

The discussion thus far has presumed the ubiquitous and persistent pressure of infectious disease on the human animal.[2] Others have done the same. N. D. Wolfe et al. similarly surmise that "human hunter/gatherer populations currently suffer, and *presumably* have suffered for millions of years, from infectious diseases similar or identical to diseases of other wild primate populations" (2007, 279, emphasis added). Some believe the presumption is mistaken. McClenon (2002), for instance, suggests that the hunter-gatherers of the Pleistocene did not suffer the robust infectious disease pressures associated with the early, agricultural communities (Neese and Williams 1996; Diamond 1997; Harari 2015). Perhaps Sapolsky's (2017) comment regarding the relatively leisurely lifestyle of contemporary hunter-gatherers applies to Paleolithic hunter-gatherers. They, too, may have been healthier and happier than the traditional farmer. Must we rest content with simple, yet possibly mistaken presumptions concerning the infectious disease burden of the environment of evolutionary adaptedness? No.

Empirical evidence for the Paleolithic disease burden can be hard to come by. Most infections affect soft tissues. Soft tissues do not fossilize. Paleolithic bodies thus present formidable obstacles for a proper autopsy and inventory of past infectious diseases. That said, some infections do leave their marks on hard tissues. Leprosy, for instance, scars bone (Robbins-Schug et al. 2013). "Surviving bone material of our distant hominid ancestors dating to over a million years ago," notes M. Singer, "shows evidence of infectious diseases" (2015, 20). Hard tissues witness to at least some infectious diseases in an ancestral past. Something else does so as well. Written into the human genome is the reality of the long-standing burden of infectious disease.

The human animal achieved anatomical modernity at least 100,000 years ago (Tooby and Cosmides 1990; Diamond 1997). Anatomical modernity reflects genomic modernity. The human genome has not changed dramatically in a hundred millenia. It is, in this regard, a record of the pressures from a Paleolithic past. Previous chapters have considered this record. We have seen how some of our genetically-coded, psychological modules reflect past selection pressures. Neurotypical humans possess a theory of mind (ToM), a hyperactive agency detection device (HADD), and a hyperactive pathogen detection device (HPDD). Our evolutionary forebears had to process correctly cues pertaining to the presence of agents and possibly infectious matter. There is yet another system for which there is coding in the genome that unmistakably attests to the robust selection pressure for which it was and remains an adaptation.

Many phenotypic traits are plastic. Plasticity reflects the differential interactions of genomes and environments (West-Eberhard 2003). Contributing directly to the range of such plasticity is allelic variation. Many phenotypic traits admit of inherent variability. For instance, and once again, while we all have genes that code for eyes, the color of the iris varies. There is a polymorphism for eye color. The system with the greatest polymorphism is the major histocompatibility complex, or MHC (Tooby 1982; Piertney and Oliver 2006).[3] The MHC is part of the physiological immune system. The MHC's pronounced polymorphism is a direct reflection of the robust threats issuing from innumerable infectious diseases over deep, evolutionary time. "The MHC is the most highly diversified part of the human genome and has been under very strong selection pressure throughout human development," writes P. Klenerman, "by maintaining a broad array of MHCs in a group, there is less chance of a pathogen overcoming the defences of an individual's or an entire population's immune system—the pathogen must tackle each person afresh" (2017, 40). The MHC polymorphism "is more frequent than expected by chance" and as such most likely reflects the "selective advantage under pathogen stress" (Wedekind and Furi 1997, 1471). "The many biochemical, physiological, and tissue-based adaptations of the human classical immune system," R. Thornhill and C. Fincher add, "are documents of past selection for traits that are defensive against parasites" (2014, 258). The human genome's complex coding for the physiological immune system attests to the fact that our evolutionary forebears had to survive repeated infections from an innumerable number of infectious diseases (Crawford 2007). Yet again, something else does so as well.

D. Dennett claimed in Chapter 2 that as soon as life gets started there is a need to differentiate between what is inside and what is outside. Living things need to be able to self-identify. How might such self-identification be achieved? Microbiologically. The ability to distinguish self from non-self is first achieved through the physiological immune system, and this even prior to birth (Cambell 1987, 825). "The vertebrate immune system," note D. J. Penn and W. K. Potts, "develops the ability to discriminate self/non-self (before birth) by randomly generating a wide diversity of T-cells with highly specific antigenic receptors and then eliminating and suppressing those that recognize self-antigens presented by MHC molecules" (1999, 150). The microbiological identification of self from non-self depends upon the MHC. R. M. Nesse and G. C. Williams liken the MHC to "a photo ID card" (1996, 40).

Sexual reproduction produces organisms with genetically distinct MHC signatures. It is this production that quite possibly accounts for the rather peculiar genetic sacrifice that is sexual reproduction. As previously noted, reproductive fitness is measured in the number of copies of one's genes that are present in future generations. Sexual reproduction only allows for half of one's genes to be passed on at any one time. This would seem to be rather maladaptive. Why did natural selection select for such a genetically prodigal process? Infectious disease (Tooby 1982; Ridley 1993; Hinde 1999).

Compared to their hosts, infectious microorganisms enjoy generation times on the order of "tens of millions" (Tooby 1982, 558). Such shortened generation time is the culprit for a persistent infection. Due to their rapid replication, infectious diseases can adapt to the host's immune system. They can achieve immunological occlusion. An infectious agent, once occluded, enjoys a most hearty environment in which to replicate. Some hosts may be able to withstand the demographic explosion of infectious microorganisms. The progeny of such hosts may not be so fortunate. Should progeny be genetically identical to the parent, the young organism's immune system will not be able to detect the immunologically occluded infection. This can be lethal. A survival advantage is gained should a species produce progeny the immune systems of which are genetically distinct from those of the parents. This is the ultimate explanation for the evolution of sexual reproduction. "Sex and recombination allow parents to diversify their offspring so that competitors, predators, and parasites cannot exploit a static competitor/prey/host genotype," N. D. Singh et al. note, "there is strong evidence that host species experiencing parasite-mediated selection pressures are more likely to evolve sexuality, increased outcrossing, and increased recombination rates" (2015, 747; Sommer 2005). Facilitating such genomic novelty, the proteins the MHC produces find their way into pheromones. Studies document female sexual preference for men whose body odors communicate MHC-dissimilarity (Wedekind and Furi 1997; Wedekind and Penn 2000). What is more, we noted in Chapter 2 that Dennett's claim about the selfish organism needed emendation. It is not a matter of me against the world. It is a matter of me and my kin against the world. The MHC similarly appears to be the source for kin altruism (Lewis 1998). The physiological immune system thus identifies both macroscopic and microscopic others. It facilitates cooperating with the former while eliminating the latter.[4]

There are two physiological immune system responses to the presence of an infectious agent. The first response is associated with what is called the innate or natural immune system. This system is found throughout the animal kingdom. Associated with inflammation, it responds to an infectious insult within seconds. The second physiological immune system response is associated with the adapted or special immune system, "the most complex of all cell-based systems of group identity" (Villarreal 2008, 49). This is a system found only in vertebrates (Damasio 2018). It can take up to a few days for it to initiate its response. It is, however, this system and its MHC proteins that enable an organism to remember its infectious disease history. Immunological memory enables a more rapid and effective response upon re-exposure to a pathogen. Vaccinations target the adapted immune system. Both systems achieve their goals through the work of a special type of blood cell.

There are two types of blood cell, the erythrocyte and the leukocyte. Erythrocytes, or more commonly, red blood cells, are the most common blood cell in the body. They are responsible for delivering oxygen from the lungs to the body's tissues and organs. These cells then return to the lungs carrying carbon dioxide which will be expelled through exhalation. The leukocytes, or, and again more commonly, white blood cells constitute one-third of the physiological immune system. The other two-thirds are the lymph organs, for instance, the thymus, lymph nodes, and spleen, and the lymphatics, the channels that contain lymph fluid. White blood cells come in two general types. One type develops in bone marrow and is called the myeloid (marrow) leukocyte. Myeloid leukocytes are also known as granulocytes or polymorphs. The three types of granulocyte are neutrophils, eosinophils, and basophils. The other type of white blood cell develops in the lymph organs and is called the lymphoid leukocyte. There are two types of lymphoid leukocyte, the monocytes and lymphocytes. Granulocytes (microphages) and monocytes (macrophages) are phagocytic cells that surround and consume invading organisms; they also dispose of dead cells and cellular debris. Phagocytic cells also secrete chemical messengers known as cytokines. Responsible for the inflammatory response, cytokines increase blood flow to an infected area, allowing thereby a greater number of leukocytes to arrive at the site of infection. Lymphocytes include T cells, B cells, and natural killer (NK) cells. Granulocytes, monocytes, and NK cells constitute the natural immune system. T and B cells constitute the adapted immune system.

There are two types of adapted immune system response. One type is cellular, the other humoral. The cellular response targets virally infected cells. T cells are primarily responsible for the cellular response. There are two types of T cell, T helper cells and T cytotoxic cells. Once an antigen has breached the body's first lines of defense and is recognized as "not-self," a macrophage presents it to a T helper cell along with the cytokine interleukin (IL) 1. IL-1 stimulates the activity of T helper cells. T helper cells secrete IL-2 which causes T helper cell proliferation. This proliferation then causes the proliferation of T cytotoxic killer cells which destroy directly the infectious agent.

The humoral response targets extracellular antigens, for instance, bacteria. B cells are primarily responsible for the humoral response. Like the cellular response, the humoral response begins with an encounter between the infectious agent and the macrophage. Also similar to the cellular response, the macrophage presents the infectious agent to T helper cells along with IL-1. In the humoral response, however, the proliferation of T helper cells leads to the secretion of B-cell growth factor. B-cell growth factor causes the proliferation of B cells. B cells make antibodies. Antibodies are a type of protein called immunoglobulin. There are five general types of immunoglobulin (Ig), that is A, E, M, G, and D. S. C. Segerstrom and G. E. Miller note, "Immunoglobulin (Ig) A is found in secretions, IgE binds to mast cells and is involved in allergy, IgM is a large molecule that clears antigen from the bloodstream, IgG is a smaller antibody that diffuses into tissue and crosses the placenta, and IgD is of unknown significance but may be produced by immature B cells" (2004, 602–3). Some suggest that IgE is associated primarily with allergies today because its original target is no longer terribly pressing, that is, helminthic infections (Nesse and Williams 1996; Klenerman 2017). IgG and IgM are also responsible for activating the set of blood proteins known as the complement system. The complement system involves proteins that can create a pore in the plasma membrane of an infectious agent, causing that agent to lyse, or break down. As components of the adapted immune system, the immunoglobulins can be spectacularly specific with respect to which antigen they target. Overall, "the body contains an incredible 3×10^9 lymphocytes," writes Crawford, "each with its own receptor that fits just one segment of a foreign protein" (2007, 26). The complexity of the physiological immune system truly reflects the robust diversity of infectious disease threats the human animal has faced, and continues to face, over its long, evolutionary trajectory.

We have now considered in some detail the behavioral, psychological, and physiological immune systems. We have also considered how religion is a manifestation of the former two. The time has come to turn our attention to the ways in which religion engages the physiological immune system. To do this, we will first turn to what some consider to be both the first religious tradition and the first medical tradition, shamanism.

Shamanism: The First Religious Tradition, the First Medical Tradition[5]

For most of human history, the healing arts have been inextricably tied to religion (McClenon 2002; McNamara 2009; Winkelman 2010). Even today, "when we observe foraging communities—glimpsing at our ancestral lifeways—we notice that a central focus of religious life has always been healing practice" (Bulbulia 2006, 91).⁶ When we observe foraging communities, we observe shamanism, or at least we do so 79 percent of the time (Peoples et al. 2016).⁷ Shamanism is the religion of hunter-gatherers. It is the religion that was developed and practised throughout the vast majority of human history and evolution. Shamanic activities may in fact have homologies among nonhuman primates, indicating thereby a deep evolutionary history. M. Winkelman, for instance, suggests that "the deeper evolutionary origins of the shamanic paradigm are derived from ancient hominin ritual capacities illustrated in the homologies of shamanic ritual with the maximal displays of chimpanzees . . . (e.g.) night-time community rituals involving drumming, emotional vocalizations, and upright displays/ dancing" (2011, 56), noting elsewhere, "they are genetically-based behaviors of the hominoid lineages" (2011, 58–9). Some propose that the shamanic paradigm reflects pan-human, biological design (McClenon 2002; Winkelman 2010). Accordingly, and "from the vantage point of cognitive architecture," Bulbulia notes, "it appears that there is only one human religion" (Bulbulia 2005, 72). Shamanism is "the primordial basis for religion" (Winkelman 2010, 58). It is "religion's earliest and most elementary form" (Sanderson 2018, 113). It is "the foundation for all later religious forms" (McClenon 2006, 150). To understand shamanism is to understand religion.

Shamanism involves perceptions, experiences, and practices based on animism (Peoples et al. 2016). Animism involves spirits that can inhabit sentient and insentient objects in this world as well as exist in realms beyond the physical. It is, in this regard, a dualistic system. It would seem that dualism underwrites virtually every religion.⁸ Some suggest that evidence of dualism can be found as early as 80,000 years ago with what appear to be intentional burials (McClenon 2002). The earliest evidence for shamanism, on the other hand, comes from Paleolithic cave art dating back at least 30,000 years (McClenon 2006). One image depicts a human body with a bird's head. This is significant because "flying ability plays an important role in many shamanistic traditions; often the 'first' shamans appeared as shape-shifting bird messengers" (Solomon et al. 2010, 100). B. Hayden also notes, "Flying to reach spirit realms is especially common, and therefore many shamans emphasize costume elements that represent feathers or birds or wings" (2003, 77). The previous chapter addressed the existential appeal of such flight fantasies. They appear particularly attractive to the existentially anxious. The Paleolithic image could depict a human in costume. Shamans are known to don theriomorphic costumes during ritual performances. There's an alternative interpretation. The image could represent an individual in an altered state of consciousness. For some, altered states of consciousness are essential to shamanic practice and healing (Winkelman 2010).[9]

Shamans interact with the spirits when experiencing an altered state of consciousness. The altered state is often a dissociative trance. Through such interaction, the shaman is able to solve problems. These problems can range from those pertaining to subsistence concerns (Hayden 2003) and the politico-legal (Lewis 1971) to the psychological and physiological (McClenon 2002; Winkelman 2010). Regarding subsistence, it is believed that shamans can divine where the game animals are, and thus assist the next hunting expedition. J. H. Turner et al. note that in some instances it is believed that the shaman must "travel in spirit to the Mother of the Sea, who out of anger keeps animals at bay" (2018, 168). It is also believed that on this journey to the Mother, the shaman must navigate his way past "dreadful monsters that hang around the edge of their reality" (Turner et al. 2018, 168). Occasionally, the shaman's job is to avoid being captured by monsters en route to appeasing an angered mother in order to wrest subsistence from her.

Concerning the politico-legal, shamans facilitate the reintegration of the free rider into the community. Shamans act in this way as arbiters between the aggrieved and the transgressor. "Shamans, in addition to their role as healers," note R. Sosis and C. Alcorta, "actively maintain social cohesion in their communities by solving disputes and easing tensions among conflicting parties" (2003, 271). Winkelman adds, "Shamanic therapies create . . . healing through confession, which relieves conflicts. . . . Confession is often followed by social forgiveness, which can reduce social stress and reestablish harmonious interpersonal relations" (2010, 207; Lewis 1971). Confession, to be sure, reestablishes the tit-for-tat reciprocity that is so essential to economic cooperation. Some game theorists have in fact identified *contrite* tit-for-tat as perhaps the evolutionarily stable strategy, or ESS (Boerlijst et al. 1997). With contrition, the aggrieved party need not follow the lead of the free rider, a behavior that has the capacity to spin out of control (Kumar 2017). Contrite tit-for-tat facultatively protects the cooperative tribe. Significantly for the present discussion, contrition rituals often involved an animal sacrifice (Girard 1977). Religion's curative violence thus attends not only the psychological immune system, as we saw toward the end of the previous chapter, but also the moral system as well. While such subsistence and economic problems needed shamanic attention, they will not occupy our attention any further here. Rather, attention will be paid to the shaman's role as healer of the psychologically and physiologically ill.

Shamans diagnose and treat the psychologically and physiologically sick individual and community using a host of techniques. The diagnosis is often achieved through dreams, either the shaman's or the patient's, and ecstatic states of consciousness. The former are especially prominent. "The activities and experiences of shamans are explicitly linked to dreams in many groups," Winkelman notes, "in some cultures shamans are explicitly thought to enter 'dreamtime'" (2010, 135). From a contemporary, medical perspective, dreams and ecstatic states are wholly unreliable diagnostics. Shamanic treatments, on the other hand, are not. Ranging from the prescription of herbal remedies to hypnosis, placebo, and collective, blood sacrifice, all but the last shamanic treatment continue to find a role in contemporary medicine.

Shamanic healing rituals routinely take place at night and often involve the donning of theriomorphic costumes, dancing, drumming, singing, and chanting. They can equally involve "stressors such as fasting, self-flagellation, and self-inflicted wounds; emotional manipulations, especially fear" (Winkelman 2010, 226). Through such behaviors, shamanic rituals induce altered states of consciousness. J. McClenon writes, "ritual may include sensory restriction or overload, fasting, ingesting drugs, repetitive movements, dancing, drumming, chanting, prayer, or prolonged postures—features inducing altered states of consciousness" (2006, 138). The induction happens for a few reasons. First, the ingestion of psychoactive substances induces hallucination. Shamanic hallucinations are directly related to communications with non-natural agents (Metzner 1998). Second, there appears to be a shift in autonomic nervous system functioning during ritual. This shift occurs when ritual behaviors beleaguer the sympathetic nervous system. As we saw in the previous chapter, the sympathetic nervous system is associated with the fight-or-flight stress response. After prolonged, ritual engagement, the system eventually shuts down, leading to parasympathetic dominance. The parasympathetic nervous system is associated with the reduction of stress, trance, and hypnosis. Third, the mind/brain is a system for processing incoming signals in order to produce the appropriate outgoing behaviors. The incoming and outgoing messages normally balance out, in which case the neuromatrix, so-called, enjoys homeostasis. However, should the incoming signals become overwhelming, the outgoing messages will cease. It is in moments of such cessation that an altered state of consciousness arises. A. Glucklich writes, "An extreme bombardment of incoming signals, in whatever sensory modality, can produce a virtual shutdown of outgoing signals, resulting in dissociative state, either trance or psychotic breakdowns" (2001, 58), noting elsewhere, "the loss of sense of self through self-hurting is based on the system's homeostatic properties (control toward balance)" (2001, 62). The opposite obtains as well. Should one forestall incoming signals, such as in certain types of meditation, the outgoing ones become more active, ultimately yielding to hallucination. In such instances, "the neuromatrix . . . overfires its output messages in the absence of stimulation from external sources (or temping feedback), and creates images—often fantastic or exaggerated—that may be experienced as real" (Glucklich 2001, 57). Altered states of consciousness appear essential to ritual healing because they are susceptible to suggestion.

Shamans are hypnotists (McClenon 2002).[10] From a combination of "hypo" and "gnosis," the hypnotic state is one in which the ratiocinative mind (gnosis) is taken offline (hypo), rendering the hypnotized often motionless (i.e., in trance) and most susceptible to suggestion. Those suffering psychological, psychosomatic, and even some physical disorders can find relief through hypnotic suggestion, "the main goal of *all* these [shamanic] techniques" (Hayden 2003, 66; Schumaker 1995). According to McClenon, "clinical studies indicate that hypnosis is particularly effective in alleviating pain, asthma, warts, headache, burns, bleeding, gastrointestinal disorders, skin disorders, insomnia, allergies, psychosomatic disorders, and minor psychological problems" (2006, 150). Winkelman also notes that hypnosis is good for treating "somatization, mild psychiatric disorders, simple gynecological conditions, gastrointestinal and respiratory disorders, self-limiting diseases, chronic pain, neurotic and hysterical conditions, and interpersonal, psychosocial, and cultural problems" (2010, 187). Under hypnotic suggestion, an individual can even control blood flow, including stoppage. "Because hunting accidents, wounds from warfare, and postpartum hemorrhage were probably major causes of mortality" (McClenon 2002, 56), this blood-stopping capability would have been a great advantage in the EEA. The capacity to direct blood flow can apparently target even cancerous growths, starving thereby the neoplasm of much-needed blood oxygen. Shaman-induced hypnosis can also facilitate sexual reproduction and childbirth.

Sexual intercourse, pregnancy, and childbirth are susceptible to a host of difficulties pertaining to coital ability, gestation, and parturition. All three are greatly compromised by stress. "Because psychopathologies influence rates of coital inability, conceptive failure, pregnancy loss, and infertility," McClenon writes, "shamanic/hypnotic treatments would be expected to affect fertility" (1997, 348). The expectation finds indirect confirmation in contemporary studies. For instance, in one study, 1,875 males were treated successfully with hypnosis for psychogenic impotency (McClenon 2002, 52). Likewise, among would-be mothers who have been trained in self-hypnosis techniques, for instance, Lamaze, there is a significant decrease in post-natal morbidity and mortality (McClenon 2002, 53). "This body of evidence," concludes McClenon, "supports the argument that spiritual healing techniques based on hypnotic processes can reduce the incidence of childbirth complications, thereby increasing survival rates of hominids" (2002, 55). It would appear that the capacity to undergo hypnosis was so adaptive that those genes that predispose the phenotype to hypnotic suggestion enjoyed a selection advantage (McClenon 1997, 2002).

Shamanic treatments are often efficacious because of hypnotic suggestions. This is not always the case, however. Some shamanic treatments may involve a certain conscious conspiracy. "Accepting the efficacy of shamanistic healing would have been particularly valuable to birthing mothers," write Sosis and Alcorta, "and thus would have directly contributed to reproductive success" (2003, 270). The efficacy of some shamanic treatments depends in part on the shaman's and patient's fully conscious expectation and acceptance of efficacy in advance. Shamans and their patients conspired for the sake of the placebo effect. A placebo is any "pharmacologically inactive substance that can have a therapeutic effect if administered to a patient who believes that he or she is receiving an effective treatment" (Bausell 2007, 30). Unlike the lack of conscious awareness during hypnotic suggestion, a placebo must be given to a recipient who is fully aware of the treatment. This is the case because a placebo is only effective if the patient wants and expects the treatment will work. If it is wholly believed to be something else, a sugar pill can do the trick.[11]

There are multiple ways one might elevate one's beliefs and expectations and thus facilitate greater success with a placebo. For instance, perhaps one has oneself recovered in the past due to shamanic treatment.[12] Similarly, if one sees others recovering due to similar treatment then the two—the treatment and the healing—begin to be correlated (Dwyer 2003). Witness enough such correlations and the two become associated through classical conditioning. R. B. Bausell notes, the "main precursors for a full-blown dose of the placebo effect" are "belief in the efficacy of the treatment, desire (or motivation) for relief, and classical conditioning" (2007, 52). Belief in the efficacy of the treatment can also be greatly enhanced if "the therapist appears authoritative, and uses powerful sounding techniques, and impressive, if incomprehensible, explanations" (Blackmore 1999, 186).[13] Shamans can appear quite authoritative.

Not everyone becomes a shaman. This role is saved for those who can overcome an "initiatory sickness" (Winkelman 2010, 113). "Mental instability" is often taken as a sign that the person is a candidate for the role of shaman (Hayden 2003, 51). This instability may find expression in initiatory "'dreams' in which the future shaman sees himself tortured and cut to pieces by demons and ghosts" (Eliade 1964, 377). In much the same way that a shaman's ecstatic journey is often beset on all sides by malevolent agents, so too does the future shaman have dreams in which he is attacked by demons and ghosts. Successfully managing the mental instability, especially through the use of ritually induced altered states of consciousness, establishes the individual as a shaman. From the time of restoration forward, the shaman has the power to enter into altered states of consciousness seemingly at will, or at least under the right ritual conditions. These altered states of consciousness, and the ecstatic behaviors often associated therewith, facilitate the healing of the sick. The shaman is, in this regard, a "wounded healer" (McClenon 2006, 141).

The shaman is equally a warrior. During trance states, the shaman travels into the spirit worlds. In the spirit world, the shaman is capable of acquiring strategic information as well as rescuing lost spirits, the latter often being the emic etiology for illness. Rescuing lost spirits is not an easy task. It often entails battles with malevolent spirits (Gibson 1986). "The military elements that are of great importance in certain types of Asian shamanism (lance, cuirass, bow, sword, etc.) are accounted for by the requirements of war against the demons, the true enemies of humanity," M. Eliade notes, "in a general way, it can be said that shamanism defends life, health, fertility, the world of 'light,' against death, diseases, sterility, disaster, and the world of 'darkness'" (1964, 508–9). Shamans are "antidemonic champions who fought spirits and disease" (Winkelman 2010, 47). Thus is the shaman's world, and by extension the shamanic community's world, populated with a host of non-natural agents committed to doing harm (Gibson 1986). The shaman's world is a demon-haunted one (Sagan 1997). The Buid, for instance, "view the cosmos as containing a hierarchy of predators," T. P. Gibson writes, "the higher up this hierarchy one goes, the more unpleasant and aggressive are the beings" (1986, 185). Elsewhere, he notes that "the spirit world is populated by a host of normally invisible beings, some of whom are men's allies, but most of whom are their predatory enemies" (Gibson 1986, 125). Shamanic communities understand that the shaman has to combat and ultimately control malevolent entities with his techniques. The shaman is, in this regard, "the master of anomaly and chaos" (Lewis 1971, 169).

As noted in the previous chapter, existential stress, and the survival disadvantages associated therewith, is directly tied to perceptions of loss of control. More often than not, the shaman does not lose control, even when faced with great odds. The shaman thus demonstrates to those around him that he is in control, even if the rest of the community is not. For some, this is his essential role. "The shaman's essential role in the defense of the psychic integrity of the community depends above all on this: men are sure that *one of them* is able to help them in the critical circumstances produced by the inhabitants of the invisible world," Eliade asserts, "it is consoling and comforting to know that a member of the community is able to *see* what is hidden and invisible to the rest and to bring back direct and reliable information from the supernatural worlds" (1964, 509). The shaman's anti-demonic violence is thus capable of curing the tribe of its anxieties and stress. "The spirit beliefs with which shamans work structure emotional life through affecting fears, stress, anxieties, and frustrations," Winkelman writes, "these emotional dynamics, which are contributary to disease, provide a general mechanism through which shamanic healing can enhance health through their reduction" (2010, 206). What is more, the shaman's ability to assert control, diagnose, and cure lends a certain sense of coherence to an otherwise chaotic world. Maintaining a sense of coherence, that is, "(a) confidence in the predictable, structured, and understandable nature of one's environment (comprehensibility); (b) belief in one's ability to successfully meet the demands of the environment (manageability); and (c) ability to interpret demands as meaningful challenges worthy of investment of energy (meaningfulness)" (Lutgendorf et al. 1999, 553), has an immunoenhancing effect. A sense of coherence in the face of life's stresses, such as a shamanic worldview affords, positively affects natural killer cell (NK) activity (Lutgendorf et al. 1999). Peoples et al. conclude, "as humans migrated out of Africa more than 60 kya . . . the shaman's curing skills and group rituals would have enhanced survival through physical and emotional healing, enforcement of group norms, and resource management" (2016, 275).

Let us pause and take stock of the aforementioned characteristics of shamanism. There is mental instability. There are psychological, psychosomatic, and physical ailments. There is dissociation, hypnosis, and placebo. There are fantasies concerning demons and malevolent spirits. There are fantasies concerning mother spirits from whom subsistence must be wrested. There is the significance of dreams. There are collective rituals involving the beleaguering of the body and mind. All of these factors constitute the world of shamanism, the world of our hunter-gatherer forebears, the world of religion. How might we account for such a world? By appealing to ontogeny.

Shamanism and Insecure-Anxious Attachments

The relevant literature is clear. Shamanic communities need someone to minister to their psychological and psychosomatic problems (we'll address the physiological problems in the next section) (McClenon 2002). It is symptomatic that the shamanic ritual often involves altered states of consciousness that incorporate fantastic struggles against predatory spirits. It is equally symptomatic that the shaman must appease spirits, often maternal ones, in order to wrest much-needed resources. Shamanic struggles look like insecure-anxious attachment struggles. As we saw in Chapter 3, insecure-anxious attachments have been directly tied to adaptive strategies for wresting provisions from an anxious and stressed parent. They have also been tied to predation anxieties. The supernatural fantasies associated with shamanism are to be expected. "Cultures characterized by 'rejecting' parenting styles," L. A. Kirkpatrick notes, "tend to believe in deities that are primarily malevolent toward man" (2005, 107). Recall, rejecting parenting styles involve "the absence or withdrawal of warmth and affection" (Rohner 1975, 45). As we also saw in Chapter 3, the pediatric style of childrearing, with its particular type of rejection, was adaptive in an ancestral past burdened with infectious disease. It nevertheless contributed to childhood trauma. A. Glucklich points out that the shaman's childhood trauma appears to reflect difficulties precisely with a parent "who withheld appropriate (ego nurturing) feedback" (2001, 103). Elsewhere, he notes that problems pertaining to the relationship with the parent include "neglect or overprotection" (2001, 124). These are the traumas associated with the pediatric style's rejection. To be sure, "deprivation to the ego is most severe when it is psychological, not directly painful to the body" (Glucklich 2001, 124). This is precisely what the ritual healing theory predicts.

> The ritual healing theory specifies that (1) childhood trauma and neglect should be positively correlated with dissociative/hypnotic capacity and frequency of anomalous experience, (2) groups claiming higher levels of anomalous experience should report higher rates of childhood trauma and neglect, (3) samples of psychic practitioners and spiritual healers should report more childhood trauma and neglect than general populations, and (4) anthropologists and sociologists who observe ritual healing will note that both spiritual practitioners and those benefitting from their treatments tend to report problems related to childhood stress and general anxiety. (McClenon 2006, 142)

Attachment trauma experienced in childhood accounts for many aspects of shamanism.

Winkelman consistently paints a picture of shamans and shamanic communities as those with insecure-anxious attachments. This is consistent with the pediatric childrearing practices most characteristic of a shamanic, hunter-gatherer past. Winkelman suggests that those disposed to trance and possession are addressing "a negative introject," that is, "a negative self-belief that the person has internalized" (2010, 220). It is "a critical self-perspective derived from internalization of an attitude from a significant other" (Winkelman 2010, 207). A negative introject is the negative self-IWM of the insecure-anxious attachment style (Kirkpatrick 2005). Addressing a negative introject often involves dissociation (McClenon 2006).

Dissociation refers to the psychological capacity to cordon off unwanted thoughts or memories from conscious awareness. It is one of the defense mechanisms of the psychological immune system. "A dominant hypothesis is that dissociation evolved as a mechanism to block awareness and memories in order to escape the intolerable stress of interpersonal situations," Winkelman writes, "for example, protecting one's self from extreme emotional stimulation and associated autonomic arousal and stress that comes from an attack or betrayal" (2010, 176). Glucklich similarly notes, "There is considerable—if not unanimous—agreement . . . that dissociation serve some defensive purpose, both preserving the adaptability of the organism under conditions of trauma by reducing stress and by maintaining minimal ego viability" (2001, 118). McClenon adds, "the incidence and severity of childhood trauma should be correlated with propensity for dissociation" (2006, 139). Dissociation protects the individual from memories of being emotionally rejected. "Dissociative people tend to become shamans" (McClenon 2006, 141).

Dissociative people experience "hysteria, conversion disorders, dissociative identity disorder, depersonalization, dissociative amnesia, hypnosis, OBE, trance possession, shamanic trance, and automatisms" (McClenon 2006, 141). Such dissociative phenomena characterize the "*shamanic syndrome*": "hypnotizability, dissociative ability, propensity for anomalous experience, fantasy proneness, temporal-lobe signs (measured by questionnaire items regarding unusual experiences associated with temporal lobe epilepsy), temporal lobe lability (measured by EEG), and thinness of cognitive boundaries" (McClenon 2002, 134). What is more, there is a positive association between insecure attachments, dissociation, and schizotypal phenotypes (Wilson and Costanzo 1996; Berry et al. 2007). Schizotypy often involves beliefs in special mental powers, magical thinking, superstitions, paranoia, apophenia, hallucination, and dissociation. "These symptoms," A. K. Willard and A. Norenzayan note, "will be positively related to over extensions of ToM measured by the cognitive biases related to supernatural belief (anthropomorphism and dualism)" (2017, 138–9). As Chapter 2 indicated, overextensions of theory of mind (ToM), anthropomorphism, and dualism are the building blocks of religion. These symptoms are found, to be sure, among both clinical *and* subclinical populations (Willard and Norenzayan 2017). Insecure-anxious attachments, dissociation, and schizotypy all reflect childhood trauma (Giesbrecht et al. 2007). The shaman's wound, his mental instability, is the psychological outcome of the pediatric style of childrearing.

Shamans minister to those suffering the symptoms associated with attachment-related traumas from childhood. Shamanic rituals afford compensations and reconstructions. "Shamanic journeying can heal these developmental traumas and reestablish contact with one's true self through 'power animals' that represent dissociated aspects of the self," Winkelman writes, "these power animal relations can nurture the traumatized aspects of the self and provide important *substitute attachment experiences*" (2010, 219, emphasis added). Through shamanic ritual, the traumatized self can remake itself. It allows one to reimagine one's attachments. "During the actual state of trance itself," Dwyer notes, "ritual participants claim to perceive changes in their physical-and-psychological condition (the phenomenal self), a process in which patients de-identify with pathological states of being and re-identify or reconstruct the self in accordance with positive feelings and conceptions"(2003, 112). Winkelman in fact likens shamanic practice to Catholic healing and possession, specifically noting that a relationship with Jesus "substitutes for absent or lost parental or spousal intimacy" (2010, 222). From the perspective of attachment theory, shamanic treatments are truly compensatory (Kirkpatrick 2005). "Shamanic ritual practices met humans' attachment needs, while using group ritual helped to fulfill fundamental human needs for belonging, comfort, and attachment to others," Winkelman concludes, "rituals integrate people, enhancing social support systems and group identity, facilitating health" (2011, 60; Baumeister and Leary 1995). Dwyer similarly notes that shamans can "engender a powerful feeling of support," noting elsewhere that "patients equally feel secure" (2003, 108).

The compensatory effects of shamanic ritual are related to the release of endogenous opioids. This is significant insofar as endogenous opioids are "implicated in mother-infant attachment; social attachment; (and) alleviating, mediating, and moderating separation distress" (Winkelman 2010, 226). They are also a natural analgesic with immunoenhancing effects. "The opioid neuropeptides," writes Winkelman, "are recognized for reduction pain, as well as for enhancing tolerance of stress, improving adaptation, and globally stimulating immune system functioning" (2010, 226). Elsewhere, he notes, "opioid release stimulates the immune system, producing a sense of euphoria, certainty and belongingness, enhancing coping skills and maintenance of bodily homeostasis, and enhancing stress tolerance and environmental adaptation" (2011, 60). Shamanic beliefs and behaviors thus provide not only compensation but healing as well. This was adaptive. J. Polimeni and J. P. Reiss suggest that "in hunting and gathering societies, individuals with schizophrenia-like symptoms may have been instrumental in initiating and maintaining spiritual ceremonies," (2002, 247), concluding, "religion appears to have meaningful connections to both shamanism and psychosis, thus supporting the notion that all three phenomena could have common origins" (2002, 245).

Altered states of consciousness are an essential aspect of shamanic healing. So are dreams. For most shamanic traditions, it is often thought that important, strategic information is imparted to the dreamer. This is a rather widespread phenomenon. "The divination of dreams," T. Smith notes, "is one of the most common, and most ancient, epistemic methods found in religion" (2019, 72). Throughout much of human history, religions have relied upon dream content for an epistemic advantage. This is especially telling because dreams are most significant for those with insecure-anxious attachments. It also appears that certain types of sleep experiences are associated with dissociation and schizotypy (Koffel and Watson 2009). What is more, and because the insecure-anxiously attached are prone to neuroticism and the attendant depression, all of which are immunosuppressing, it is not only telling that dreams are most significant for this group but that dreams take place during sleep.

A good night's rest is a wonderful thing. It is, all the same, quite peculiar. The peculiarity reflects the risks and lost opportunities associated with sleep. The greatest risk posed to a sleeping animal is predation. Without a wakeful, watchful companion, a sleeping animal is at great risk of being the victim of a predatory attack. Similarly, and from a life-history perspective, a sleeping animal is losing time that could perhaps be better spent on acquiring necessary resources, attracting mates, or raising young. B. T. Preston et al. thus note, "To outweigh these costs, the benefits of sleep must be substantial" (2009, 7). The substantial benefits of sleep are twofold.

The physiological immune system is one of the most calorically expensive systems in the body. This is one of the reasons natural selection selected the behavioral immune system. The behavioral immune system prophylactically protects the animal's limited reserves of calories by forestalling the contraction of disease, thereby allowing what little calories the animal does have to be allocated to other life-history tasks. When it is not allocating its caloric reserves to the life-history tasks pursued during waking hours, an animal enjoys the luxury of shunting that energy to the immune system during sleep. Studies indicate that animals that sleep longer enjoy a greater population of circulating leukocytes. What is more, when sleep deprived, an animal's antibody production in response to vaccination can be diminished by half. In this regard, sleep doesn't conserve energy (Berger and Phillips 1995). It spends it strategically (Schmidt 2014). Preston et al. conclude, "evolutionary increases in sleep are associated with increased investment in the immune system" (2009, 10), noting elsewhere, "our results are consistent with parasite resistance having played an important role in the evolution of sleep" (2009, 11). The function of sleep is to enhance an animal's parasite resistance. The function of dreams is to enhance an animal's predator resistance.

An animal has two prominent strategies for defending itself against predation. It can seek out proximity to a stronger, wiser other, that is, an attachment figure. It can also physically defend itself through fight-or-flight behaviors. Threat simulation theory proposes that dreams can improve both strategies. "The immune system has evolved to protect us from microscopic pathogens," notes A. Revonsuo, "whereas the dream-production system (along with a number of other systems) has evolved to protect us from dangerous macroscopic enemies and events in the environment" (2000, 895). How might dreams protect us from dangerous macroscopic enemies? By facilitating practice. Dreams present opportunities for an animal to rehearse threatening situations in a safe environment. Although the motor system is dampened during sleep, the cognitive processing of information continues as if nothing has changed. The brain does not differentiate between the dream scenario and a real one. Motor patterns in dreams are the same motor patterns in waking life. "Rehearsing threat-avoidance skills in the simulated environment of dreams," notes Revonsuo, "is likely to lead to improved performance in real threat-avoidance situations in exactly the same way as mental training and implicit learning have been shown to lead to improved performance in a wide variety of tasks" (2000, 891; Valli et al. 2005). For instance, most everyday dreams, as well as nightmares, tend to involve threats to the dream-self and those social others who are of reproductive value to the self. The dreamer also often engages in behaviors that are survival relevant. Unlike the recurrent dream that often involves fantastic scenarios, everyday dreams and nightmares realistically portray threatening events (Zadra et al. 2006). Dreaming is, in this regard, similar to pretend play. F. F. Steen and

S. A. Owens (2001) propose that common forms of play among children are equally geared toward honing skills in safe spaces. They write, "in pretend play, evolution has produced a suite of cognitive adaptations designed to make use of surplus resources in a safe environment to train strategies for dealing with dangerous or expensive situations that have not yet occurred" (2001, 292). As it is with dreams, so too with play, chase and evasion are over-represented themes. "Chase play is," Steen and Owens propose, "a form of pretend predation" (2001, 296). They further note that even when we are engaged in activities for the sheer pleasure of it, we are likely engaged in some form of learning. "Certain forms of popular and mass entertainment, such as theatrical performances and movies," they suggest, "appear to involve culturally elaborate forms of pretend play" (Steen and Owens 2001, 294). Might shamanic/religious rituals be such a theatrical performance as well? There is reason to believe so. Although often performed with great gravitas, shamanic ritual may be pretend play.

P. Boyer and P. Lienard have identified what they believe to be the stereotyped themes associated with ritualized behavior. These themes are captured by what they call the "Hazard-Precaution System" (Boyer and Lienard 2006, 595). This system identifies the hazards our evolutionary forebears would have had to negotiate as well as the precautions they could have taken in advance of a direct threat. The hazards include contagion and contamination (e.g., micropredation), intrusion (e.g., macropredation), social offense (e.g., risk of ostracism), and resource scarcity and depletion. These hazards are most pronounced for the insecure-anxiously attached. The precautions, on the other hand, include securing a habitat free of micro- and macropredators through washing and checking, scrupulosity to avoid social offense, and resource hoarding to avoid resource deprivation. As it is with dissociative phenomena, so too with the Hazard-Precaution System, both are related to childhood experiences. "Our model implies specific claims about the Hazard-Precaution system in children," Boyer and Lienard note, "early childhood is a period of calibration of the system" (2006, 607). The pediatric style of childrearing and its associated insecure-anxious attachments hyperactivates the Evolutionary Hazard-Precaution System.

Dreams, play, and ritual afford opportunities to rehearse survival strategies. They also afford opportunities to address attachment concerns. "Dreaming shapes daytime behaviors," McNamara et al. note, "through activation and processing of persistent attachment related themes in dream content" (2001, 125). McClenon (2002) notes that many paranormal dreams, so-called, include anxieties regarding the death of attachment figures. This is consistent with the threat simulation theory as well. The theory points out that the threats faced in dreams are toward the self and "people on whom the reproductive success of the dreamer is most dependent: close relatives and friends rather than people or physical resources only remotely related to the future success of the dreamer" (Zadra et al. 2006, 453). The "diagnosis" of schizotypal, insecure-anxious attachments in an ancestral past enjoys corroborating support from the fact that dream recall and intensity—phenomena associated with shamanism—are greatest among those whose attachment style is insecure anxious. "Participants who were classified as 'high' on the 'insecure attachment' scale were significantly more likely to (a) report a dream, (b) dream 'frequently,' and (c) evidence emotional intensity in their dreams as compared with participants who scored low on the insecure attachment scale," McNamara et al. write, "participants whose attachment style was classified as 'preoccupied' were significantly more likely to report a dream and tended to report dreams with higher mean number of words per dream as compared to participants classified as 'securely' attached or as 'avoidant' or as 'dismissing'" (2001, 125). The facultative benefits of sleep and dreams appear to be most utilized by the insecure-anxious, that is, by most shamanic communities, our first religious communities.

Shamans were the first to engage in "indigenous psychotherapy" (McClenon 2002, 52; Dwyer 2003). They were equally the first to take a shot at being physicians. The former treats a sick mind, and the psychosomatic troubles associated therewith. The latter treats a sick body. Shamans were the first to address systematically a biologically based disease. They did this in a few ways. As noted earlier, shamans employ hypnosis and the placebo effect. Both are effective against certain types of physical malady. Shamans also often prescribe certain herbal remedies (Winkelman 2010), a tactic shared by many species of animal (Hart 1990). Occasionally an herbal remedy will contain an actual, bioactive substance (Bulbulia 2006). Hart (2011), for instance, reports that evidence has been found of the presence of anti-inflammatory plants in what appears to be a 60,000-year-old cave. He similarly reports that a 5,300-year-old man was unearthed in the Italian Alps in 1991. The man had in his possession birch fungus, presumably an antibiotic or laxative. Animals, human and otherwise, have used herbal remedies for millennia.

The shamanic employment of herbal interventions, dissociative hypnosis, placebo effects, and immunoenhancing, endogenous opioid manipulation to address psychosomatic and physical maladies is widely attested and perhaps intuitive. In each case, the intended result was the reduction of the illness and the stress associated therewith. This was not always the case, however. Bulbulia draws attention to the issue that we must now address. Presuming the salubrious effects of hypnosis and placebo, he writes, "we also need to understand whether this explanation can generalize to cover the hard cases of religious expression—instances where religious practice appears to be deliberately risky or terrifying" (2006, 92), noting elsewhere, "terror is incompatible with stress reduction, this fact is frequently overlooked in discussions of religious healing" (2006, 104). Bulbulia implies, as might McCauley and Graham (2020) and McNamara (2009), that ritual healing theory cannot handle religion's stress-inducing rituals. "When we consider the costs that religion brings," Bulbulia observes, "many of them involve willing exposure to supplementary health risks . . . blood sacrifices . . . these are far from healthful modes of acting" (2006, 104). And yet, blood sacrifices are often performed precisely when someone in the tribe contracts a biologically based disease. How is it possible that killing cattle can cure people?

The Immunology of Curative Violence

Many ethnographic and historic accounts detail the use of a blood sacrifice when a member of the local community/tribe contracts a biologically based disease (Bloch 1992). The explanation for the illness often rests on the exacting nature of capricious, non-natural agents. It is widely held that the previous actions of the infected had offended the spirits, or ancestors. To atone for the offense, and thus be rid of the illness, a shaman would perform a blood sacrifice. Because an exhaustive documentation of such practices would clearly exceed what can be accomplished here, we will have to rest content with a consideration of five cases of religion's curative violence.

The Tamils of South India recognize a pantheon of deities. Within this pantheon resides Mariyamman. Although her associations are changing today, in the past she was closely linked with infectious disease, especially small pox (Egnor 1984). When someone came under her possession, that is, fell ill, the local community gathered to perform a blood sacrifice. W. Harmon describes one such sacrificial scene, "Dancing and frenetic physical and audible expressions typical of possession will characterize the person designated to perform the act of severing a goat's head, a cock's head, or, rarely, a water buffalo's head. . . . Male blood presented in an ecstatic context constitutes for her (i.e., Mariyamman) a form of appeasement" (2011, 192). Harmon also notes that "devotees emphasize her unpredictable, capricious nature" (2011, 186). Mariyamman's unpredictable, capricious nature likely corresponds with the behavior of pediatric parents who appear unpredictable and capricious to a young child.[14] Additionally, the goddess is unpredictable and capricious because infectious disease is equally unpredictable and capricious. "When capricious gods are present," W. W. Lambert notes, "there are significantly more frequent sacrifices" (1992, 228). Perhaps sharing the dismay of McCauley, Graham, McNamara, and Bulbulia, Harmon admits, "Strangely, when illness, physical affliction, and certain other misfortunes strike, earnestly performing rituals pleasing to Mariyamman can be the wisest and most effective recourse for healing" (2011, 193).

The Buid of the Philippines similarly perform blood sacrifices for sick members of their community (Gibson 1986). They see the controlled nature of the sacrifice as a means of driving off predatory spirits. "Sacrifices ... involve the controlled appropriation of animal vitality," Gibson writes. "They are performed when the vitality of men is under direct threat of appropriation by predatory spirits, and they are used to counter that threat. . . . The controlled release of that vitality is said to frighten the predatory spirits away" (1986, 157). The sacrificial act is both provocative and frightening. Gibson writes of one sacrificial ritual,

> The swinging of the pig . . . constitutes a controlled indication of animation which frightens the predatory spirits. The pig's throat was then cut where it hung above the children, its death struggles providing further cause for alarm to the evil spirits. . . . Next, two chickens were grasped by the legs and swung over the heads of the children. . . . The chickens were then bound to the floor by one leg and their throats cut. They were left to flutter freely about until they died. The medium said that by now all the evil spirits would be so thoroughly alarmed that they would be fleeing from the house in all directions. (1986, 158)

The evil spirits were likely not the only ones who were thoroughly alarmed.

Like the Buid and Tamils, the Wana of Indonesia take recourse to sacrificial rituals when sickness descends upon one of their members. J. M. Atkinson writes, "In Wana terms, one of these gifts—the chicken or chickens slaughtered in payment of the vow—is singled out explicitly as a sacrificial victim whose life is substituted for the patient's" (1989, 184). She recorded the following from a Wana shaman: "Three chickens I'm going to slaughter over the feet of that parent and child . . . That's what I am doing, cutting the neck of a chicken over their feet. . . . Surrogate for Joni's body, along with Neli's. That's what the chicken is. . . . Three chickens I cut" (1989, 184–6). Similar acts are performed by the Zinacantecos of southern Mexico. Descendants of the Maya, the Zinacantecos slaughter animals to effect a cure. Fabrega Jr. and Silver observed the following ritual healing ceremony:

Then he (i.e., the h'ilol/shaman) kills the k'esholil (i.e., sacrificial chicken) and tosses it onto the patient to see how it performs. If it performs well—that is, jumps around a lot while dying—the patient will get better. If the patient is going to live, the chicken's head will fall to the east; and if the patient is to die, the head will fall to the west. If the chicken's head falls to the west, the h'ilol turns it to the east and puts it next to the patient's head. . . . The chicken remains for one day [usually hung head down from a hook on the outside of the bed enclosure]. (1973, 185).

A similar diagnostic ritual is performed by the Azande of north-central Africa. Reynolds and Turner note, "by killing a chicken and seeing how it ran as it died, he [i.e., the shaman] interpreted how best to approach the problem, both socially and medicinally" (1995, 137). There are many more such accounts of blood sacrifice and healing in the ethnographic and historic records.

Different cultures on different continents have stumbled upon the use of curative violence. Until now, ethnographers and anthropologists alike have simply been unable to arrive at an explanation of why such practices are so widespread, and quite possibly persistent, depending on the level of medical care available. Equally confounding is the fact that many of these sacrificial practices required the presence of the local group. Gathering around a sick individual exposes the group to potential infection. This, according to Bulbulia, can only find an explanation in costly-signaling theory. "From a patient's vantage point, the gathering of the community is a hard-to-fake signal of support . . . because contact at such close quarters increases the risk of pathogen infection," he writes, "This is a costly signal of commitment to him or her" (2006, 112).[15] Perhaps that is the case. There is, however, another explanation.

Religion manages stress. It induces stress when it seeks to assess the trustworthiness or health of a would-be partner. It reduces the stress associated with existential and attachment anxieties. Bulbulia suggests the former is associated with moral religiosity, the latter with healing religiosity. The induction of stress is thought to be an antipathetic goal for a healing ritual. And yet, that is what blood sacrifice does. Why does killing cattle cure people? Because acute-stress inductions are immunoenhancing (Dhabhar 2018). Blood sacrifice is immunoenhancing. For this to happen, everyone attending the blood sacrifice should become acutely stressed. On this point, some have demurred. They have done so because of the seemingly routine nature of blood sacrifices in certain communities. Capricious deities, after all, require repeated sacrifices. Although anecdotal, I have routinely come across those, especially cultural anthropologists, who argue that one can become habituated to blood sacrifices such that they no longer have a stress-inducing capacity. They are wrong.

The habituation hypothesis places too much confidence in the central nervous system's ability to override the body's adaptive, *autonomic* reactions. Like the disgust response's ability to override cognition, so, too, can acute-stress override habituation. "From the point of view of the individual psyche, this sort of victim sacrifice must have had profound effects," McNamara observes, "it is *impossible* to observe the dismemberment of even a chicken or bird without some discomfort—*even for the most practiced of executioners*" (2009, 223, emphases added). The discomfort one feels when witnessing the dismemberment of even a chicken reflects the acute-stress induction. Corroborating evidence comes from a consideration of novice and experienced skydivers (Sapolsky 2004, 2017).

All novice skydivers show a stress response prior to and during a jump. This is not the case for the experienced. Experienced skydivers are generally stress-free *prior* to the jump. This all changes during the jump. Even the most experienced of divers show a stress response during the dive. If the analogy holds, then even the most seasoned of executioners, not to mention their audience, experience acute stress *during* the actual ritual. Perhaps even more troubling for those who wish to play the habituation card, it turns out that one doesn't even need to be consciously aware of the stimulus for an acute-stress response to be induced. "If an organism is anesthetized," Sapolsky notes, "it still gets a stress-response when a surgical incision is made" (2004, 254). Shamanic communities expose themselves to psychological stress when they perform blood sacrifices in much the same way that "some individuals deliberately expose themselves to a form of psychological stress, such as watching a horror movie" (Mian et al. 2003, 41). Observing the slaughter of cattle is psychologically stressful. Killing cattle is immunoenhancing.

Several studies demonstrate that acute stress potentiates the physiological immune system (Jonsdottir et al. 1997; Dhabhar 2002; Sapolsky 2004; Edwards et al. 2007; Dhabhar 2008; Sapolsky 2017; Dhabhar 2018). This applies to both the natural and the adapted systems (Dhabhar 2002). When experiencing acute stress, an organism's T cells, B cells, and monocytes are deployed to possible sites of infection—for instance the skin, oro-digestive tract, or urogenital tract—directly leading to a measurable decrease in blood leukocyte subpopulations (Dhabhar and McEwan 1996; Bowers et al. 2008, Dhabhar et al. 2012). F. Dhabhar believes that "the ability of short-term stress to induce changes in leukocyte distribution within different body compartments is perhaps one of the most under-appreciated effects of stress and stress hormones on the immune system" (2014, 197). Such distribution has been identified in a host of species, ranging from fish and hamsters to horses and primates, human and nonhuman (Dhabhar 2009). According to Dhabhar, "This suggests that the phenomenon of stress-induced leukocyte redistribution has a long evolutionary lineage, and has important functional significance" (2018, 178). The proposed functional significance of this preemptive redistribution is to prepare the organism for potential injury resulting from an agonistic encounter with another organism. Dhabhar believes natural selection would not select for an animal's exquisite fight-or-flight response, only to have that same animal perish due to infected wounds. Acute stress readies in this way the immune system for any potential insult.

There are two primary threats to an animal's health and thus inclusive fitness. An animal must be prepared for agonistic encounters with other animals. It must also be prepared to respond appropriately to the presence of pathogens and parasites. These threats induce two separate affective responses, fear and disgust. Both emotions are immunoenhancing.

Disgust motivates behavioral immune system responses such as withdrawal and avoidance. It similarly potentiates the physiological immune system (Schaller and Park 2011). Curtis and de Barra assert, "the disgust response is now known to be functionally integrated with the immune system, with disgust elicitation resulting in short-term pre-emptive immune upregulation" (2018, 2). Disgust is equally pyrogenic (Stevenson et al. 2011). Fever stimulates immune system activity. It also provides a hostile environment for further infectious disease replication. Acute stressors may thus be either terrifying or disgusting, and in the case of blood sacrifice, quite possibly both. Of course, the brain that dreams and plays is the same brain that registers a threatening or disgusting stimulus. A dreaming brain and a playing brain do not make distinctions between the simulation and reality. Neither does the blood-sacrificing brain. A brain that perceives a fictional, acute stressor is a brain that produces a bodily response as if the stressor was real. R. Mian et al. write,

> If the human mind cannot dissociate observation of fictional stressful situations from personal psychological experience, then the results have implications for anyone witnessing a stressful event. Witnessing a stressful event could well be sufficient to alter the number and activation state of circulating leukocytes. Indeed, the percentage of activated leukocytes remained high even though many of the other variables such as the number of circulating leukocytes . . . had returned to basal (prestress) levels. (2003, 46)

Merely perceiving a threatening or disgusting stimulus, whether fictional or otherwise, is enough to induce an acute-stress response and the accompanying upregulation of both the innate and adapted immune systems. Mian et al. observe elsewhere, "Watching a psychosocial stressful event that by definition has no objective effect on survival can thus affect immune reactivity" (2005, 65). The ancestral past was replete with actual stressors. The contemporary world is replete with fictional ones. The stress response cannot tell the difference.

In an ancestral past, the threat system would have been stimulated repeatedly by real stressors. This is no longer the case. In the present environment, and despite persistent dream content, we seldom find ourselves trying to flee and escape adverse situations. For most populations, lions, tigers, and bears are animals one might run into only at a zoo. We watch horror movies, instead (Mian et al. 2003, 2005). Valli and Revonsuo note, "horror movies, television, and other sources of fantasy and fiction, might, in the present environment, provide the threat simulation system with repeated, powerful perceptual stimulation associated with stronger negative emotions than everyday life events" (2006, 467). Sapolsky adds, "We activate the classical physiology of vigilance while watching a scary movie" (2017, 11). The brain that dreams is, of course, the same brain that watches scary movies. There is, all the same, a significant difference. Unlike dreams where the dream-self often fails to notice that the scenario, or dream, is wholly fictional, movie audiences know fully well that what is happening on the screen is totally detached from reality. Such conscious awareness *cannot* override the stress response. This incapacity attends not only stress responses to visual cues. Even hearing a stressful story is enough to induce an acute-stress response (Sapolsky 2004). Empirical evidence bears all of this out.

The acute-stress response that is associated with the activation of the threat simulation system induces a physiological immune system response. In one study, test subjects were assayed for immunological markers before and after viewing the horror film, *The Texas Chain Saw Massacre*. The results were as expected. Test subjects had clearly mounted an immune response to the movie (Mian et al. 2005). Similar results were found in a study in which test subjects watched an eleven-minute surgical video (Bosch et al. 2001). Schaller et al. (2010) also report a study in which test subjects mounted an immune response after watching a slideshow of disease-connoting images. Steptoe et al. (2001) observe that circulating cytokines appeared more elevated two hours after a stressor than forty-five minutes after. Perhaps to be expected from the foregoing, Herz (2012), Schaller et al. (2010), and Schaller and Park (2011) report studies that show how our immune systems initiate a response when we simply see someone who appears ill. "Mere visual perception of other people's disease symptoms," notes S. L. Neuberg et al., "causes perceivers' white blood cells to respond more aggressively to bacterial infection by producing greater quantities of the pro-inflammatory cytokine interleukin-6" (2011, 1047). This widespread ability to mount an immune response based upon mere visual and aural cues suggests that this would have been an adaptive advantage for our evolutionary forebears. Those incapable of such a perception-based activation would have succumbed to far more infections and the attending morbidity, subfecundity, and mortality (Schaller et al. 2010).

The acute-stress response is now considered to be "mother nature's endogenous adjuvant" (Dhabhar 2018, 180). From the Latin "adjuvare," meaning to help, adjuvants are often substances, organic or inorganic, that enhance the physiological immune system response (Klenerman 2017). For instance, dead cells release an adjuvant in order to stimulate the immune system to clear the debris (Rock et al. 2005). That is an instance of an endogenous adjuvant. External adjuvants are often added to vaccines to enhance the immunological response. K. M. Edwards et al. note,

> A common method of maximizing vaccine efficacy involves the use of adjuvants. Adjuvants act to increase the efficacy of the vaccine response by stimulating the innate immune system, which provides for a rapid response of the first line of defense against infection. Among the many effects of the innate response are a rapid burst of inflammatory cytokines and activation of antigen-presenting cells, which prepare the immune system for subsequent development of specific adaptive immune response to the vaccine. (2007, 154)

Dead cells and certain chemicals can act as adjuvants. Certain psychological states can similarly so act. Acute stress acts not only as an immunoenhancing stimulus for the innate immune system. It can equally contribute to enhanced long-term immunity through the adapted immune system. Vishwanathan et al. write, "acute stress increases the efficacy of critical processes that occur during a primary immune response. This may in turn increase immunologic memory formation resulting in subsequent immunoenhancement at the time of secondary antigen exposure" (2005, 1060). In one study, it was shown that acute stress experienced prior to vaccination led to an enhanced response upon re-exposure to the antigen nine months later (Dhabhar 2014). What is more, an acute-stress induction at the time of secondary exposure equally enhances the adapted response (Dhabhar 2009). "The neuroendocrine stress response," asserts Dhabhar, "is nature's adjuvant that could be *psychologically* and/or pharmacologically manipulated to safely increase vaccine efficacy" (2009, 225, emphasis added). Here is where the immune response to horror films, surgical videos, and slides with disgusting images suggests an interesting analogy with shamanic ritual. "The terrifying experiences enacted by the shaman" (Winkelman 2010, 226) psychologically manipulates the neuroendocrine stress response and as such acts as an adjuvant.

Shamans engage in ritual behaviors that induce an acute-stress response. If watching something get hacked to pieces on a movie screen can induce the stress response, being in the presence of an ecstatic shaman mutilating chickens over sick people's bodies would equally do the same. Paraphrasing McNamara, it is simply impossible to witness a blood sacrifice without some stress induction, and this even for the most seasoned shaman. Here is the mechanism about which McCauley and Graham (2020) remained doubtful. Here is the answer to Bulbulia's consternation concerning why a community would gather around a sick individual during a shamanic ritual. Being in close proximity to the sick does indeed run the risk of exposing oneself to the disease. Today, most people rightly try to stay as far away as possible from infected individuals. Such behavior, however, may not have been wise in an ancestral past. "Long before the recent advent of vaccines," Hart writes, "immunity to local pathogens in both animals and humans was acquired through exposure to potentially pathogenic organisms sufficient to evoke antibody production but in doses that did not cause disease," noting elsewhere, "prior to vaccines, any predisposition of humans to 'intentionally' expose vulnerable family or group members to small, immune-sensitizing doses of foreign pathogens . . . certainly would be expected" (2011, 3413). Gathering around a sick member of the tribe indeed exposes one to possible infection. That is the point.

Shamanic healing practices often resort to blood sacrifices and other stress-inducing behaviors. The shaman's induction of acute stress in not only the patient but in the community as well enhances the immune response of all. This enhanced response can either be directed toward novel exposure or secondary exposure. Either way, the acute-stress-induced enhancement facilitates healing in the sick individual as well as serving as a pre-pharmacological, indigenous vaccination opportunity for the tribe. If the sick individual presents with a novel infection, then a group that gathers around that individual and undergoes an acute-stress induction—the adjuvant—will in effect expose themselves to a low dose of the pathogen. Blood sacrifices were indigenous vaccination clinics. Facilitating further these indigenous vaccinations is the fact that a close-knit group of people can share emotional experiences. Studies indicate that if you see a loved one undergoing a stressful experience, you, too, will experience the stress. Known as the shared arousal hypothesis, such emotional contagion has been documented in mice, dogs, chimpanzees, and humans (Konvalinka et al. 2011). A shamanic community engaged in blood sacrifice potentiates a shared immunoenhancing response. The immunoenhancement which results from the acute-stress-inducing nature of horror and disgust, as found in a shaman's blood sacrifice, is the mechanism which to this point has eluded many. Killing cattle cures people.

We have now come to the end of our discussion of religion's positive role in mitigating the burdens of infectious disease threats. We have seen that the behavioral immune system is calibrated to forestall the transmission and contraction of infectious disease by encouraging highly conservative, social behaviors, the behaviors associated with traditional religions. These behaviors include the beliefs and values of tribal living. Tribal living is living collectively. We saw that the collectivist adult is most likely characterized as being insecure-anxiously attached. This is the case because of the predominant mode of childrearing in robust infectious disease ecologies, that is, the pediatric style. Recalling that that particular style would seem to be characterized by low emotional investment, we can now add that "individuals with low social support . . . may mount a more robust immunological stress response" (Dhabhar 2014, 200). Truly, no one need be conscious of all the facultative aspects of their behavior.

We have also seen that part of religion's attempt to mitigate disease threat is through abiding vital lies and illusions of control. Because chronic stress is associated with hypervigilance toward threats, a characteristic most common to the insecure anxious, religion would have needed to combat such stress. Religion reduces chronic, existential stress through stories and fantasies about lives everlasting. Equally, religion creates perceptions of control when in reality there is none. The perception of control can either relate to one's own abilities or to the abilities of another. The shaman was one such other. Fostering illusions of control, the shaman was/is able to reduce the tribe's chronic stress and the associated morbidity and subfecundity. Additionally, through dissociated states, states most associated with schizotypal, insecure-anxious attachments, shamans are able to minister to those with attachment needs. Religion is indeed a manifestation of the psychological immune system.

Finally, this chapter demonstrated how religion manipulates the acute-stress response in order to potentiate the physiological immune system. Shamanic traditions do so through the use of terrifying, not to mention, disgusting rituals, that is, blood sacrifices. Such sacrifices help heal the sick. It equally affords an indigenous vaccination clinic for the healthy. The shaman was/is an indigenous psychotherapist and physician. Although our focus in this chapter has been on shamanism, it should be noted that the shaman is not alone when it comes to such ministrations. We find similar stress-inducing rituals among Catholic priests and revival-tent healers. They equally induce acute stress as they ecstatically shout and command that the evil spirits are to depart from the possessed, from the sick. Healing religiosity involves both reductions and inductions of stress. Religion's violence cures.

It is now time to turn to our final substantive discussion. As is the case with all discussions pertaining to immunology, we must now address autoimmunity. We must address those moments when religion becomes the infection. In a world of advanced medical and subsistence technologies, it is possible that religions "now persist as auto-immune diseases" (Wiebe 2016, 62).

6

At War with the Body

When Religion Becomes the Infection

Over the past four chapters, we have considered how certain religious perceptions, behaviors, and experiences contribute to the human animal's pursuit and maintenance of its inclusive fitness. We've seen how religion facilitates vital, extra-genetic cooperation and fair exchange, both economic and reproductive. We've also seen the various ways religion keeps the mind and body healthy through the facilitation of the integrated immune system, that is, the behavioral, psychological, and physiological immune systems. It is only fitting that we turn now, in this final, substantive chapter, to the problems arising from autoimmunity.

Most considerations of autoimmunity have dealt with the problems attending the physiological immune system. Autoimmune disorders typically arise when the physiological immune system targets for destruction healthy tissues and organs in the body (Cohen and Herbert 1996). What was once rightly perceived as safe is now incorrectly perceived as dangerous (Matzinger 2002). Autoimmune disorders can similarly affect the other two branches of the integrated immune system. This chapter will consider those moments when religious perceptions and beliefs lead the practitioner to inflict physical harm on herself. It will also consider those moments when religion leads someone to inflict harm on their progeny and occasionally on others. Religion possesses the capacity to threaten inclusive fitness, a capacity it would seem no other species of animal suffers.[1] "Religious belief and practice is very often unhealthy, for it exposes agents to risk, harm, opportunity cost, disease, and, in some instances, early death and celibacy," J. Bulbulia observes, "such effects are not healthful to individuals and their germ lines, and selection should have weeded them out" (2006, 114). That natural selection has not so weeded suggests that there must be something other than genes motivating such self-destructive behaviors. As we will see in what follows, religion occasionally becomes a memetic infection.

The chapter first addresses memetics. Memetics attempts to account for cultural evolution (Dawkins 1976; Dennett 1991; Blackmore 1999; Bloch 2001; Aunger 2002; Richerson and Boyd 2005; Boudry and Hofhuis 2018; Stewart-Williams 2018). Like genes, memes compete with one another for the resources necessary for their replication. This resource has primarily been the human brain (Dennett 1991, 1995). Human animals are cyborgs in this regard, that is, part gene machine, part meme machine (Blackmore 1999). Also like genes, some memes simply outcompete other memes in their replication. Prolific memes generally tend to be those that promote the inclusive fitness interests of their host. Memes and genes often work toward a common, adaptive goal. They are often mutualistic. This is not always the case. Genes are not the only selfish replicators. Memes, too, are selfish. The meme's interests will not only occasionally conflict with the gene's interests, but they may actually override the latter. Cultures that promote the meme's interests to the detriment of the gene's interests are usually the ones that end up collapsing (Diamond 2015). An infectious gene can lead to the destruction of the host. An infectious meme can be equally destructive.

Memetics is largely an issue of cognition. There is, however, more to the meme machine than cognition. Affect is never far behind. Following a consideration of memetics, the chapter returns to a topic first addressed in Chapter 4. It returns to animal-nature disgust. As we saw previously, reminders of our animality disgust us. This is the case because we know that all animals are destined to die, a fate we wish not for ourselves. As noted in Chapter 4, animal-nature disgust often motivates us to engage in self-deception. It motivates us to adopt a religious worldview. The standard content of this worldview is dualism. Although philosophically problematic, dualism—religious or otherwise—promotes a worldview in which there is an essential difference between the mind/soul/spirit and the brain/body/matter. Bodies die and decay. They can thus arouse our animal-nature disgust. Souls do not die and decay. No one feels disgusted by the idea of a soul. Fortunately for the body and its genetic interests, most of those who adopt such religious worldviews abide détente dualism. Détente dualism encourages a certain rapprochement between body and soul. This type of dualism is not the subject matter of the present chapter. Militant dualism is.

Some religious practitioners are dissatisfied with détente dualism. The body remains too threatening. In such instances, recognition must cede to dominion. Militant dualism encourages the violent performance of the mind over matter. It encourages "hurting the body for the sake of the soul" (Glucklich 2001). Performing the mind's dominion over the body often involves intentionally insulting the body and its naturally selected interests. The ultimate of such insults is suicide. Militant dualism occasionally becomes suicidal dualism. "In certain instances, suicide is part of a culturally approved script," S. Solomon et al. note, "devoutly religious people sometimes book their own passage from a transient earthly existence to a heavenly afterlife" (2015, 202). Most militant dualists do not take the war with the body to such an extreme. Rather, they engage in behaviors that a genetically determined organism never would, never could. From refusing vaccinations to consuming pathogen-rich exuviae, memetic infections offend their hosts' genetic interests. There is perhaps no better manifestation of the memetic infection than we find in *classical* Hindu Yoga and Tantra, topics for the final section of this chapter.

Memetics

The scientific image is correct. Humans are animals. We do not possess souls (Flanagan 2002). Though deflationary, this truth does not preclude the fact that humans are quite distinctive in one respect. Humans possess the capacities and motivations for complex culture (Dennett 1995). The complexity distinguishes human culture from the rudiments of culture we might perceive in other species. We can thank our capacity for language for this grand distinction (Pennock 1999; Bering 2011). Language uniquely facilitates the rapid communication and accumulation of information. It is the premium medium of the cognitive niche (see Chapter 2). As "a collection of ideas, beliefs, and values that can be abstracted from individuals and considered as a pool of information at the population level" (Aunger 2002, 30), culture is a collection of memes.

Richard Dawkins (1976) was the first to propose the concept of the meme.[2] Derived from the Greek *mimeme*, meaning to imitate, a meme is a unit of information capable of being replicated, that is, imitated with both a modicum of fidelity and differential fecundity. What happens to a culture's pool of memes over time is similar to what happens to the genes of a population over time. The same Darwinian algorithm applies. Memes evolve. Cultures evolve (Aunger 2002; Richerson and Boyd 2006). Some have their doubts.

Some have questioned the reality of the meme. Difficulties arise for memetics when it comes to determining precisely what a meme is. Similarly, doubts arise regarding where one meme ends and another begins. Although self-described as being well-disposed to the idea, M. Bloch contends, "The memeticist must believe that there ultimately *are* discrete memes on which natural selection acts, whether these form clusters or not. In reality, culture simply does not normally divide up into naturally discernible bits" (2001, 194). Bloch adopts here a certain holism seemingly hostile to memetics. Aunger's suggestion that culture is *a* pool of information is similarly holistic. Does cultural holism upend memetics? I don't believe so.

Culture may not divide cleanly at the joints in the way genes do. We can, all the same, isolate parts of culture from one another. For instance, who would want to debate the claim that subsistence ideas and practices are distinct from aesthetic ideas and values? How one farms in all likelihood does not inform how one dances.[3] The pool of information that is *a* culture is composed of any number of smaller pools. How discrete a pool is depends on one's interests. One could be interested in religion as such. One could be interested in Hinduism only. One could be interested in yoga and tantra, as we will be shortly. In other words, there is good reason to believe that one can isolate certain elements of a culture from other of its elements. What is more, any one culture necessarily admits of having various, and sometimes competing, pools of ideas, beliefs, and values. Republicans and democrats in the United States belong to the same American culture, despite their often mutual exclusivity. In this regard, I believe we would be right to beware *"the philosopher's trap"* (Stewart-Williams 2018, 294). The trap pertains to getting so hung up with problems of precise definition and delimitation that one never starts getting any work done.[4] We can thus follow the behavioral ecologists. Recall, behavioral ecologists run the phenotypic and behavioral gambits: they study phenotypes and behaviors without being caught up with their precise genetic and neural bases, respectively (Nettle et al. 2013). This chapter runs "the memetic gambit." This gambit is willing to argue that there is socially transmitted information inducive of imitative beliefs and behaviors even if we cannot precisely identify the substrate or exact dimensions of such transmission. The memetic gambit follows in this way M. Boudry and S. Hofhuis's counsel. "We . . . sidestep fruitless debates over the ontological status or physical substrate of memes, or other cultural units," they argue, "some measure of pragmatism and tolerance for fuzziness is called for here" (2018, 157). S. Blackmore seemingly concurs, "As long as . . . information can be copied by a process we may broadly call 'imitation,' then it counts as a meme" (1999, 66).

Memes were late to the game of life. They had to await the evolution of an animal that possessed the capacity to learn by imitating. They had to await the evolution of an animal that possessed a theory of mind. Memes had to await the neuroanatomically modern, human animal. In order to imitate what another is doing, one has to be able to take his perspective on the matter to understand what is being done (Blackmore 1999). The meme's original environment of evolutionary adaptedness was the human brain (Dennett 1995). In other words, the human brain was the meme's original niche. This niche presented an immediate selection pressure. Because memes are replicators, the lifetime of any one particular brain placed a limit on the meme's longevity. Memetic replication and differential fecundity thus selected for memes that encouraged their host to engage in behaviors that would facilitate their transmission and reception from one brain to the next. "Memetic lineages" (Aunger 2002, 244) radically depend on their extended phenotypes. "The proximate, or first-order, memetic phenotype would be the neural spike," R. Aunger proposes, "the 'extended' phenotype of a meme, then, would be the *result* of the spike, such as host behavior ... that goes about its business *outside* the host body" (2002, 239). A. Rosenberg similarly notes, "People are the environments in which [memetic] strategies are selected for, owing to whether their effects on people who play them and on whom they are played by others effect the probability or frequency with which they are copied or not copied.... A bit of strategic behavior is the meme's 'phenotypic' effect" (2017, 360). For these reasons, the emergence of memes changed the environment of evolutionary adaptedness for the human animal. "Once imitation evolved and memes appeared," Blackmore writes, "the memes changed the environment in which genes were selected and so forced them to provide better and better meme-spreading apparatus" (1999, 93). The selective advantage of being able to share memes produced what is known as the Baldwin Effect.

The Baldwin Effect describes the moment when an organism can learn a new behavior as a response to a pressure in the environment.[5] Should that behavior lead to an increase in inclusive fitness, then organisms possessing the capacity for learning that behavior will enjoy an adaptive advantage over others. In time, the population will become more populated with organisms with that capacity. Memes provided the perfect selection pressure for the Baldwin Effect. Those brains that were better at transmitting and receiving memes enjoyed a pronounced fitness advantage. After all, and as we noted in Chapter 2, the cooperative exchange of information is the vital resource within the cognitive niche. It is quite possible that memes drove the selection for a larger and thereby more capable human brain, that is, a brain that can store ever-larger collections of memes and that can transmit these memes with greater fidelity and fecundity. A meme's phenotypic effect, for instance, "ideas, the brain structures that instantiate those ideas, the behaviors these brain structures produce, and their versions in books, recipes, maps and written music" (Blackmore 1999,

66), ultimately affects that meme's chances of winning out in the Darwinian competition with other memes.

There are two primary means for transmitting memes. Memes can be transmitted either through behavior or artifacts. Behaviors transmit memes in the immediate present. Foremost among such behaviors is spoken language. Language is the surest medium for memetic transmission. Behavioral transmission enjoys the capacity to correct errors. One can always say, "no, that's not how I did it." Behaviors are, all the same, limited in the audience they can reach. You have to be present. Artifacts, on the other hand, have the capacity to transmit memes even when the original emitter is long dead. We saw this in Chapter 2 with the descendant-leaving hypothesis and the Golden Rule, itself clearly a meme. "Memes have an either/or choice," observes Aunger, "either produce a brain spike that escapes into the macroenvironment as a social signal (in the form of photon or phoneme streams), or produce a physical template—an artifact—that can catalyze signals at some later time. It's basically a choice between current or later transmission" (2002, 288). If language is the foremost behavior for propagating memes, the foremost artifact is the written word. The trouble for all artifactual transmission is that it cannot ensure the fidelity of the transmission. One can never be sure that one's written work, or any other artifact for that matter, will be imitated with the modicum of fidelity necessary for a successful memetic lineage. All artifacts are open to interpretation. Interpretation is not quite the same thing as imitation. Once interpretation gets into the business of transmitting memes, we really can never know if fidelity to the original intention has been maintained. This may not always be a bad thing. In fact, a modicum of information infidelity may contribute to memetic, and by extension cultural, evolution (Gadamer 2004 [1960]). If imitation were always and wholly accurate, culture would become static. No culture is static.

Memetic lineages evolve. The evolutionary question thus pertains to both genes and memes, that is, *cui bono* (Dennett 1995)? Who, or what, benefits in the process? Do genes benefit, or do memes? Dennett identifies this question as the one to ask. Others have suggested alternatives. For instance, Boudry and Hofhuis ask not *cui bono*, but rather *cui malo* (2018, 158)? Instead of figuring out who benefits, perhaps we should ask who or what ultimately suffers. There is yet a third option. "The more appropriate question to ask . . . is *cui impellor*? Who drives the cultural evolutionary process or sets it in motion? In other words, Who's in control?" Aunger argues, "It's not who benefits but *whose interest is being expressed* that needs to be asked when you're attempting to explain what happens in a *coevolutionary* system, as when the dynamics of genes and memes interact in ways that determine what happens to either of them" (2002, 62). It is in answering this third question that memetics comes into its own. Are memes capable of making their hosts act against their inclusive fitness interests? Can memes become parasitic? Can they be infectious?

Dawkins (1976) suggests that what makes something parasitic depends on the replication cycles of the potential-parasite and the potential-host. If the one entity can replicate without hindering the other entity's replication, then we have at least a commensal relationship between the two. For instance, if my memetic interests in listening to John Coltrane's music do not stand in the way of my genetic interests in sexual reproduction then my genes and memes, in this particular situation, enjoy a commensal relationship. Of course, should my listening to John Coltrane be a sexual ornament, then my genes and memes enjoy a mutualism. It is for this reason that talk of memes as solely infectious mind viruses is not entirely accurate (Brodie 2011). In fact, perhaps the virus metaphor is altogether wrong. Maybe memes are more like bacteria. "Admittedly, memeticists do sometimes describe memes as mind viruses," Stewart-Williams observes, "a more apt analogy would be with bacteria. Some bacteria are bad for us, but plenty of bacteria are good: We couldn't survive without them. Ditto memes" (2018, 302). Boudry and Hofhuis similarly remark, "some [i.e., memes] are mutualists (enhancing the fitness of the host), others are commensal (neutral to the host) and still others are parasites (fitness-reducing)" (2018, 158). Previous chapters documented the mutualism between religious memes and human genes. Here we are interested in the religious memes that have become parasitic.

One can intentionally transmit memes. One can engage in instruction. One can also transmit memes unintentionally. If you happen to hear me humming a certain tune, say, the first four notes of Coltrane's *A Love Supreme* and then you proceed to hum the same four notes, I have successfully, although unintentionally, passed to you the meme that is the opening to Coltrane's masterpiece. This may be a pleasant experience. I hope it would be. Occasionally, however, we find that we are humming a tune, or thinking a thought, that we would rather not hum, or think. For the life of us, we simply cannot stop humming that damn tune. In such circumstances, it would seem that a meme has commandeered our brains. We have acquired an auricular helminth, or ear worm. It is this phenomenon that is the true subject of the science of memetics, that is, "this startling idea—that thoughts can think themselves" (Aunger 2002, 2). Of course, being unable to stop singing a particularly annoying refrain, such as the one to Britany Spears's "Oops! . . . I Did It Again," is largely inconsequential. It is annoying, but it seldom leads to destructive behaviors. For good or ill, there are times when this is not the case. There are times when it would appear that some memes motivate behaviors that benefit the replication of the meme to the detriment of the gene. This is the memetic infection. This is the "memetic theory of religion": "religious beliefs spread purely because they're good *for themselves*" (Stewart-Williams 2018, 295).

When Religion Becomes the Memetic Infection

The amount and speed with which we can acquire new information through social learning makes genetically generated novelty seem glacial. Culture evolves at a pace with which genes simply cannot keep up. Such rapidity can lead to adaptive changes in behavior as environments and contexts change. There may, however, be an occasional drawback to social, imitative learning. "Opening our minds to ideas in the environment allows rapid adaptation," P. J. Richerson and R. Boyd note, "but it also leads to the evolution of pathological cultural maladaptations" (2005, 14). "A potential downside to social learning," Nettle adds, "is ending up with a pattern of behaviour that does not serve one's interests" (2009, 231). Social learning always comes with the "risk of catching pathological superstitions" (Richerson and Boyd 2006, 162). Pathological superstitions are "cognitive infections" (Pinker 2021, 321). The risk of contracting cognitive infections counsels similar strategies to the ones associated with the behavioral immune system. It is sometimes best to stay away from social others who may be harboring pathogenic genes and/or memes (Richerson and Boyd 2006, 188). Occasionally, it may be best to stay away from the religious.

Some suggest that religion is nothing but a memetic infection (Ray 2009). "The costs of religion are so extreme that a vocal minority of naturalists view religion as itself a variety of illness," Bulbulia observes, "on their view, religion is a form of mental harm—barking madness—caused when our brains become infected by compelling but rationally disabling ideas or 'memes'" (2006, 89). The vocal minority's view is surely exaggerated. Religion has had its adaptive functions. As previous chapters have demonstrated, it was mostly adaptive for our evolutionary ancestors. This is what the "biomeme hypothesis" suggests. A. Y. Panchin et al. write, "various religious practices could represent biomemes: manifestations of a symbiosis between informational memes and biological organisms" (2014, 4). Take for instance the pronatalist characteristic of many, if not in fact all, conservative religions. As we saw in Chapter 2, religions often counsel behaviors and values conducive to having and nurturing children. Some traditions, in fact, encourage their followers to produce a "quiver full" (Psalm 127, 3–5). This would seem to be a winning combination for both the genes and the memes. Having more children means there will be more copies of one's genes in the next generation. Having more children means there will be more hosts for the transmission of one's memes. There is always a risk, of course, that what was once adaptive may be no more. Producing more children in the environment of evolutionary adaptedness would have been adaptive due to the high morbidity and mortality rate of infants and children. Today, however, some modesty in family planning might be wise, given the ballooning population of the planet. Roman Catholicism's condemnation of contraception is quite possibly maladaptive today. It is especially maladaptive in those countries suffering greatly from sexually transmitted diseases, such as HIV/AIDS (Hitchens 2012). That said, D. S. Wilson rightly notes, "What will *not* be observed, or rather seldom observed, are major beliefs . . . that actually handicap the believer by motivating dysfunctional behaviors" (2002, 156). Stewart-Williams similarly remarks, "It is true that *highly* virulent, fitness-diminishing memes, such as suicide bombing and celibacy, are rare. . . . The more virulent a meme is, the less common that meme will be" (2018, 303). As we will see shortly, some of the most virulent religious memes and the behaviors they encourage, like classical Hindu Yoga and Tantra, are truly limited to a heroic few.

Medical interventions are generally oriented toward relieving the sick and ill of their symptoms and diseases (Fabrega Jr. 1997). The eradication of sickness and disease is beneficial for genes. It is deleterious for religious memes. Religious memes appear to flourish among populations of hurting and sick people. "The more people suffer," K. Gray and D. M. Wegner write, "the more they appear to believe in God" (2010, 7). Elsewhere, they note, "If bad is indeed stronger than good, then God should not thrive in times of plenty but in times of pain, with disease and trauma fueling his perception" (2010, 11). This appears to be the case. Gray and Wegner found that when education, income, and healthcare are of high quality, religious memes suffer. What is more, they observed that "suffering and belief are significantly correlated . . . and remain so even after controlling for both median income and education" (Gray and Wegner 2010, 11). In other words, health status appears singularly influential for the viability of religious memes. A sick population is most susceptible to religio-memetic infections. "From a memetic point of view," Gray and Wegner conclude, "it makes sense for religion to encourage its adherents both to come to harm and to encourage moral interpretations of such harm. . . . Seen in this light, it is understandable why some religions discourage their members from seeking orthodox medical treatment—the more harm that comes to them and their family, the more they believe. . . . The mind of God would seem to thrive under such circumstances" (2010, 14). The irony, cruel or not, is that what appears to have started out as a system for maintaining health amid robust disease ecologies has now become a system for maintaining sickness amid robust allopathic medical ecologies. How might religion achieve such maintenance?

Religious memes fail to thrive in communities with high-quality health care, education, and income. Big governments provide these resources. Big governments and Big Gods are interchangeable (Zuckerman et al. 2018). They may even be mutually exclusive. There is a separation of church and state when it comes to infectious diseases. Certain forms of religion appear interested in destabilizing government and its ability to provision the masses. "Theoconservative opinion and practice" (Paul 2009, 423) seems particularly poised to fight against "big government." A. C. Kay et al. similarly note, "contexts that weaken beliefs in governmental stability can strengthen faith in the existence of a controlling God" (2010, 725). Elsewhere, they write, "conditions of political instability lead to increased belief in a controlling God via decreased faith in the government's ability to maintain order" (2010, 733). "Religious beliefs," V. Reynolds and R. Tanner add, "have a greater opportunity to survive and thrive where Western technical modernity has not made much impact" (1995, 32). G. Paul (2009) points out that many religiously conservative groups oppose government assistance programs and prefer to engage in social work through faith-based charities. Unfortunately for those truly needing such services, faith-based charities fail to provide adequately. Memetically speaking, this is no accident.

Faith-based charities simply lack the resources and logistical structures necessary to do an adequate job of provisioning and healing the masses. This, too, may be part of the memetic infection. If religious memes need sick populations, then an ineffective, faith-based charity is just what the preacher ordered. "High levels of conservative theism," Paul writes, "directly contribute to the poor societal circumstances and faith-based charitable work that encourage popular religiosity and creationist opinion" (2009, 423). Clarity is most warranted here. Some religious groups seek to destabilize government not because such destabilization and the attendant faith-based charity work is actually better for the masses; rather, it is better for religious memes. "Conditions of political instability," Kay et al. write, "lead to increased belief in a controlling God via decreased faith in the government's ability to maintain order" (2010, 733). Of significance for the recent political history in the United States, Kay et al. note that simply questioning the validity of a routine election is capable of inducing perceptions of political instability. "Perceptions of political instability were simply heightened by the presence of, or the possibility of, a national election," they write. "Such common instances of instability, which are of no real threat to people's lives, are sufficient to at least temporarily increase people's reported belief in a controlling God" (2010, 734). Is it not telling that the insurrection at the Capitol building in the United States on January 6, 2021, was undertaken by a right-wing, conservative Christian group, willing to pause for a moment to hold up a Bible in congress chambers and say a prayer of gratitude before resuming their insurrectional behaviors?

Sick populations need God. Religious memes need sick populations. Religious memes can encourage a host of behaviors conducive to the maintenance of "disease and trauma" (Gray and Wegner 2010, 11). For instance, the religious right opposes universal healthcare. "America's high levels of adult and especially juvenile mortality," Paul notes, "are probably due to the lack of the comprehensive medical system that is opposed by most elements of the creationist right" (2009, 422). Although the United States passed Obamacare after Paul had penned those words, the theoconservative right has consistently fought to overturn this piece of secularly welcomed legislation. Opposing universal health care is not the only strategy religions counsel when it comes to keeping religious memes salient. Religious memes equally promote anti-vaccination beliefs and behaviors (Koenig et al. 2001). Religiosity "best predicts vaccination skepticism" (Rutjens et al. 2018, 384); "vaccine skepticism was consistently predicted by religiosity" (Rutjens et al. 2018, 396). Biological antigens are not the only things vaccines kill. Vaccines kill religious memes. So great is the significance of a sick population for religion's relevance that some religious memes are willing to, as the meme goes, "lawyer up."

Many court cases were considered in the twentieth century in which religious plaintiffs argued for the right to forego compulsory vaccination. This was especially the case for public school attendance. Many religious parents claimed that the state had no right to demand that their children be vaccinated in order to attend. The argument in each case was much the same: the First Amendment protected the free exercise of religion and that included the right to deny on religious grounds the required vaccination. Fortunately for public health, "the judges . . . ruled that the right to practice religion freely hadn't been violated because vaccination was required of all religions, without discrimination" (Offit 2011, 140). Unfortunately for public health, in 1966, the state of New York set the precedent for a dubious reversal of this salubrious fortune.

In 1966, New York State passed a bill that required all children receive the polio vaccine prior to attending school, with a grave exception. "The bill excluded children whose parents' religion forbade vaccination," P. A. Offit notes, "a direct result of lobbying by what was then one of the most powerful religious groups in the United States: Christian Scientists" (2011, 140–1). According to Christian Scientists, disease is not a physical issue, but rather a psychological one. "Mary Baker Eddy, the founder of the Christian Science church," note Reynolds and Tanner, "taught that 'materialist' healing was unnecessary for believers as only the action of the divine mind on the human mind could cure disease" (1995, 257). Prayer was to supplant vaccines. Memetic manipulation was to supplant genetic intervention. Perhaps to be expected, those Christian Scientists who suffered the most from such memetic infection were the children. Offit (2011, 141) reports that there was a polio outbreak in a Christian Scientist high school in 1972 in Greenwich, Connecticut; in 1982, a nine-year-old died of diphtheria while attending a Christian Scientist camp in Colorado; in 1985, three children contracted measles and died at a Christian Scientist school in Elsah, Missouri; and between 1985 and 1994, there were four outbreaks of measles among Christian Scientist students in the St. Louis area.

Anti-vaccination ideologies predicated on religious positions are not limited to Christian Scientists. Offit points out that "the successful lobbying of Christian Scientists to include a religious exemption in New York State changed the strategy of those who wanted to avoid vaccines" (2011, 141–2). He reports two cases—one in New York and one in Massachusetts—brought before the court by two families unaffiliated with the Church of Christ, Scientist. In both cases, the argument was made that the Bible forbids violating the sanctity of the human body. Vaccinations so violate. Purity and pollution memes dictate that a vaccinated body is an unclean body and thus unacceptable to God. According to the plaintiffs, if one religion can be exempt, any religion can be exempt. Both judges agreed. The memes won. "By 2009, forty-eight states allowed exemptions to vaccination" (Offit 2011, 142). The result? H. G. Koenig et al. (2001) report outbreaks of measles, pertussis, rubella, and poliovirus among various religious groups who failed to vaccinate their children.

Other religions similarly put their members at risk of morbidity and mortality. As it is with the former, so too with the latter, it would appear that children are often the most vulnerable. For instance, there are several reports of children of Jehovah's Witnesses dying due to a refusal to accept a blood transfusion (Koenig et al. 2001). Some estimates suggest that upward of 1,000 Witnesses die each year from such refusals. Similarly, many Pentecostals have seen their children die due to their beliefs in the laying on of hands as a means of healing, that is, faith healing. "Believers are urged to refuse medical treatment for themselves and their families," note S. Solomon et al., "resulting in fatalities from conditions that, when treated, have survival rates of over 90 percent" (2015, 182). Similarly, "prayer . . . may also be dysfunctional if it causes the person to avoid actively seeking to confront the predicament by trusting passively in God to solve the dilemma" (Spilka et al. 2003, 482; Thornhill and Fincher 2014b). In such cases where the children of religious parents die, genetic interests and memetic interests both seem to take a hit. When one sacrifices one's child for religion not only do the genes lose out, but it would also seem that the memes lose too because they are losing a potential host. How might this be adaptive for the memes? It can be adaptive because memetic success, unlike genetic success, doesn't depend on the number of children one or one's family members have. One's memes can find replicative success in genetically unrelated others. In fact, allowing one's child to die because of faith may just serve as a credibility-enhancing device, or CRED (see Chapter 2). Witnessing another's devout faith—and what could be more impressively devotional than watching a parent forsake the life of their own child for religious reasons (a phenomenon not unknown to the Jewish and Christian communities)—may in fact encourage another's, thereby making the other the better replication machine for the religious memes. Of course, allowing a child to die is one thing. Intentionally killing children because of one's memetic interests is another. "The fact that some parents disown, abandon, or even murder offspring who stray from their own beliefs suggests that passing on the symbols we cherish can even be more important than passing on our genes" (Solomon et al. 2015, 104). In such cases, the memetic infection has truly commandeered its genetic host.

Other facets of religion facilitate the transmission of infectious disease (Panchin et al. 2014). For instance, we noted in Chapter 3 that religions often abide purity and pollution codes. We also saw that thinking about dirty and sinful things lead people to want to wash. Almost all religions have certain rituals intended to purify the body. These are called ablutions. Washing after contact with something potentially infectious is wise biological counsel. Ablution wells and sites, however, can become sources of infection (Panchin et al. 2014). M. C. Inhorn and P. J. Brown report that schistosomiasis infections were more prevalent among a Muslim population than a Christian one, "owing to the frequent Islamic practice of *wudu*, or ritual ablution before prayer" (1997, 45; Nations 1986). Reynolds and Tanner add, "in mosques in rural areas of Yemen and Bangladesh, the water for washing comes from water storage tanks, and all those who wash before prayer run the risk of contracting infections from guinea worms, schistosomes, or other disease agents present in the water" (1995, 279). A. Y. Panchin et al. similarly note that "'Holy springs' and 'holy water' have been found to contain numerous microorganisms, including strains that are pathogenic to humans. The Ganges River probably tops the list . . . bathing in this water is associated with the development of multiple diseases, including cholera" (2014, 3). J. Zias et al. (2005) found evidence to suggest that the ancient Essene community in Israel had a rather peculiar morbidity and mortality rate. They note that entrants to the Essene community tended to be robust, healthy young adults. They found evidence that many of these entrants were dying within just a few years of admission. What could so drastically alter the trajectory of their health? J. Tabor and Zias suggest that it had something to do with Essene defecation practices. They showed that the Essene community followed strictly Hebrew biblical injunctions for toilets to be placed at a certain distance from their dwelling space. What the Essenes apparently didn't realize at the time was that their practice of burying fecal matter actually preserved the bacteria found therein. If this were in fact the case, then every time someone went to the toilet, they exposed themselves to bacteria which they transported back to their ablution wells just outside their dwelling, facilitating thereby bacterial infections. Zias hypothesizes that it is such bacterial infections that ultimately account for "the extreme differences in early mortality between Qumran and the contemporary Jericho" (Siegel-Itzkovich 2006).

Bathing in infected waters is one way religions may unknowingly promote the contraction of a disease. There are other ways. Many religions have sacred relics to which multiple people will apply their lips, thereby establishing a disease vector (Panchin et al. 2014). Although not itself considered a relic, the communion chalice in Christian rituals may equally serve as a disease vector (Panchin et al. 2014; Pellerin and Edmond 2013; Reynolds and Tanner 1995). Another religious practice seemingly quite conducive to infectious disease spread is a pilgrimage. Often a massive gathering of people within a limited space, pilgrimage has been linked to a variety of infections. For instance, "in India the propagation of cholera was (and is) largely a function of religious pilgrimage" (McNeill 1976, 65). S. Tewari et al. note that long-duration, collective rituals, like the Hajj of Islam, pose "significant risks to well-being and health. Some risks concern the dangers posed by communicable disease" (2012, 1). J. Pellerin and M. B. Edmond (2013) also note that the Hajj has been associated with flu, Hepatitis A, B, and C, poliovirus, and Mycobacterium tuberculosis. They similarly suggest that the Hindu sideroll, a ritual wherein men will roll on their sides around temples and shrines, exposes the practitioner to hook worm infection. Although not en route to a special destination, the penitents of the Middle Ages served as vectors for the plague, moving as they did from village to village (Reynolds and Tanner 1995). Of course, anyone on the move eventually returns home, "spreading the infection into areas not previously touched" (Reynolds and Tanner 1995, 268). Lastly, the practice of Metzitzah b'peh, wherein the mohel will suck on the freshly circumcised penis, has been associated with the transmission and contraction of Herpes simplex type I (Pellerin and Edmond 2013). Religio-memetically driven behaviors can thus serve as infectious disease vectors, keeping the religious communities sick and thereby in need of God, or at least, in need of religious memes.

The antiestablishment clause in the First Amendment to the Constitution of the United States proclaims that no government entity shall promote or demote a religious position. There is to be a separation of church and state. American citizens are free to practice the religion of their choosing. There is something private about one's religion. The trouble, however, is that some religious memes motivate behaviors, the ramifications of which spill into the public sphere. There may have once been an advantageous, public health dimension to religion. This may no longer be the case. It may be maladaptive to allow religion to determine public health policy. One person's religiously motivated decision to forego vaccination is something that cannot be kept to oneself. An outbreak is an outbreak. Regardless of religious perspective, everyone is susceptible in such a situation. Of course, one's decision not to get the vaccine is not intended to affect negatively the other, but that is clearly a possible by-product. It's one thing if you and your family are Jehovah's Witnesses and you all choose accordingly to forego lifesaving blood transfusions. One could argue that that is your business. It is another thing, however, for you to rely on your religious memes to affect national policies, especially policies that could positively increase the well-being of others. Religiously caused suffering need not respect tribal boundaries. It would seem that we have a rather significant breach of the separation of church and state when a religious position can negatively influence a national policy that holds out hope for great improvements in human well-being. This is the case when it comes to something as promising as embryonic stem (ES) cell research.

ES cells are pluripotent. Pluripotency refers to the capacity of a stem cell to become any number of specific tissues or organs. With the technology now in place, biomedical researchers can manipulate ES pluripotency to produce a host of cures for many of the human animal's worst diseases and conditions. Couple stem cell technology with embryonic cloning and "the remarkable potential for an entirely new array of medical therapies may be achieved" (Silver 2006, 129). Stem cell research in nonhuman animals has produced results that appear to treat Parkinson's disease, paralysis, multiple sclerosis, and heart disease. There is even some promise that a cure for diabetes is on the horizon. Equally, stem cells can be converted into all types of blood cells, which can in turn be used to address a range of blood disorders. "With the combined use of stem cell and genetic modification technologies, clever scientists could someday attack every human disease, including brain disorders," notes L. Silver, "a new age of biomedical innovation may be coming, but only if science, religion, and politics can find common ground" (2006, 130). Finding common ground has proved quite elusive.

There is radical disagreement over the nature of a one-cell embryo. The disagreement is over the presence, or not, of the soul. Many religious practitioners will argue that the embryo is ensouled and as such deserves the dignity we extend to a fully developed human organism. Silver notes that "a potent code phrase used today is *culture of life*, which stands for the fundamentalist belief that each and every microscopic human embryo is ensouled by God and has an absolute right to life, equivalent to yours or mine" (2006, 119). Such a position is wholly memetically determined. There is no empirical reason to believe in a soul, including whether or not stem cells possess one (Flanagan 2002). For someone like Silver, religious memes have no place at the scientific table. "According to the physicalist worldview, if an organism does not have a cerebral cortex capable of conscious thought," Silver argues, "it cannot have the kind of intrinsic value that human beings attribute to themselves" (2006, 111). This is not how many religious people see it. From the religious meme's perspective, it is best if not only the local religious community suffers, but that the whole community, religious and secular alike, suffers. Insofar as religious opposition to ES research "has no basis in science" (Silver 2006, 110), it would seem that certain iterations of religion are memetic infections today. Religion can become an autoimmune disorder of the behavioral and psychological immune systems.

Religious memes are capable of catalyzing unhygienic and even fatal behaviors. These behaviors keep the religio-memetic lineages alive and kicking, despite the potentially debilitated constitution of their hosts. Most of these practices are honestly intended to help the failing body. Christian Scientists believe prayer is more efficacious than pharmacological intervention. It is equally understood by some that vaccinations do more harm than good, especially when it comes to appeasing God. Some ritual behaviors also *inadvertently* act as vectors for infections. No one goes on pilgrimage with the expressed intent to contract and transmit viruses and bacteria. Lastly, some religious memes encourage the suffering of not only their own but everyone by forestalling technologically advanced, biomedical research and interventions. They do this in order to save the other's soul. In this regard, everything considered up to this point regarding the role religious memes play in maladaptive behavior appear to be by-products of détente dualism. The beliefs and practices just reviewed are *consciously* undertaken for the benefit of soul and body. No one has deliberately *attacked* a perfectly healthy body, not yet at least. It is now time to turn to those religio-memetic lineages that encourage the host to attack intentionally its own body and its inclusive fitness interests. Deliberately attacking one's own body results from a combination of religious memes and a hypertrophied animal-nature disgust.

Animal-nature Disgust and Militant Dualism

Animal-nature disgust *can be* associated with the adoption of détente dualism. It clearly informs militant dualism. Militant dualists find no existential relief with the mere recognition of a duality between soul and body. Perhaps exemplary of the militant dualist mindset, St. Paul of the Christian tradition(s) counseled the Romans thusly, "For if you live according to the flesh, you will die; but if by the Spirit you put to death the misdeeds of the body, you will live" (Romans 8:13). Militant dualists must put to death the so-called misdeeds of the body. Militant dualists want their spirits to live. If they can perform the dominion of spirit over body then, perhaps, they can finally convince themselves that their precarious worldview is in fact true. "The belief that the physical and animal nature of humans is a weakness to be controlled or transcended is a prominent theme cutting across cultures, historical epochs, and philosophical and religious traditions," J. Goldenberg observes, "the soul or spirit is favored over the body, intellectual life over passion, human will over temptation; and the capacity to exert these formers over the latter is viewed as proof of human superiority over animals" (2005, 225).

Animals die. All species of animal, except one, are unaware of this fate. The human animal is not so unaware. "We know" (Pyszczynski et al. 2003, 16). We are disgusted, and terrified to be sure, at the thought of being mere animals. Those things that our biological body was naturally selected to accomplish can be sources of great disgust. "Sensitivity to disgust may be understood as originating in human beings' need to convince themselves that they are different from animals," write V. Saroglou and L. Anciaux, "and so in the need to keep a distance from everything that reminds them of animal life: eating, excreting, reproduction, injury, death, and decay" (2004, 262). Religion's purity and pollution codes address just those reminders of animal life. They are all sources of pollution. Militant dualists must proactively address these issues. For instance, members of the Chagga Tribe of Mt. Kilimanjaro are known for wearing butt plugs, "as if they never needed to defecate" (Solomon et al. 2015, 150). The Luguru of Tanzania shave off all of their auxiliary hair, including pubic hair, to reduce their musky odors (Cox et al. 2007, 505). The Hindus believe that during the *Satya Yuga*, from which we have now fallen greatly, people reproduced asexually (Parry 1989). It is precisely due to such a fallen nature that we are now fated to reproduce sexually and thus we have the *Kama Sutra*, as noted in Chapter 4. For almost all religious virtuosi, that is, militant dualists, the one act that must be abandoned first and foremost is the one that is most essential to the type of animal we are, that is, sexual intercourse. Monks and nuns do not conceive.

Wearing butt plugs, shaving hair, and refraining from sexual intercourse may be rather mild reactions to animal-nature disgust. Others are a bit more extreme. "If a human being is to reach spiritual heights," Solomon et al. note, "then the corrupt body needed to be dominated and punished like the animal it was" (2015, 154). This is the essence of militant dualism. Hayden observes, "Remarkable instances of *the mind's mastery over the flesh* are part of some religious practices in the world . . . spirit mediums use these mortifications of the flesh as an indication that they harbor powerful spirits" (2003, 58, emphasis added). He notes elsewhere, "Eyewitnesses, scientists, artists, and photographers have often documented extreme instances of the mastery of the flesh through self-inflicted wounds. . . . Shamans use these accounts and feats to impress others with their supernatural abilities or connections" (Hayden 2003, 58). Perhaps impressive and thus inducing of charisma, both contributing to the shaman's ability to manipulate the placebo effect (see Chapter 5), such displays do not abide biological counsel. Intentionally opening the flesh is an invitation for infection. There are more extreme performances.

The true performance of the dominion of mind over matter is suicide. It would seem that many have willingly gone to the grave in an attempt to free their spirits from the existential dungeon that is life in the world (Solomon et al. 2015). Some harbor in this way not only animal-nature disgust but also a certain "disgust with life in general" (Finlay-Jones 1983). Occasionally militant dualism mutates into suicidal dualism. The anxiety of an impending doom is simply too much for some to bear. These individuals must beat death to the punch. One

Hindu text puts it this way: "When [the yogi] considers all . . . experience to be repulsive, he relinquishes his own body and proceeds to the state of no return" (White 2009, 116). Suicidal dualism is tragic. It becomes even more so when it takes place in a group.

The historic record presents moments when mass suicide was undertaken. Perhaps the most infamous of such tragedies took place in 1978 in Jonestown, Guyana, when over 900 parishioners of Reverend Jim Jones's People's Temple, some of whom were infants and children, committed suicide (Guinn 2018). In 1993, seventy-two Branch Davidians went to their death in Waco, Texas, because they refused to renounce their ties to their religious leader, David Koresh (Wright 1995). A similar number of people committed suicide on four separate occasions between 1994 and 1997; they were members of the Solar Temple cult located in Canada, France, and Switzerland (Koenig et al. 2001). Thirty-nine members of the Heaven's Gate cult committed suicide in 1997, believing that their souls would awaken aboard an alien spaceship that was hiding in the tale of the Hale-Bopp comet (Zeller 2014). In all such cases, "if people are armed with the wrong hypotheses, abduction can easily lead them to adopt false and often deleterious beliefs" (Richerson and Boyd 2006, 167). The wrong hypothesis is, in these cases, a pathological superstition, a parasitic meme, a cognitive infection. Infected with a religious meme, the suicidal dualist opts out of the meme pool. This turns out to be a good thing for religious memes. Religiously motivated suicide, like religiously motivated infanticide, can act as a CRED (see Chapter 2). For instance, early Christian martyrdom is a qualified form of suicide. It is also a CRED. A. Norenzayan writes, "By their willing martyrdom, they became potent cultural exemplars and encouraged the cultural spread of Christian beliefs. What better way to prove one's sincerity than the willingness to die for those beliefs? And what better way to transmit these beliefs to others than to hold them with irrefutable sincerity?" (2013, 99). As many an apologist will note, because so many were willing to die for their Christian beliefs, the beliefs must be true. That itself is an example of a successful, infectious meme. It need not be true. There wasn't a mothership in the tail of the Hale-Bopp comet. Most who suffer from animal-nature disgust, and quite possibly a disgust with life in general as well, are seldom so certain. Lacking the certainty necessary to take one's own life, many are still willing to attack their bodies and their bodies' interests.

There are numerous ways one can offend the body and its inclusive fitness interests. As mentioned earlier, celibacy is clearly a memetic offense against the body. No other sexually reproducing animal on the planet self-selects to forego sexual reproduction. A celibate priest is the religious meme's ideal host.

Blackmore (1999) notes that a celibate priest is free to devote all his time and energy toward spreading religious memes. Such a commitment is deleterious for the priest's genes, assuming that in his free time he isn't helping his siblings or cousins raise children. It turns out that the celibate priest may be a genetic altruist. In other words, there are some genes that tend to benefit from the priest's memes. People genetically unrelated to the priest are memetically related. As noted in Chapter 2, the deployment of fictive kin ties to identify who is in the religious tribe and who isn't tends to promote cooperation. Fictive families attend churches, mosques, synagogues, or temples. Doing so exposes them to their religious leader's memes. The tragic cases reviewed above notwithstanding, most religious leaders promote worldviews which the congregants accept. A priest promotes confidence in the worldview. This facilitates the reduction of existential stress. This reduction facilitates, in turn, reproductive success of the laity. A celibate priest propagates the set of memes that constitutes the fitness-enhancing worldview for the laity.

Celibacy is one way to offend the biological body's selection for sexual intercourse. There is another. At any moment the celibate priest could forego his/her vows and reenter the stream of sexual reproduction. Only memes keep the celibate celibate, certain psychopathological conditions notwithstanding. As it perhaps is with the religious worldview, so too is it with any set of memes: they can never guarantee that their interests will outweigh genetic ones. This lingering possibility can apparently be quite troubling for some. So troubling that it must be dealt with once and for all. This is accomplished through castration. The Galli, for instance, who were Roman devotees of Cybele, castrated themselves. "The Galli . . . practiced the ritual of self-castration . . . in the hope of throwing out their animal-like physical nature to bring out the spiritual instead" (Mordeniz and Verit 2009, 399). A similar ritual modification of the genitalia was practised by the Skoptzy whereby "both men and women did away with their genitalia in an effort to achieve sexual purity and facilitate the second coming of Christ" (Norenzayan 2013, 96). C. Mordeniz and A. Verit (2009) suggest that an ithyphallic male figure from Gobekli Tepe is noticeably missing his testicles. If, as the terror management theorists argue, Gobekli Tepe was erected to manage anxieties surrounding death, and animal-nature disgust attends death anxieties, then perhaps the castrated male figure represents one of our earliest artifacts communicating the religio-memetically driven renunciation of sexuality.[6]

We have considered up to this point groupwide practices. If, for instance, your religion encourages circumcision, then all male members will tend to be circumcised. As Chapter 2 suggested, circumcision facilitates economic and reproductive cooperation among the men of the tribe. This is a good thing. If your religion refuses medical treatment, then most will decline a visit to the doctor (Fincher and Thornhill 2012). This is a bad thing. Most religious groups will also have those who are variously described as charismatics, virtuosi, or ascetics. These are individuals who adopt practices that would seem to take the dominion over the body to new heights. Charismatics are true, militant dualists. A. Glucklich notes, "The only way to purify this disgusting flesh is to discipline it harshly and mercilessly by means of asceticism—extreme mortification" (2001, 27). J. M. Masson similarly notes, "the ascetic wishes to abandon his physical self for a better, more purified self; in order to do this, he engages in an activity that is nothing less than a form of hypochondria—a total and often exclusive preoccupation with the body" (1976, 622). According to Masson, it is as if the ascetic suffers a certain counterphobia, that is, being obsessed with the very thing that causes the most disgust and existential anxiety. "It is by an absolute mastery of his own body," notes J. Parry, "that the ascetic attains salvation" (1989, 501). In keeping with our discussion of shamans in the previous chapter, it is quite likely that our true militant dualists may actually present schizotypal phenotypes (Polimeni and Reiss 2002; Berry et al. 2007; Crespi and Summers 2014). "Disgust for the putrid feces of humans or mammalian carnivores is virtually universal," P. Rozin and A. E. Fallon note, "the only exceptions that we know of among adults involve consumption in ritual contexts or consumption by mentally disturbed individuals" (1987, 290). Rozin and Fallon's disjunction may be unwarranted. It is perhaps the case that the ritualists and the mentally disturbed are one and the same. For some militant dualists, the disgusting body must first be ritually bound before it can be ritually consumed. Classical Hindu Yoga binds the body. Classical Hindu Tantra consumes it.

The Memetic Lineages of Classical Hindu Yoga and Tantra

Yoga is often perceived today as a practice to strengthen the body and to integrate it with the mind (Singleton 2010; Jain 2014). It has generated a multi-billion-dollar industry. Yoga's origins, however, testify to a different goal. Yoga once reflected the desire to perform the mind's "absolute mastery over it [i.e., the body]" (Parry 1989, 511). M. Winkelman proposes in fact that "cross-cultural research and linguistic evidence . . . suggest shamanism was the basis from which the yogic and meditative traditions developed" (2010, 72). If Winkelman is right, then the shamans were the first yogis, the first ascetics. This makes good psychological sense. We noted in Chapter 3 that the predominant style of childrearing in our evolutionary past would most likely have been pediatric in nature. We also noted that that style tends to produce those with insecure-anxious attachments. Such attachment styles are adaptive for collectivist living. Collectivism is a survival strategy in a hostile environment. In the previous chapter, we saw that insecure-anxious collectivism leaves some dissatisfied, and possibly depressed. According to J. M. Masson, "the ascetic is originally in the grip of a potential depression" (1976, 620), noting elsewhere, "all ascetics must have suffered from harsh and unloving parents . . . *all* ascetics suffered massive traumas in their childhood" (1976, 623). As the prototypical yogi, the shaman is perhaps the one for whom the pediatric practices were most influential, psychologically speaking. If we can cautiously look to contemporary hunter-gatherers to get a sense of the economic and sexual practices of our evolutionary forebears, perhaps in a similar way we can look to the psychological profiles of those raised in pediatric conditions—such as we find in certain segments of Hindu India (Ellis 2015)—to provide a window onto the psychology of the shaman, the psychology of the yogi, the psychology of those who established the first religion.

"Yoga" is a rather prevalent meme in our midst these days. It is currently part of "spiritual urban cool" (Singleton 2010, 32). The meme is often associated with practices of bending and stretching, fancy clothing, and bourgeois retreats. This is a modern invention of those who are wont to establish a direct connection to the yoga practised on the Indian subcontinent prior to the modern period. M. Singleton suggests that the yoga of today is merely a homonym with the yoga of an Indian past (2010, 15). "The bedrock of the West's modern-day, billion-dollar yoga industry, with its celebrity gurus . . . glossy journals, fashion accessories, trademarks, franchises, and lawsuits, is Indian yoga," notes D. G. White, "but a reinvented Indian yoga that dates from no earlier than the 1930s" (2009, 247).

"Tantra" has similarly captivated a modern, transnational audience. It too has had a face lift. The popular perception of tantra is that it is a practice intended to enhance the sexual pleasures of both men and women (Sovatsky 2014). "New Age 'Tantric sex' is a Western fabrication, whose greatest promise, if one takes its Internet advertising at face value, is longer sexual staying power for men and more sustained and frequent orgasms for women," White observes, "none of this has ever been the subject matter of any authentic Tantric teaching" (2003, xiv), "to say nothing of yoga for pets and other inanities that yoga entrepreneurs are continuously inventing" (2009, xiii). The contemporary understanding of yoga and tantra is that they are good for our minds *and* our bodies. Contemporary yogic and tantric memes are at the very least commensal, if not in fact mutualistic with the biological body's genes. This hasn't always been the case. While it can certainly prove difficult to capture the original meanings of these memes as they are communicated through visual and written artifacts, they are, all the same, quite explicit in their counsel. Original yoga and tantra may have been good for the mind, but not so much for the body.

Singleton and White tend to emphasize the substantive difference between contemporary yoga and classical yoga. There is, however, one rather telling continuity. Yoga has been consistently, not to mention fantastically, associated with both curing and preventing disease. For instance, K. V. Iyer, a prominent proponent and sculptor of contemporary yoga, suggested that *hatha* yoga contributes directly to immunity to disease. Singleton points out that "Iyer . . . had a widespread reputation for healing disease through yoga" (2010, 124). Yogi Ramacharaka's *Hatha Yoga* (1904) similarly afforded counsel on how to cultivate the capacity to eradicate disease through certain mental skills. Such claims resonate not only with those of the Christian Scientists we considered earlier but also with the classical, fifteenth-century text on *hatha* yoga, *The Hatha Yoga Pradipika* (HYP). Credited to Svatmarama (Akers 2002), the text identifies the eradication of disease as a goal of the practice. For instance, HYP 1.31 proposes that the practice "overcomes defects and quickly destroys all diseases"; HYP 1.44: "This is Padmasana. It destroys the sickness of those who practice it"; HYP 1.54: "destroyer of all diseases"; HYP 2.34: "crown of Hatha practices . . . dries up all defects and diseases."[7] What is more, a seventeenth-century account from Khajuraho describes an encampment of yogis and suggests that "whoever is subjected to a disease like leprosy or elephantiasis lives with them for a long period of time and is cured by the permission of God" (cited in White 2009, 218).

Practicing yoga ostensibly cures one's own diseases. The one who practices yoga can similarly cure others. Winkelman is right to note in this regard that the yogic traditions do resemble shamanic ones. The resemblances pertain to both the practices and the functions. Like shamans, yogis were spiritual warriors. "Down to the present day," notes White,

> yogis are called upon as exorcists, driving away disease and evil spirits with their traditional tools: spells, amulets, salves, blood, red ochre, threads, earrings, drums, ashes, fire-tongs, peacock feather fans, and so on. . . . Their powers extended to control over nature as well, with yogis reputed, down to the present day, for their capacity to control wild animals and serpents, divert hailstorms

and other natural calamities, and ensure fertility in livestock as well as human women. (2009, 232)

If there is a significant difference between the yogi and the shaman, we are not finding it here. Similarly, if there is a significant difference between the yogi/shaman and quite possibly the world's most popular religious figure in history, that is, Jesus of Nazareth, that, too, is not found here.

Derived from the Sanskrit verb *yuj*, yoga is often taken to mean "to yoke" or "to bind." That which is yoked or bound is a matter of some dispute. The yogi was originally associated with a warrior and his horses who were yoked to the chariot, readied for battle. The yogi was "the model for the warrior" (White 2009, 60). This martial aspect of yoga accounts for its cognate, joust (White 2009). According to S. Sarbacker's (2005) categories, martial yoga is "numinous" yoga. Numinous yogis are often known to have powers to take over other peoples' bodies (White 2009). Numinous yogis bind the bodies of others. Cessative yogis bind their own minds in order to bind their own bodies.

Cessative yoga is the yoga of meditation. It attempts to bind the wondering mind so as to achieve a clear distinction between the subject and the phenomenal world. Perhaps the most famous text in the tradition of yoga, Patanjali's *Yoga Sutras* claims just that: "Yoga is the cessation of the turnings of thought. When thought ceases, the spirit stands in its true identity as observer of the world" (Miller 1995, 29). Classical compendiums of Indian philosophy associate this type of yoga with the system known as Samkhya. The oldest of the Indian philosophical systems, Samkhya is staunchly dualistic (Halbfass 1990). Samkhya maintains that there is an unbridgeable gap between the spirit (*purusa*) and matter (*prakriti*). Practicing yoga ostensibly enables a direct realization of such duality. For some yogis, such a realization appears to be the end goal. These yogis are détente dualists. For others, however, the true goal of yoga cannot be achieved without its militant complement.

Many coefficients have qualified the meme, yoga. "Raja" and "hatha" are perhaps the most common. Raja means "king." Hatha means "forceful," "violent," "oppressive." Svatmarama's claim that "the unification of mind (citta) is called Raja Yoga" (HYP 4.77) suggests that Patanjali's yoga is raja yoga. His text repeatedly draws a direct connection between raja yoga and hatha yoga: "The science of Hatha for one reason—Raja Yoga" (HYP1.2); "Raja Yoga will not be complete without Hatha, nor Hatha without Raja Yoga" (HYP2.76); "All the methods of Hatha ... are for achieving Raja Yoga" (HYP 4.103). The methods of hatha yoga are the methods of the militant dualist.

A mutation within the memetic lineage of yoga effected a redirection of the violence. No longer interested in the conquest of the other, that is, numinous yoga, the hatha yogi turned his martial intentions against his own body. Hatha yoga's militant dualism has both sexual and masochistic dimensions. Regarding the former, the hatha yogi is to retain his semen. If sexually active, he is to suck the emitted semen back into his urethra, bringing with it any vaginal emissions as well. For instance, "The knower of this Yoga practice should draw upwards with the penis to preserve his own semen and even the seminal fluid of a woman who has just completed menstruation" (HYP 3.91). There is yet another way of incorporating menstrual fluid, a topic to which we return shortly. For now, and according to the yogic traditions, it is important to recover lost semen, or even better to retain it in perpetuity. Emitted semen leads to death. This is a fantasy clearly informed by animal-nature disgust: "The knower of Yoga should preserve his semen and thereby conquer death; preservation of semen is life" (HYP 3.88). Perhaps even better than reclaiming emitted semen, the yogi is to develop a disinterest in sexual intercourse altogether. The sincerity of such a disinterest was attested to by a hard-to-fake sign. The sign was detumescence in the presence of sexual provocation. White, for instance, relays how Marco Polo wrote of yogis who would subject a fellow monk to the wiles of the devadasis, that is, temple prostitutes. If he showed any sign of arousal, he was ostracized (White 2009, 207–8). What is more, some yogis would apparently fasten iron rings around their penises in order to forestall intercourse with women (White 2009, 203). Such methods for the retention of semen insult the body's genotype. Other aspects of hatha yoga insult the body's phenotype. Today's hatha yoga is salubrious for the body. Yesterday's yoga was not.

European travel accounts of hatha yoga are insightful regarding the premodern practice. Although often couched in an idiom of disgust coupled with Orientalist self-congratulation (Inden 1990), such accounts are full of descriptions of self-mortifying practices resulting in a beleaguered body. These descriptions include such austerities as prolonged exposure to the elements, especially the sun; carrying chains meant for elephants; spending hours on end in a handstand; and, assuming painful and difficult contortions of the body, which one author characterized as "unnatural" (quoted in Singleton 2010, 38). The previous chapter indicated that shamans would often engage in self-flagellation and prolonged postures, the behaviors and postures now associated with classical hatha yoga. Singleton also relays a report from 1698 describing "overgrown nails that pierce the flesh of the hand, dislocated arms, and excruciating postures held for so long that the limbs in question became ossified and shriveled" (2010, 39).

White similarly presents the account of Jean de Thevenot from 1666: "Their penance consists in forbearing to eat for many days, to keep constantly standing upon a Stone for several weeks, or several months; to hold their Arms a cross behind their head, as long as they live, or to bury themselves in Pits for a certain space of time" (2009, 214). As attested here, classical hatha yogic practices are contrary to the best interests of anyone's body. Both classical raja and hatha yoga took counsel from a certain animal-nature disgust and its accompanying somatophobic memeplex. There was yet another memetic mutation within the yogic lineage that led to an even more severe dominion of mind over matter.

At the heart, or better yet "gut," of hard-core tantra is the generation and consumption of "clan nectar" or *kulamrta* (White 2003, 76).[8] The tantric practitioner consumes, or occasionally dons, a concoction of "jewels" (*ratna*) or "moons" (*candra*) more often than not identified as menstrual blood, semen, urine, feces, and phlegm (McDaniel 1989, Jha 1995, White 1996; Kinsley 1997; Openshaw 2002; White 2003). According to the ninth- to tenth-century *Kaulajnananirnaya*, the practitioner is enjoined to consume "poison, menstrual blood (*dharamrtam*), semen, blood, and marrow. . . . One should practice the drinking of [their] menstrual blood (*dharapana*). . . . One should constantly drink blood and semen" (quoted in White 2003, 76). Likewise, the *Kaulavalinirnaya*, dating approximately to the sixteenth century, instructs the practitioner to "worship the Goddess with the nectar of vulva and penis . . . by drinking of the virile fluid" (quoted in White 2003, 74). The tantric practitioner is to consume in this way pathogen-rich exuviae. The source of these moons or jewels varies. Some practitioners employ the categories of *ekak* or *yugal* (Jha 1995, 69). *Ekak* (oneself/alone) moons are either one's own or those of the guru and/or the guru's wife. *Yugal* (other/with partner) moons are either *svakiya*, that is, one's spouse's, or *parakiya*, that is, moons of any indiscriminate-member-of-the-opposite-sex. Further qualifying these moons is the timing of consumption. The moons could be consumed immediately upon issuance from the body or after they had been exposed to the heat of the sun. Finally, and quite possibly for the "faint-of-will," the moons may be consumed on their own or diluted with other substances so as to make them "more palatable" (Openshaw 2002, 227).

Choosing the source of the moons appears to be an open issue. Some of the more striking examples of tantric practice fall into the *"yugal-parakiya"* class. For instance, the "hagiography" of the tantric saint, Ramakrishna, relates how he went to the riverbank and found a pile of human feces to which he applied his tongue. The hagiographer Swami Nikhilananda notes that Ramakrishna "felt no disgust" (quoted in Kripal 1995, 270). In another striking example, S.

N. Jha relates an instance when the tantric practitioners not only sought out and consumed "random moons," but actually bloody feces. Bloody feces are indicative of dysentery (1995, 91). Both instances exemplify *yugal-parakiya sadhana*, with the added element of "exposed to heat." The consumption of pathogen-rich excreta constitutes the first of the two limbs of hard-core tantric *sadhana*, or practice (White 2003, 13).

"Typical Tantric disgustingness" (Wedemeyer 2007, 391) applies to the generation and oral consumption of the moons. It equally applies to *maithuna*, or sexual intercourse. Tantric sex typically involves a tantric hero (*vira*) and his mystical lover (*yogini*). The *yogini* is thought to be a goddess as well as a mother-substitute. J. J. Kripal suggests that tantric sex is, in this regard, "a form of mystical incest" (1995, 90). J. Openshaw similarly notes that *bartaman panthis*—for all intents and purposes a type of hard-core tantric practitioner—conflate the two roles, that is, the lover and the mother (2002, 178). What is more, the mother-substitute ought to be menstruating. She is also to ride astride the male partner during intercourse (Kinsley 1997, 7; Openshaw 2002, 199). Finally, the hero's *yogini* often issues from a lower caste (a qualification confounding the incestuous intention). It is this admittedly overdetermined combination of mystically incestuous intercourse with a menstruating, riding-astride, out-of-caste woman and the consumption of the attendant bodily fluids and other excreta that constitutes hard-core tantric practice. "The four moons practices, whether performed alone or with a partner," observes Openshaw, "involve a shift or erasure of boundaries between self and not-self" (2002, 247). This erasure of boundaries between self and not-self is recognizably the denouement of tantric practice. The practice appears perfectly calibrated to achieve just such a goal. As the previous chapter noted, the first mechanism to establish a distinction between self and not-self is the major histocompatibility complex. Tantra intentionally offends the MHC. Tantra equally enjoins those activities that most remind us of our animality. Tantric practitioners are often exhorted to behave like animals (Haidt et al. 1994, 712; Jha 1995, 90; Openshaw 2002, 209).

Although animal-nature disgust makes being animal-like and being religious seem antithetical, such a constellation constitutes hard-core tantra. By celebrating, albeit alchemically (White 1996) and thus fantastically, bodily excreta as well as sexual intercourse with menstruating, esoterically incestuous, out-of-caste women, tantra confounds—whether genuinely or counterphobically (Fenichel 1945; Kakar 1981; Langner 2002)—the results of those social-psychological studies that document a widespread, robust animal-nature disgust. Although it may be seen as evoking animal-nature disgust, tantra more accurately evokes core disgust. It is not simply that tantric practitioners are acting like animals, and thus remind us that we too are animals and thus doomed to death and decay, that disgusts us. Likewise, it is not the case that we find tantra disgusting because of some confusion of arbitrary, macro-social divisions and boundaries as Mary Douglas would have us believe. Tantra is disgusting because it subverts biological wisdom. The biological disgust we have for tantra is the same core disgust we ultimately have for religion when it is pushed to its logical conclusion.

The natural body can be a source of great anxiety for many. It is one of the reasons people are religious. It is also one of the primary reasons people practice hard-core tantra. Hard-core tantra's militant dualism attempts to defeat bodily realities, not to deny them fantastically as idealism is often wont to do. The two practices constitutive of hard-core tantra—the consumption of pathogen-rich excreta and maximally suboptimal sexual intercourse with an out-of-caste and thus parasitologically strange partner—are not accidental cultural constructions. Rather, it is precisely *these* two practices, *not* others, that most offend the biological realities of the human organism. To convince oneself of one's bodily transcendence may just require intentionally participating in activities most offensive to this body.

The human body is well adapted. Enjoying the integrated immune system and the primary emotion of disgust, it comes predisposed to prosper biologically. Biological prosperity entails the accomplishment of two goals. First, the body must fight against the ingression of pathogens that could possibly lead to premature death. Premature death is death-before-reproductive-success. Once reproductive maturity is reached—the first goal—the human animal seeks an appropriate partner with whom to engage in sexual intercourse, an activity primarily in the service of producing viable progeny—the second goal (Bittles and Neel 1994). A lifelong avoidance of pathogen-rich materials en route to nonincestuous, heterosexual intercourse with a nonmenstruating, sexually mature female is *the* biological goal of the human male. These twin goals constitute "the enemy" against which militantly dualistic, tantric heroes— who are men (Openshaw 2002, 14; White 2003, 160)—fight. Transcending the embodied condition requires abiding by a repertoire of infectious memes that encourage the confounding of the biological condition. It is no accident that "the tongue is *the* Tantric organ" (Kripal 1995, 305). Tantra employs the very organ used to expel pathogens for the exact opposite end. Tantra's tongue relishes the pathogenic: "Kali's tongue . . . is not about shame but about the destruction of disgust" (Kripal 1995, 305). In its attempt to destroy disgust, Kali's tongue, tantra's tongue approaches the destruction of the body itself. Tantra's tongue consumes the other's moons. It offends the very reason for an immune system. Likewise, sexual intercourse with an incestuous, menstruating, riding-astride, out-of-caste partner appears to be the *most* suboptimal, intraspecific, heterosexual union of which the human animal is capable.[9] A menstruating woman is temporarily infertile. The woman-astride position is the least conducive to insemination.[10] What is more, even if progeny were to issue from the union, the antibiological intention behind the admittedly fantasied incestuous act is one of producing a lethal allele homozygous child or a child with an MHC too similar to the parents', both conditions contributing to the likelihood of premature death. To be sure, tantric practice is meant to "reverse the flow of life" (Openshaw 2002, 199).

White suggests that tantric sex was always primarily in the service of generating the moons, not sexual ecstasy. As we saw earlier, the source of these moons varies. What we now realize is that the emic classification Jha presents occludes elements of biological significance. V. Curtis and A. Biran (2001) point out that the pathogenicity of others' moons varies. Reporting the results of empirical research on 40,000 participants, Curtis et al. conclude, "sharing a person's bodily fluids becomes more disgusting as that person becomes less familiar because strangers are more likely to carry novel pathogens and hence present a greater disease threat to a naïve immune system" (2004, S132). Jha's esoteric identification of one's moons with one's guru's and/or guru's wife similarly occludes the significance of this biological distinction. The guru and the guru's wife are in effect "parasitological strangers," that is, potential carriers of novel and thus offensive pathogens. Similarly, placing one's spouse's moons in the *yugal* category obscures the fact that one's spouse's moon is more parasitologically familiar than is the guru's, guru's wife's, or any indiscriminate other's and are thus less biologically dangerous and less disgusting. These concerns ultimately inform the biologically transgressive nature of the *yogini's* out-of-caste status. Like the guru and guru's wife, the *yogini* is parasitologically strange. It isn't an accident that the *yogini* was often associated with birds. Birds may be attractive to the existentially anxious (see Chapter 4). They are, all the same, animals associated with the transmission of disease (White 2003, 58). Tantric heroes actively sought out "cracks in the human immune system" (White 2003, 52).

Courting the biologically dangerous is where we locate the perfected, militant dualism of tantra. Tantric practice is about the erasure of distinctions between self and non-self. To erase the distinction between self and non-self requires not the overcoming of arbitrary, cultural divisions or the mental gymnastics of meditative regimens. The erasure results from the intentional ingestion of pathogenic substances. If self-other distinctions begin with the major histocompatibility complex (see Chapter 5), then to erase dualistic boundaries requires offending the immune system, that is, finding the cracks in the human immune system. Offending the immune system is the performative gustatory act of hard-core tantra and it is only this act that truly realizes the dominion of mind over matter. In its attempt to be liberated from the only conclusion the body promises, that is, death, tantra becomes maladaptive.

The purity and pollution codes of south Asian culture that tantra flouts are not arbitrary constructions of an accidental, social institution. Rather, the codes, as we saw in Chapter 3, address what is universally found disgusting and are thus reflective of evoked culture. The Lawbook of Manu (5:135)—a Hindu text pertaining to purity and pollution—states unequivocally that one is to avoid contact with "oily exudations, semen, blood, urine, feces, the mucous of the nose, ear wax, phlegm, tears, the rheum of the eyes and sweat" (Doniger 1991). It is, thus, irrevocably relevant that tantric practitioners consume precisely the substances they do and not others. It is equally irrevocably relevant that tantric practitioners engage precisely the sexual unions they do, pursuing, as one *sadhaka* most tellingly put it, "the [antibiological] ideal of non-procreation" (Openshaw 2002, 243). "From ancient times," Jha notes, "these *sadhaks* are against childbirth" (1995, 98). To the extent that this is the case, these *sadhaks* memetically and performatively pursue genetic extinction. The consumption of pathogen-rich bio-toxins and the performance of maximally suboptimal sexual intercourse strike at the very raison d'etre of the naturally selected human body. What better way for the mind/soul and its memes to win the universally religious war against the body and its genes than by intentionally offending the body precisely in those arenas naturally selected for its success? Hard-core tantra memetically sanctions the confounding of the core disgust mechanism on the gustatory, sexual, and social fronts. Tantra is literally and universally disgusting because it is positively maladaptive. As an antibiological attempt to "reverse the flow of life" (Openshaw 2002, 199; Bloch 1992), tantra may just be the denouement of the universal, religio-martial campaign against the biological body.[11] In this regard, and despite any initial revulsion, the core disgusting bodies and sexual activities constituting hard-core tantric practice make of this particular, memetic tradition a disgusting, though quite possibly "perfected," religion. Tantra's infectious memes promote a militant dualism that spells doom for the body. Tantra is an autoimmune disorder.

It is an exaggeration to suggest that religion is nothing but a memetic infection, an autoimmune disorder. Religion was selected over deep, evolutionary time as a fitness advantage in the war against suboptimal behaviors. But as it is with any population, be it genetic or memetic, mutations inevitably arise. Some religious traditions encourage biologically deleterious behaviors. Through a combination of exaggerated animal-nature disgust and memetic lineages ministering to such disgust, we get religious traditions that appear antithetical to the biological body's naturally selected, genetic interests. It appears to be the case that a meme can occasionally motivate its host to engage in behaviors the sole benefit of which accrues to the meme. As we have seen in this chapter, religious memes perhaps enjoy the greatest replication among human hosts who are sick and depressed. When two replicators compete for the resources to replicate, and when the replication cycle of one benefits at the expense of the other, then we are dealing with a parasitic relationship. There are moments, perhaps fewer and farther between, when religious memes replicate at the expense of their genetic hosts. Religions have the capacity to become parasitic. They can become memetic infections.

7

Conclusion

In 1975, E. O. Wilson held out the prospect that biology would eventually render religion transparent. He wasn't mistaken. Although full transparency has yet to be achieved, much progress in the biology of religion has since been made. We now have convincing empirical evidence and theoretical arguments for a host of selection pressures that led to the emergence and evolution of religion. As we have seen, many authors propose, as did Wilson, that religion solved the fundamental problem of cooperation. It devised mechanisms for rooting out the free and promiscuous riders. It did this through costly and hard-to-fake signs of commitment. Religion also helped steer the human animal away from fast and short-term reproductive strategies to slow and long-term strategies. The latter enhanced inclusive fitness. Religious practitioners often enjoy greater reproductive success. What is more, religious practitioners tend to leave more descendants. Generations of descendants carry one's genes far into the future. This is reproductive success. Reproductive success is the only metric by which the life sciences determine if a life has been well lived. What we have seen in the preceding chapters is that religion also helps mitigate the selection pressures issuing from infectious diseases. Religion's opacity is waning.

Economic and reproductive successes are the adaptive goals of the human animal. There is a persistent and ubiquitous problem that threatens such success, infectious disease. As we noted in Chapter 3, a sick population is a population on sick leave. Natural selection's answer to this persistent and ubiquitous problem is the integrated immune system. The integrated immune system is composed of the behavioral, psychological, and physiological immune systems. Religion is a manifestation of the former two.

The behavioral immune system encourages religious tribalism. Tribalism is a reflection of the geography of immunocompetence. Because local communities can develop an immunity to the local disease pool, it was advantageous to be suspicious of extra-tribal others, that is, others who were quite likely vectors for a novel infection. Novel infections can decimate a local community. To ward off such threats, the behavioral immune system incentivizes collectivism. Religion's tribalism is collectivism. Collectivism is often characterized by ethnocentrism and xenophobia, traits routinely associated with traditional religions.

Religious tribes routinely abide by purity and pollution codes. These codes are prophylactic in nature. They counsel physical purity. Those who do not abide by such codes, for instance extra-tribal others, elicit our disgust. Although we saw in Chapter 2 that those who cheat on economic agreements disgust us, the emotion was originally selected to motivate prophylactic behaviors. Successful collectivism ultimately depends upon an incentivized population. An incentive for collective living emerges through an adult personality profile. The adult personality profile most suited for religious tribalism, for collectivism appears to be a product of childrearing practices. In robust disease ecologies, parents tend to adopt the pediatric style of childrearing. This style places its emphasis on physical, not emotional, investment. Such parent-child interactions tend to nurture an insecure-anxious attachment style. Although facultative for interdependent living, we noted that there are a few psychological ramifications, such as neuroticism, especially anxiety and depression. Here is where the psychological immune system comes into play.

Economic and reproductive activities do indeed presume healthy bodies. They equally presume healthy minds. An anxious and depressed animal suffers not only immunosuppression but also subfecundity. Successful reproduction requires a mind that is not chronically stressed. Insecure-anxious attachments are particularly susceptible to both attachment depressions and existential anxieties. These conditions can result in behavioral paralysis, if left unmanaged. Terror management theory proposes that the human animal must construct cultural worldviews that hold out the hope for immortality in order to manage existential anxieties. There are two types of immortality, the symbolic and literal. Only religion promises the much-desired latter. Religion tells anxiolytic tales about lives everlasting. Religion also mitigates chronic stress and depression by promoting adaptive illusions of qualified, internal control. Through ritual performance, the human animal believes it can wield a modicum of control over objectively uncontrollable situations by appealing to gods or thwarting devils. Religion is, in this way, a manifestation of the psychological immune system.

The first two arms of the integrated immune system are prophylactic. The third and final arm is eradicative. The physiological immune system identifies and destroys parasitic microorganisms that have found their way beyond the body's first two lines of defense, the skin and mucosal membranes. Our concern in Chapter 5 was to determine the extent to which religion can facilitate the functioning of the physiological immune system. We turned to shamanism to make such a determination. Shamanism appears to be both the first religion and the prototype for future religions. The shaman was the first therapist as well as a physician. He was, and remains, in certain hunter-gather communities, responsible for solving a host of problems. We briefly noted the problems pertaining to subsistence and the politico-legal; we focused on the psychological and physiological. The relevant literature attests to the prevalence of attachment anxieties within shamanic communities. It is quite possible that shamans, themselves, were schizotypal, insecure-anxiously attached. The shaman's induction of dissociated states of consciousness appears calibrated to adjust the negative self-introject associated with insecure-anxious attachments. A new self emerges with the help of the shaman's therapeutic work. The shaman also treated biologically based disease, a point about which many have had their doubts. Shamanic treatments for disease were manifold. The shaman manipulates the placebo effect. The shaman prescribes herbal remedies, some of which contain bioactive ingredients. Lastly, and perhaps most counterintuitively, the shaman induces an acute-stress response through blood sacrifices. Here is where religion facilitates physiological immune system success.

The historic and ethnographic records attest to the practice of blood sacrifice when someone in the local community has contracted a disease. The connection between the two has eluded most authors to date. Many suggest that the acute stress associated with blood sacrifice is antithetical to healing. This is not the case. When experiencing acute stress, the physiological immune system is potentiated. Potentiating the immune system is helpful for those who are not only sick but also for those who would wish to be immunized. When a member of the religious tribe contracts a disease, it is salubrious for all to gather around the sick individual and witness a blood sacrifice. The acute stress that results from witnessing such a terrifying and disgusting display enhances the immune system response. For the one who is already sick, acute stress promotes an already-engaged physiological immune system. For those who are healthy and in attendance, they experience a low-dose exposure to the novel pathogen. A low-dose exposure to an antigen while acutely stressed amounts to an indigenous vaccination clinic. Blood sacrifice enhances physiological immune system functioning.

We concluded our discussion with autoimmunity. We asked to what extent has religion become a memetic infection. Memetic infections promote behaviors that are biologically maladaptive. Originally a system for health promotion, religion occasionally appears to be a system for health demotion. Religious memes wax while biological genes wane. Contemporary medical and subsistence technologies may render religion unnecessary. They are better at doing all the things religions once did, the only exception being promises of everlasting life. Religious participation declines wherever there is a big, provisioning government. Some religious practitioners therefore behave in ways that are detrimental to their biological health, but beneficial to their memetic health. We see this, especially today, in religiously inspired anti-vaccination ideologies.

We also saw that the human animal is prone to animal-nature disgust. This type of disgust emerged as a reaction to reminders that we are at the mercy of the second law of thermodynamics. Like all animals, we are fated to die. Reminders of our animality disgust us. Animal-nature disgust often motivates the adoption of a religious worldview. Religious worldviews often adopt some iteration of dualism. Animal bodies die, but souls live on. Most religious practitioners adopt this dualism and get on with the business of living, respecting, and satisfying the body's biological agenda of staying healthy and engaging in productive reproduction. This is détente dualism. Militant dualism is a more radical response to animal-nature disgust. The militant dualist does not find existential solace with a simple commitment to mind-body dualism. Rather, the militant dualist must perform the dualism by demonstrating to one and all that the mind is truly divorced from the body. This demonstration often takes the form of masochism. The militant dualist punishes the body for the sake of the soul. The extreme iteration of such militancy is suicidal dualism. Some religious traditions accommodate suicide. Most militant dualists, however, do not carry their disgust to that extreme. Despite their bowdlerized iterations today, the militant dualisms of classical Hindu Yoga and Tantra involved beleaguering the body through contortionism and ingesting pathogen-rich excreta. What is more, the sexual escapades associated with classical tantra were maximally suboptimal. Tantra, in effect, thumbs its nose, or even better, sticks out its tongue at wise, biological counsel. Some religions counsel a war with the body. Some religions can become the infection.

D. Wiebe (2016) suggests that religions today may persist as autoimmune disorders. He particularly draws attention to religion's ability to promote tribalistic ethnocentrism and xenophobia, phenomena we addressed in Chapter 3. He may be onto something. Religious tribalism's ethnocentrism and xenophobia were facultative in protecting the geographies of immunocompetence. Such geography no longer obtains. International travel breaches daily immunological borders.[1] That genie simply cannot be put back into that bottle. "With our present propensity for international travel . . . wherever a new microbe emerges in the future it cannot be regarded as just a local problem," D. Crawford writes, "in our globalized world . . . only global cooperation can prevent the looming catastrophe of a flu pandemic" (2007, 215). Prescient words. In today's world, there can only be one tribe. We are all implicated in global health politics. Does this mean that we must resort to draconian policies when it comes to vaccinations? Maybe. "Individuals have the freedom to resort to the healing tradition of their choice," admits H. Fabrega Jr., "however, if the needs of society are to be given significant weight in health decisions, individuals should in fairness be held responsible when the standardized package of medical information of the society is not heeded" (1997, 306). There are many, perhaps too many, who wish not to heed the standardized package of medical information. Those who heed not eventually get sick. This is a problem. It is a problem because the sick need antibiotics. This is unsustainable. "We have a huge global problem," Crawford further notes, "increasing numbers of microbes are acquiring resistance to multiple drugs, the natural source of antibiotics has virtually run dry, and there are few new drugs in the pipeline" (Crawford 2007, 193). In other words, the best way forward is through vaccinations. Crawford writes elsewhere, "when a pneumococcal vaccine was introduced in 2000, few antibiotics were needed, the selection pressure was removed and the incidence of resistance fell" (Crawford 2007, 214). Whether religiously motivated or not, an international, public health policy is what the doctors order. Thus are we faced with yet another cooperation problem: we need international cooperation. Although difficult, it isn't impossible. To do otherwise just might expedite the fate guaranteed to us by the second law of thermodynamics. Indeed, "there is a very real danger that we humans will be the first form of life to be responsible for our own extinction" (Solomon et al. 2015, 149).

Rudolf Otto proposed that religion is predicated on a rarefied experience of the holy. He openly recognized that the experience is not had by all. Only the privileged were invited to read his book. This volume similarly suggests that religion is predicated on an experience, but it is an experience that has been had by all. Its audience is not privileged. Everyone has experienced the pain and suffering associated with the contraction of an infectious disease. Throughout most of history, it was religion's job to manage this persistent and ubiquitous problem. Religion's integrated, immunological benefits greatly enhanced our ancestors' inclusive fitness. We are perhaps here today because of our religions of yesterday. To what extent will religion be adaptive for us tomorrow? This is a question concerning which the proverbial jury remains hung.

Notes

Chapter 1

1 In addition to being a marketing nightmare, Otto's counsel may in fact exclude a majority of those people who would rightly consider themselves religious. The philosopher of science Susan Haack observes, "For most people, if religious experience is to warrant belief in God, it will have to be other peoples' religious experience. Many of us have [sic] rely on the assurances of others that they have seen black swans; but in the case of religious experience, most of us will have to rely on a relatively few others who claim to have had experiences of a kind radically different from any that we—the unprivileged majority—have ever had" (2003, 285). In other words, one's religious commitment can be attributed to another's religious experience.
2 Even if you are an artificial lifeform, you, too, probably ought to beware of the common computer virus.
3 Subfecundity is the failure to achieve optimal reproductive success.
4 The other Horsemen are, to be sure, Famine, War, and Death.

Chapter 2

1 An allele is a variation of a gene. For instance, all sighted animals have genes that code for the production of eyes. The particular look of the eye, however, reflects variations in those genes. Some eyes are blue, some brown. Variation in eye color reflects allelic variation, that is, polymorphism. For the sake of convenience and convention, we will use the term "gene" when talking about biologically inherited traits.
2 S. Stewart-Williams suggests that anthropology and sociology are ultimately "specialist branches of zoology" (2010, 155).
3 Evolution is a substrate-neutral algorithm. All it needs is a population of replicators that replicate with a modicum of fidelity in an environment in which the materials necessary for such replication are scarce, that is, the replicators must compete to replicate. While evolution by natural selection is rightly associated with the biological world, it is equally applicable to the cultural and artificial ones as well.

4 Dennett overstates the case. P. Matzinger (2002) argues that it is not necessarily an issue of distinguishing between self and non-self as much as it is distinguishing between self and a parasitic, as opposed to a mutualist or commensal, non-self.
5 In similar fashion, infants expect that two solid objects cannot take up the same space in time; there can be no action at a distance (e.g., the eight ball will not move until the cue ball makes contact); objects move as cohesive units; and there is a difference between things that are alive and things that are not (Kirkpatrick 2005; Slingerland 2008).
6 We now know that such a radical distinction between what is living and what is not is a mistake. There are intermediate categories, for instance, viruses (Stewart-Williams 2010).
7 In much the same way that there isn't a radical distinction between what is living and what is not, there similarly is no such distinction between what is a human and what is a nonhuman animal (Stewart-Williams 2010).
8 Folk biology cognitively accounts for our capacities for racism and anti-Semitism.
9 P. Boyer realizes how intuitive such distinctions are; he also provocatively argues that they are wrong. "When we try to explain why people do what they do, our natural inclination is to see them as persons. . . . We assume that people's behavior is caused by their intentions," he argues, "that is just as wrong for a science of people as it was for the science of rivers and trees" (2018, 24). As is evident from our inveterate tendency to anthropomorphize (Guthrie 1993), it will remain quite difficult to shake the influence of folk psychology.
10 Folk economics, like the other folk sciences, appears to be present at birth, and if not, then very soon thereafter (Gredeback and Melinder 2011; Barrett 2015).
11 Although some contest rational choice theory (Kahneman 2011), Pinker suggests that the artificial scenarios by which test subjects are assessed for rational choosing in the laboratory do not adequately reflect real life conundrums. In other words, laboratory results suggesting that people do not choose rationally are simply artifacts of experimental design. On the whole, people, and animals generally, are rational choosers. R. Stark and R. Finke are correct: "Given their information and options, humans generally act in a rational way, is the preferable starting point for all theories of human action, including their religious actions" (2000, 21).
12 So important is this capacity to reason about mental states for the religious life that some authors entertain the possibility that autism spectrum disorders (ASD), which are now being considered disorders in the theory of mind module, may render the sufferer incapable of understanding a great bit of religion (Baron-Cohen 1995; McCauley and Graham 2020). If you cannot imagine another physical system as possessing a mind, that is, if you cannot impute agency to a naturally occurring object such as a human body, an incapacity associated with ASD, then imagining

the existence of a God, that is, a disembodied mind (more on that below), may simply be out of the question (Bering 2005).

13 Although it may be the case that cooperation presents a robust conundrum for evolutionary biology—so much so that evolution is often popularly characterized as the "survival of the fittest," an idiom of competition—we seem to see it at all levels of life. Some suggest that life began as a cooperative project (Margulis 1997). Even bacteria appear capable of a certain type of cooperation (Nettle 2009). Ridley notes, "cells are collectives . . . formed from the symbiotic collaboration between bacteria" (1996, 16). J. Greene also observes, "from simple cells to supersocial animals like us, the story of life on Earth is the story of increasingly complex cooperation" (2013, 59). Gaining control and the ability to cooperate appear co-constitutive.

14 My use of "perceive," and perhaps not the usual, "believe," is intentional. To perceive something is real is more compelling than simply believing. "Calling God a belief is a misnomer," claims M. Graziano, "it is more than a belief; it is more than a theory; it is more than imagination; it is a perception" (2010, 47), a "perceptual illusion" (2010, 50). Where belief appears motivated by some desire—we want it to be the case (Freud 1927)—perception appears to be a natural, default position, cognitively speaking (Bering 2011).

15 While gods modeled upon a father or king are surely widespread throughout many religious traditions, we would be remiss if we did not immediately include mothers in the range of models (Rizzuto 1979).

16 Even the exclusion of animals from the pantheon of *gods* is a bit off the mark; after all, Hinduism's pantheon of gods clearly includes theriomorphic deities, for example, Hanuman and Ganesha.

17 It should be noted that a woman's reproductive strategy is often contingent on ecological circumstances. Ecologies that are stressful and have high mortality rates tend to encourage women to adopt a more permissive, promiscuous strategy for reproduction. High stress ecologies tend to encourage fast strategies (Schmitt and Fuller 2015).

18 Indirectly corroborating this line of thought is the fact that some cultures apparently practice sexual promiscuity as a means of contraception. "The Muria themselves alleged that conception was prevented by the supernatural protection of the tribal gods over the village dormitories," note Reynolds and Tanner, "they had a number of folk ideas about achieving contraception, such as the need for *frequent change of partners*, and they believed it helped to restrict intercourse to once or twice a week" (1995, 137–8, emphasis added). Elsewhere, they note, "Whereas emphasis was heavily laid on sex in marriage for some small-scale societies, in others adolescent sex was the approved norm. In the latter case, we found that widespread promiscuity did not inevitably lead to the expected high premarital

birth rates" (1995, 146). Promiscuity can be, perhaps ironically, a birth control strategy.

Chapter 3

1 Chapter 5 will also address those religious conventions calibrated to eradicate infectious disease.
2 The "anxious" in "insecure-anxious" has been variously replaced with "preoccupied," "resistant," and "ambivalent."
3 The infectious diseases that appear to have posed the greatest risk to human survival throughout history, especially infant and child survival, have been primarily nonzoonotic. Nonzoonotic diseases are passed between humans (Thornhill and Fincher 2014b). There are six possible means of transmitting and contracting a nonzoonotic disease: direct interpersonal contact; exposure to aerosolized droplets of infectious matter; sexual contact; contact with a secondary host or vector, for example, a rodent or insect; ingestion of contaminated food or water; and contact with a fomite, that is, an object that carries a viable pathogen (Curtis and da Barra 2018, 2).
4 The opposite of collectivism is individualism. Cross-cultural research indicates that certain cultures are predominantly characterized by one or the other.
5 Douglas is similarly mistaken when she suggests that what is impure is what is anomalous. Such a position cannot account for the fact that anomalous entities, say, in the plant kingdom do not disgust us the way animal anomalies do (Rozin et al. 2000). Anomaly is neither sufficient nor necessary for us to feel something is dirty or polluted. What is sufficient is the presence of an infectious agent. Sources of infection disgust us, or so the "parasite avoidance theory of disgust" would have us believe (Sarabian et al. 2018; Curtis and da Barra 2018).
6 An example of such a word-stem task might be the following: Complete the stem, s _ _ p. Test subjects primed with religious images and ideas were more likely to spell "soap" as opposed to a control group who were just as likely to spell "ship."
7 M. B. Petersen recently suggested that the outgroup other may not enjoy some cognitively unique status in the mind of the ingroup member. Rather, it appears that when an ingroup member comes across an outgroup other, that other is cognitively placed in the same category as an infected ingroup member. He writes, "when in-group members showed signs of manifest infection, they were more often processed as belonging to the same mental category as out-group members" (2017, 1860), noting elsewhere, "the association between out-groups and pathogens seems to be a by-product of a general hypervigilance against deviations from the expected phenotype, such that physical (and potentially cultural and behavioral) differences

are processed as signs of manifest infection in the same way as is a rash on the face of an in-group member" (2017, 1862).

8 The "Red Queen's race" refers to the scene in Lewis Carroll's *Through the Looking Glass* where Alice and the Red Queen are racing each other but neither can move ahead. The phrase is now a euphemism in evolutionary biology for any relationship between two organisms that are trying to outcompete one another but cannot.

9 Prezygotic isolating mechanisms include ecological, temporal, behavioral, mechanical, and gametic isolation. Postzygotic isolating mechanisms ultimately amount to the zygote failing to survive and/or thrive. Such failure may be due to genetic incompatibilities or sterility (Mayr 2001).

10 A recent study suggests that infectious disease may have been one of the more significant factors in the decline of the Indus Civilization (Robbins-Schug et al. 2013).

11 In GIDEON online. Retrieved from http://www.gideononline.com on June 6, 2013.

12 The eleven world regions studied were Anglo, Middle East, Confucian Asia, Eastern Europe, Germanic Europe, Latin America, Latin Europe, Nordic Europe, southern Asia, and sub-Saharan Africa. The cluster that scored highest for collectivist values was Latin America. Tellingly, the cluster that scored lowest for collectivism practices was Nordic Europe and the cluster that scored lowest for values was Germanic Europe (Gelfand et al. 2004).

13 The complement to altricial is precocial. A precocial animal, for instance, a horse, is born relatively mature and is able to function in the world without immediate assistance.

14 Before we get into the details of the pediatric/pedagogical taxonomy, it is perhaps best to dispense with the normative concern up front, that is, which strategy of childrearing practice is best. There isn't one. "That any form of phenotypic variation is in and of itself positive or negative is an anathema to biology," T. Y. Zhang et al. note, "The merit of any variation in phenotype is understandable only in terms of the degree to which it serves to enhance adaptation to environmental demands with respect to reproductive fitness" (2006, 73). Thus, the differences we find in childrearing ethnographies "may betoken adaptive variation rather than deficiency or defect" (LeVine 2007, 249). Truly, "there is no single ideal form of parenting" (Zhang et al. 2006, 75). In the same way that there is no single ideal form of parenting, there is no single ideal outcome of such practices for the child's and eventually the adult's personality.

15 In a critical review of the ethnographies of childrearing practices, B. S. Hewlett et al. (2000) problematize LeVine's sense of "indulgence." They suggest that they don't see such indulgence in the agrarian community they studied, an expectation one would apparently draw from LeVine's work. I'm not sure I find the criticism persuasive. Hewlett et al. do not address the difference between physical and emotional indulgence, nor do they take stock that for LeVine it is not so much the mode of

subsistence that determines which childrearing practice will be most prevalent. Rather, it is the degree to which the local disease ecology is robust or not. I don't believe Hewlett et al. adequately address this distinction.

16 Another characteristic of the pediatric model would seem to be polymatry, or allomothering. In many hunter-gatherer tribes an infant is often cared for by a host of mothers in the group. "Although sexual intercourse may take place with only two partaking, successful survival of small offspring in our species has almost never been a matter of an isolated pair, but of social networks" (Blume 2015, 64). While Kurtz (1992) believes such a practice helps mitigate the infant's primary attachment to the mother, thus preparing the child for attachment to the group—more on that shortly—there may be another reason for such polymatry. Hart (1990, 2011) and Freeland (1976) witness the same intentional passing of the infant around the group in several animal species. It would appear that such behavior "is an example of immune system priming." To be sure, a "newborn of primate groups must acquire immunity to the group's potential pathogens.... The behavior of mothers ... in intentionally passing their infants around to the group members ... is an example of immune system priming" (Hart 2011, 3410–11).

17 In the psychoanalytic traditions this is also known as the transference (Jones 1991).

18 An unfortunate consequence of the language used to identify and characterize these attachment styles is that they seem to convey a certain normativity. One gets the impression from the early work on attachment that the secure style is the rightfully desired one (Bowlby 1969; Ainsworth et al. 1978). As previously noted, such judgments may be misleading, especially when viewed in an evolutionary light. Perhaps secure attachments are normative in industrial and post-industrial cultures, like the ones in which J. Bowlby worked. "A prototypically secure attachment strategy of open emotional experience and interpersonal trust," L. M. Diamond suggests, "should prove beneficial only in relatively safe and nurturant environments in which stressors are manageable and reliable caregiving is available" (2015, 110). Employing a history and sociology of science perspective, F. Rothbaum et al. also point out, "If attachment research had its origins in cultures that prioritize interdependent selves, and if those cultures enjoyed the scientific dominance that the West currently enjoys, it is possible that current theories would hypothesize that qualities like proper demeanor and accommodation, rather than autonomy and exploration, are universal consequences of security" (2011, 169). In other words, "security" can be inherently ethnocentric. The same may be said for the term, "adaptive." Diamond notes, "We can no longer casually use the word *adaptive*: *Adaptive* is a fundamentally relative construct, defined with respect to the challenges and environments at hand" (2015, 110).

19 Maunder and Hunter (2001) suggest that 35–40 percent of the population are insecure anxious.

20 There is some nuance here. E. E. Noftle and P. R. Shaver note, for instance, that "attachment anxiety is negatively related to only the dominance aspect of Extraversion, but not the sociability aspect," after all, the insecure-anxiously attached are "highly interested in social relationships" (2006, 200).

21 For an opposing view, see Tybur et al. 2018.

Chapter 4

1 This paragraph and the one preceding rely upon the presentation in Campbell (1987, 897–8).

2 This is the reason why a glucocorticoid is often used to treat autoimmune disorders, in which the immune system starts to attack the body's own organs and tissues. The steroid can indeed suppress the immune response, but in so doing it renders the organism more vulnerable to infectious diseases.

3 Depression is not always a bad thing (Nesse and Williams 1996). There are moments when it might in fact be adaptive. L. A. Kirkpatrick and B. J. Ellis suggest that a certain "depressive realism" might be "a behavioral strategy for taking time out to reassess one's situation and/or to wait for better times . . . a behavioral strategy activated by low self-esteem in one or more domains" (2004, 53). P. Gilbert similarly proposes that "despair is . . . designed to make an animal *stop signaling* and moving in the environment (hunker down/demobilize) when not to do so is dangerous" (2006, 290). Mild and short-lived depression may help the organism occasionally navigate successfully scenarios in which it would be deleterious to be outspoken, vibrant, and ambitious.

4 Other psychological stressors include a lack of outlets for the expression of frustration, the perception of no social support, and the perception that life is only going to get worse (Sapolsky 2004).

5 The bulk of this paragraph and the previous one draw upon the presentation in Solomon et al. (2015, 75–8).

6 While TMT claims that we are primarily afraid of annihilation, this may be inaccurate. This is the case because death anxiety is actually multidimensional (Mikulincer et al. 1990; Ellis 2008). There are three such dimensions. The first dimension, and the one that TMT presupposes, reflects fears of annihilation. This is called "intrapersonal death anxiety." A second dimension is known as "transpersonal death anxiety." This anxiety is not as alarming as the intrapersonal type in that it doesn't really attend to one's personal death as much as it does philosophical musings on the nature of life and death, abstractly considered. The third dimension, and the one that seems to get the highest "return rate" on death anxiety surveys is called, "interpersonal death anxiety." This anxiety reflects the

fear that when one dies, one's soul will carry on, but it will do so in perpetual social isolation. Regardless of dimension, death anxiety must be managed.

7   It may seem obvious on first pass that no one wants to die. S. Kagan (2012) suggests, however, that if we stop to think about it, maybe we really don't want to live forever after all. The tedium that would attend life everlasting could itself be terrifying.

8   Thanatocentric theories propose that religion originates with the need to manage existential anxieties through denials of death.

9   It should be noted here that there are some religions that seem to celebrate the natural world rather than denigrating it and wishing to transcend it. Upon close inspection, however, these religions are not really celebrating nature. J. Goldenberg et al. note in this regard, "Cultures that construe human life as closely connected to other animals and the natural environment tend to imbue all of nature with supernatural power and significance. Animals, plants, and physical objects like mountains and rivers are seen as sources of great spiritual power. Although humans may be construed as being 'one with nature' within the context of these cultural worldviews, the nature they are one with is supernatural rather than natural. Natural entities are anthropomorphized into something far beyond their basic physical qualities, rather than viewed as the consequence of physical and biochemical processes, as in Western culture's scientific worldview" (2000, 214).

10 I include under this one term, "exorcism," all rituals that are intended to keep a non-natural agent at bay. For instance, exorcism, strictly speaking, is intended to drive out of an individual or object the invading, malevolent, non-natural agent. Propitiation, on the other hand, is intended to keep such an agent, whose intention could become to possess someone or something, at bay. Thus, for sake of economy, I will use "exorcism" to connote any ritual performance the outcome of which is either to expel or keep at bay a malevolent, non-natural agent.

11 This constitutes the central claim of the preeminent Jewish theologian/philosopher Maimonides's theodicy (1995).

12 It is this sense of agential contingency in the intentional stance that seemingly, not to mention conveniently for many apologists, eludes disconfirmation. Prayer and worship enjoy what J. Barrett calls, "conceptual control," that is, "a ritual's ability to withstand evidence of failure... (they) cannot be easily falsified" (2004, 70–1).

13 I say, "often," because I do not want to exclude the reality that sometimes demons and devils are anthropomorphically based and so, occasionally, certain social manipulations will animate an exorcism (Cohen 2007).

14 The pronounced concern with free will animating most religious traditions attests to this. Of course, even Calvinism's fatalism (i.e., predestination) did not preclude people from behaving in ways that indicated a residue of the illusion of control.

15 To be sure, I am aware of reports of people who have in fact flatlined and then been resuscitated. While such reports are indeed intriguing, they do not truly count as evidence of coming back from the dead. This is the case because the resuscitation

often happens within minutes of flatlining (although I do believe I came across a story of a person who was resuscitated several hours later, but that person had peculiar circumstances, such as low temperatures). If someone were to present convincing evidence that someone was resuscitated seventy-two hours after passing away, they would have my attention.

16 One can make the argument that such a dynamic informs the world's most widely practiced religion, Christianity.

Chapter 5

1 We can note here that the world's most widely practised religion, Christianity, has as its central theological claim that the blood of the sacrificed Christ heals the sinner.
2 N. D. Wolfe, C. P. Dunavan, and J. Diamond (2007) have identified the twenty-five diseases that have caused the greatest morbidity and mortality for the human animal over time. Seventeen of these diseases continue to impose "the heaviest world burdens today (they have the highest disability-adjusted life years [DALY] scores)" (Wolfe et al. 2007, 279–80). Eight of these diseases are temperate, the other nine, tropical. The temperate diseases include hepatitis B, influenza A, measles, pertussis, rotavirus A, syphilis, tetanus, and tuberculosis. The tropical diseases are AIDS, Chagas' disease, cholera, dengue fever, East African sleeping sickness, West African sleeping sickness, *vivax* malaria, *falciparum* malaria, and visceral leishmaniasis. The remaining eight diseases are those that appear to be no longer burdensome today but surely were in an ancestral past. They are temperate diphtheria, mumps, plague, rubella, smallpox, typhoid, typhus, and tropical yellow fever (Wolfe et al. 2007). Oaten et al. (2009) identified the transmission routes for these twenty-five diseases. They note that typhus, rotavirus, and cholera are passed via the fecal-oral route. This generally means that contaminated fecal matter finds its way into the local water reservoir, awaiting consumption by an unwary host. Smallpox, influenza, measles, pertussis, tuberculosis, diphtheria, mumps, and rubella are transmitted through aerosolized droplets in saliva or nasal discharge, or upon direct contact with a contaminated object such as a hand. Ten diseases have their transmission routes through an arthropod vector with reservoirs in rodents. M. Oaten et al. write, "Lice were the vector in 2 cases (plague and typhus), biting flies and bugs in 4 cases (East and West African sleeping sickness, visceral leishmaniasis, and Chagas disease), and mosquitoes in a further 4 cases (falciparum and vivax malarias, yellow fever, and dengue fever)" (2009, 307). They also note that AIDS, syphilis, and hepatitis B are transmitted through the exchange of sexual fluids and blood. Oaten et al. also note that twenty of the twenty-five identified diseases are disgust elicitors. To this assessment, M. Singer (2015) adds that six

diseases are responsible for ninety percent of deaths today, that is, "HIV disease, malaria, diarrhea, measles, pneumonia, and tuberculosis" (2015, 71).
3   In the human animal, the MHC is sometimes called the HLA, or the human leukocyte antigen complex.
4   There are instances in which the body's immune system tolerates foreign matter. The human animal, as all animals do, plays host to what is called the microbiome. The microbiome is the set of bacterial species that have adapted to the animal's biochemistry. "Our gastrointestinal, respiratory, and reproductive tracts, and our skin, are normally colonized by communities of microorganisms, which are known collectively as the human microbiome," R. L. Perlman writes, "the microbiome is made up of thousands of bacterial species, which together comprise roughly ten times as many cells (approximately 100 trillion vs 10 trillion) and contain more than 100 times as many genes (roughly 3 million vs 21 thousand) than are present in 'our own' bodies" (2013, 77). The microbiome is composed of commensal and mutualistic communities of microorganisms. Where the former's survival and replication does not result in debilitation for the host, the latter not only does not debilitate the host, but it actually is beneficial to the host. "Host-microbe interactions are essential to many aspects of normal 'mammalian' physiology," note L. Dethlefson et al., "ranging from metabolic activity to immune homeostasis" (2007, 811). Accordingly, and as we've seen previously, the immune system actually operates on the danger model, not the stranger model (Matzinger 2002).
5   Many anthropologists argue that shamanism is not a religion (Hayden 2003; King 2007; Winkelman 2010; Peoples et al. 2016). They do so for two reasons. First, shamanism is not a religion because it is a technique for communicating with and manipulating spirits. According to the definition presented in Chapters 2 and 4, this would clearly make shamanism a religion. Intentional and mechanistic relationships between this world and a spirit world are the stuff of religion. The second claim is that shamanism cannot be religion because the shaman wields power over the spirit world; spirits cannot reciprocate in kind. Like the first contention, this second one is also unpersuasive. "Shamans . . . allow their bodies to be taken over by spirits" (McClenon 2002, 6). D. Sperber has the appropriate reply to such anthropological concerns: "Because both religion and magic are family resemblance notions, the agentive and nonagentive character of the supernatural powers involved is not an automatic and absolute criterion: Many religious practices (e.g., the use of relics) are somewhat magical, and many magical practices (e.g., the conjuring of demons) are somewhat religious by that criterion" (2004, 751). If it enjoys collective sanction, as shamanism clearly does, communicating with the spirit world is religion.
6   Some suggest that the comparison between contemporary hunter-gatherer groups and ancestral communities is tenuous at best, and misleading at worst. M. Bloch, for instance, writes, "modern hunters and gatherers live in conditions quite unlike those of our ancestors, precisely because they are surrounded by non-foragers. This

means that it is unlikely that what goes for contemporary groups of hunters and gatherers applied also in the past" (2001, 195–6), noting elsewhere, for example, "there is absolutely no reason to believe that the New Guinea highlanders have somehow been frozen in time and are thus 'living fossils' retaining unchanged customs of thousands of years ago . . . this is simply not so" (2001, 196). While that may be true, H. Peoples et al. note, "Although present-day hunter-gatherers are not direct analogues of those early societies and may not be direct, unbroken descendants of ancestral hunter-gatherers, they can provide a window onto traits selected for in the Pleistocene, including traits of early religion" (2016, 263).

7 Corroborating Norenzayan's point that tribal communities do not need Big Gods because they are small enough to police each other (see Chapter 2), Peoples et al. (2016) note that among a sample of thirty-three HG communities only 15 percent had active, Big Gods.

8 If a religion is not dualistic, then it is most likely idealistic. Idealism is a metaphysical position that denies the fundamental reality of the physical. No religion seems to adopt physicalism. Physicalism disallows the existence of souls (Flanagan 2002) and is strongly agnostic (Ellis 2008) or weakly atheistic (Kitcher 2015). According to physicalism, all religions are purely inventions of the human mind.

9 It would appear that there is a genetic mutation associated with capacities for altered states of consciousness and that this mutation occurred approximately 30,000–50,000 years ago. The mutation produced a highly active form of the DRD4 gene, that is, the dopamine receptor D4. Those with the highly active form are more prone to religious beliefs, explanations, and experiences. In fact, some have called this, "the God gene" (Hamer 2005). Artificial upregulation of the DRD4 gene can induce religious sensibilities. Similarly, drugs that block the DRD4, such as clozapine, can reduce religious sensibilities. Significantly for what follows, the presence of DRD4 in the schizophrenic's brain appears "500 percent higher than normal" (Silver 2006, 77). Perhaps the first shamans were the first people to "enjoy" this genetic mutation. That said, not everyone agrees that an altered state of consciousness is essential to shamanism. Gibson notes that some authors do "not see trance as essential, so long as the shaman 'is thought to control spirits by ritual techniques'" (1986, 143).

10 The fact that the capacity for hypnotic-like states is found throughout the animal kingdom, for instance, the Totstell reflex, attests to the survival advantages accruing thereto (McClenon 2006).

11 Of particular importance for shamanism's psychotherapeutic goals, one study found that among efficacious antidepressants, 75 percent of the efficacy could be attributed to placebo (Winkelman 2010).

12 J. Bulbulia suggests that by recovering due to a placebo one can signal one's sincere commitment to collective action: "Actually getting well in the presence of a religious placebo is a hard-to-fake signal capable of authenticating intention to cooperative

exchange. . . . Defectors can verbally express commitment, but without genuine belief they cannot benefit from religious placebos" (2006, 112). We'll see in the fourth section that Bulbulia equally deploys costly-signaling theory to account for certain aspects of blood sacrifice.

13 The same applies to those engaged in complementary and alternative medicine (CAM), the majority of which rely solely on the placebo effect for their efficacy (Bausell 2007).

14 The pediatric style of childrearing associated with the robust infectious disease ecology of south Asia has been previously documented (Ellis 2015).

15 It should be noted that H. Whitehouse has argued that exposure to imagistic rituals, such as blood sacrifice, can in fact bond a community together. "The imagistic mode first appeared among Upper Paleolithic hunter-gatherers through processes of religious experimentation that turned out to be highly adaptive in conditions of intensified competition for resources, not least because they fostered forms of especially intense local cohesion, facilitating more effective forms of group defence" (Whitehouse 2000, 3).

Chapter 6

1 There are, of course, other species of animal that can engage in self-directed hurt as well as inflict harm on offspring. We can be sure, though, that when such events occur there is, all the same, an inclusive fitness algorithm afoot. For instance, sometimes a parent may invite injury to self if it leads to the survival of offspring. Similarly, many species of animal will engage in infanticide if the survival of the infant would lead to a decrease in inclusive fitness, as when a runt would drain too many calories from the resource pool, a drain the runt will never be able to repay.

2 While Dawkins was the first to use "meme," others have suggested something quite similar. For instance, Lumsden and Wilson (1981) proposed, "culturgen"; Richerson and Boyd (2005) proposed, "cultural variant"; and Sperber (1990) proposed, "shared representation." Despite the troubles some have tried to make for memetics, there is something simply intuitive about the idea that information is passed between individuals such that one individual thinks and behaves in a way that is so similar to the source that something must be replicating.

3 This is not to deny that sometimes a culture may engage in dance for the sake of the crops (Buttree 1930).

4 The same troubles with discrete identities bedeviled the early evolutionary scientists. When Mendel first proposed the gene as a unit of inheritance, he really had no idea what the gene was and was not. Had those scientists in the first few decades after Darwin and Mendel, and before the discovery of the actual

composition of the gene, put on hold their research on evolutionary theory, our arrival at the modern synthesis would have been greatly delayed (see Chapter 2). In other words, productive work was accomplished in advance of knowing the exact contours and nature of the gene. Perhaps the same can be said for the meme.

5 The effect is named after the American psychologist, James Mark Baldwin.
6 Religious traditions that engage in castration rituals are seemingly things of the past. A residue of such practices remains. Especially among Jews and Christians, circumcision is still widely practiced. Circumcision is symbolic castration. "One of the world's oldest and most frequently performed surgical procedures with a high rate in the USA and worldwide (70 and 33%, respectively).... Circumcision is a modified ritual of the ancient sacrifice of castration" (Mordeniz and Verit 2009, 402).
7 All references to the *Hatha Yoga Pradipika* (HYP) are from Akers (2002).
8 It should be noted that the qualifying coefficient "hard-core" has not been universally adopted by those working on tantra. The phrase seems to have a certain pornographic ring in Western cultures. The extent to which D. G. White wishes to incorporate such allusions is both unclear and ultimately unimportant.
9 It should be noted that the incestuous component of the paradigm seldom, if ever, plays out in reality. Indeed, the hero's partner is generally from out-of-caste and thus cannot be his mother or sister. That said, the hero actually ingests orally pathogenic substances. Also, and not to seem homophobic but merely descriptive, the most suboptimal sexual union is the homosexual one.
10 The woman-astride position either intentionally or unintentionally employs gravity to aid in forestalling successful fertilization.
11 Other religious traditions follow suit. For instance, the consumption of heavy metals in the Daoist tradition of *wai-tan* appears comparable. So too, some of the reports concerning St. Francis of Assisi kissing the open sores of a leper and eating from a bowl mixed with the blood from a leper's fingers clearly offends immunological wisdom.

Chapter 7

1 We could, of course, suggest that fundamentalist religion has seen a comeback over the course of the twentieth and twenty-first centuries precisely as reactions to this expanded exposure to potentially infected others.

References

Abramson, L. Y., G. I. Metalsky, and L. B. Alloy. (1989). "Hopelessness Depression: A Theory-based Subtype of Depression." *Psychological Review* 96(2):358–72.

Ainsworth, M. D. S. (1969). "Object Relations, Dependency, and Attachment: A Theoretical Review of the Infant-Mother Relationship." *Child Development* 40:969–1025.

Ainsworth, M. D. S., M. C. Blehar, E. Waters, and S. Wall. (1978). *Patterns of Attachment: A Psychological Study of the Strange Situation*. Hillsdale: Lawrence Erlbaum Associates.

Akers, B. D. (trans.) (2002). *The Hatha Yoga Pradipika (The Original Sanskrit Svatmarama)*. Woodstock: YogaVidya.com.

Alexander, R. D. (1990). "Epigenetic Rules and Darwinian Algorithms." *Ethology and Sociobiology* 11:241–303.

Alloy, L. B. and C. M. Clements. (1992). "Illusion of Control: Invulnerability to Negative Affect and Depressive Symptoms After Laboratory and Natural Stressors." *Journal of Abnormal Psychology* 101(2):234–45.

Alvarado, K. A., D. I. Templer, C. Bresler, and S. Thomas-Dobson. (1995). "The Relationship of Religious Variables to Death Depression and Death Anxiety." *Journal of Clinical Psychology* 51(2):202–4.

Arthur, S. (2013). *Early Daoist Dietary Practices: Examining Ways to Health and Longevity*. Washington, DC: Lexington Books.

Atkinson, J. M. (1989). *The Art and Politics of Wana Shamanship*. Berkeley: University of California Press.

Atran, S. (2002). *In Gods We Trust: The Evolutionary Landscape of Religion*. New York: Oxford University Press.

Aunger, R. (Ed.). (2001). *Darwinizing Culture: The Status of Memetics as a Science*. New York: Oxford University Press.

Aunger, R. (2002). *The Electric Meme: A New Theory of How We Think*. New York: The Free Press.

Aunger, R. and V. Curtis. (2015). *Gaining Control: How Human Behavior Evolved*. New York: Oxford University Press.

Axelrod, A. (1984). *The Evolution of Cooperation*. New York: Basic Books.

Ayub, Q. and C. Tyler-Smith. (2009). "Genetic Variation in South Asia: Assessing the Influences of Geography, Language and Ethnicity for Understanding History and Disease Risk." *Briefings in Functional Genomics & Proteomics* 8(5):395–404.

Badcock, P. B. T. and N. B. Allen. (2007). "Evolution, Social Cognition, and Depressed Mood: Exploring the Relationship Between Depression and Social Risk Taking." In J.

P. Forgas, M. G. Haselton, and W. von Hippel (Eds.), *Evolution and the Social Mind: Evolutionary Psychology and Social Cognition* (pp. 125–42). New York: Psychology Press.

Balon, R. (2007). "Depression, Antidepressants, and Human Sexuality." *Primary Psychiatry* 14(2):42–50.

Bamshad, M., T. Kivisild, and W. S. Watkins. (2001). "Genetic Evidence on the Origins of Indian Caste Populations." *Genome Research* 11(6):994–1004.

Barkow, J. H., L. Cosmides, and J. Tooby (Eds.). (1992). *The Adapted Mind: Evolutionary Psychology and the Generation of Culture*. New York: Oxford University Press.

Baron-Cohen, S. (1995). *Mindblindness: An Essay on Autism and Theory of Mind*. Cambridge: The MIT Press.

Barrett, H. C. (2005). "Adaptations to Predators and Prey." In D. M. Buss (Ed.), *The Handbook of Evolutionary Psychology* (pp. 200–23). New York: Wiley.

Barrett, H. C. (2015). *The Shape of Thought: How Mental Adaptations Evolve*. New York: Oxford University Press.

Barrett, J. L. (2004). *Why Would Anyone Believe in God?* Lanham: AltaMira Press.

Barrett, J. L. (2012). *Born Believers: The Science of Children's Religious Belief*. Miami: Atria Books.

Bartholomew, K. (1990). "Avoidance of Intimacy: An Attachment Perspective." *Journal of Social and Personal Relationships* 7:147–78.

Basu, A., N. Mukherjee, S. Roy, S. Sengupta, S. Banerjee, M. Chakraborty, B. Dey, M. Roy, N. P. Bhattacharya, S. Roychoudhury, and P. P. Majumder. (2003). "Ethnic India: A Genomic View, with Special Reference to Peopling and Structure." *Genome Research* 13(10):2277–90.

Baumard, N. and C. Chevallier. (2015). "The Nature and Dynamics of World Religions: A Life-History Approach." *Proceedings of the Royal Society B* 282: n. pg.

Baumeister, R. F. and M. R. Leary. (1995). "The Need to Belong: Desire for Interpersonal Attachments as a Fundamental Human Motivation." *Psychological Bulletin* 117(3):497–529.

Bausell, R. B. (2007). *Snake Oil Science: The Truth About Complementary and Alternative Medicine*. New York: Oxford University Press.

Becker, E. (1973). *The Denial of Death*. New York: Simon & Schuster.

Becker, E. (1975). *Escape from Evil*. New York: Free Press.

Bell, D. (2015). "Fathering, Rituals, and Mating: Exploring Parental Stability and Sexual Strategies in Early Religious Practices." In D. J. Slone and J. A. Van Slyke (Eds.), *The Attraction of Religion: A New Evolutionary Psychology of Religion* (pp. 169–87). London: Bloomsbury.

Belsky, Jay. (1999). "Modern Evolutionary Theory and Patterns of Attachment." In Jude Cassidy and Phillip R. Shaver (Eds.), *Handbook of Attachment: Theory, Research, and Clinical Applications* (pp. 249–64). New York: The Guilford Press.

Berger, S. A. (2012). *Infectious Diseases of India*, Gideon e-books, http://www.gideononline.com/ebooks/country/infectious-diseases-of-india/.

Berger, R. J. and N. H. Phillips. (1995). "Energy Conservation and Sleep." *Behavioral Brain Research* 69(1–2):65–73.

Bering, J. (2005). "The Evolutionary History of an Illusion: Religious Causal Beliefs in Children and Adults." In B. J. Ellis & D. F. Bjorklund (Eds.), *Origins of the Social Mind: Evolutionary Psychology and Child Development* (pp. 411–37). New York: Guilford Press.

Bering, J. (2011). *The Belief Instinct: The Psychology of Souls, Destiny, and the Meaning of Life*. New York: W. W. Norton & Company.

Berman, E. (2009). *Radical, Religious, and Violent: The New Economics of Terrorism*. Cambridge: The MIT Press.

Berry, K., R. Band, R. Corcoran, C. Barrowclough, and A. Wearden. (2007). "Attachment Styles, Interpersonal Relationships and Schizotypy in a Non-Clinical Sample." *Psychology and Psychotherapy* 80(4):563–76.

Bittles, A. H. and J. V. Neel. (1994). "The Costs of Human Inbreeding and Their Implications for Variations at the DNA Level." *Nature Genetics* 8(2):117–21.

Black, R. E., L. H. Allen, Z. A. Bhutta, L. E. Caulfield, M. D. Onis, M. Ezzati, C. Mathers, and J. Rivera. (2008). "Maternal and Child Undernutrition: Global and Regional Exposures and Health Consequences." *The Lancet* 371(9608):243–60.

Blackmore, S. (1999). *The Meme Machine*. New York: Oxford University Press.

Bloch, M. (1992). *Prey into Hunter: The Politics of Religious Experience*. Cambridge: Cambridge University Press.

Bloch, M. (2001). "A Well-Disposed Social Anthropologist's Problems with Memes." In R. Aunger (Ed.), *Darwinizing Culture: The Status of Memetics as a Science* (pp. 189–203). New York: Oxford University Press.

Bloch, M. (2005). *Essays on Cultural Transmission*. Oxford: Berg Publishers.

Bloom, P. (2004). *Descartes' Baby: How the Science of Child Development Explains What Makes Us Human*. New York: Basic Books.

Blume, M. (2015). "How Is't With Thy Religion, Pray? Selection of Religiosity Among Individuals and Groups." In D. J. Slone and J. A. Van Slyke (Eds.), *The Attraction of Religion: A New Evolutionary Psychology of Religion* (pp. 63–71). London: Bloomsbury.

Boehm, C. (1993). "Egalitarian Behavior and Reverse Dominance Hierarchy." *Current Anthropology* 34(3):227–40.

Boerlijst, M. C., M. A. Nowak, and K. Sigmund. (1997). "The Logic of Contrition." *Journal of Theoretical Biology* 185:281–93.

Bosch, J. A., E. J. C. de Geus, A. Kelder, E. C. I. Veerman, J. Hoogstraten, and A. V. N. Amerongen. (2001). "Differential Effects of Active Versus Passive Coping on Secretory Immunity." *Psychophysiology* 38:836–46.

Boudry, M. and S. Hofhuis. (2018). "Parasites of the Mind. Why Cultural Theorists Need the Meme's Eye View." *Cognitive Systems Research* 52:155–67.

Bowers, S. L., S. D. Bilbo, F. S. Dhabhar, and R. J. Nelson. (2008). "Stressor-Specific Alterations in Corticosterone and Immune Responses in Mice." *Brain, Behavior, and Immunity* 22(1):105–13.

Bowlby, J. (1969). *Attachment*. New York: Basic Books.
Bowlby, J. (1973). *Separation: Anxiety and Anger*. New York: Basic Books.
Bowlby, J. (1980). *Loss: Sadness and Depression*. New York: Basic Books.
Boyer, P. (2001). *Religion Explained: The Evolutionary Origins of Religious Thought*. New York: Basic Books.
Boyer, P. (2018). *Minds Make Societies: How Cognition Explains the World Humans Create*. New Haven: Yale University Press.
Boyer, P. and P. Lienard. (2006). "Why Ritualized Behavior? Precaution Systems and Action Parsing in Developmental, Pathological and Cultural Rituals." *Behavioral and Brain Sciences* 29:595–650.
Boyer, P. and B. Bergstrom. (2008). "Evolutionary Perspectives on Religion." *Annual Review of Anthropology* 37:111–30.
Boyer, P., R. Firat, and F. van Leeuwen. (2015). "Safety, Threat, and Stress in Intergroup Relations: A Coalitional Index Model." *Perspectives in Psychological Science* 10(4):434–50.
Bretherton, I. (1985). "Attachment Theory: Retrospect and Prospect." In I. Bretheron and E. Waters (Eds.), *Growing Points in Attachment Theory and Research. Monographs of the Society for Research in Child Development* 50(1–2, Serial no. 209):3–35.
Brodie, R. (2011). *Virus of the Mind: The New Science of the Meme*. New York: Hay House.
Bulbulia, J. (2005). "Are There Any Religions?: An Evolutionary Exploration." *Method & Theory in the Study of Religion* 17:71–100.
Bulbulia, J. (2006). "Nature's Medicine: Religiosity as an Adaptation for Health and Cooperation." In P. McNamara (Ed.), *Where God and Science Meet*, vol. 1 (pp. 87–121). Westport: Praeger.
Bulbulia, J. and E. Slingerland. (2012). "Religious Studies as a Life Science." *Numen* 59:564–613.
Bulbulia, J., J. Shaver, L. Greaves, R. Sosis, and C. G. Sibley. (2015). "Religion and Parental Cooperation: An Empirical Test of Slone's Sexual Signaling Model." In D. J. Slone and J. A. van Slyke (Eds.), *The Attraction of Religion: A New Evolutionary Psychology of Religion* (pp. 29–53). London: Bloomsbury.
Burkert, W. (1996). *Creation of the Sacred: Tracks of Biology in Early Religions*. Cambridge: Harvard University Press.
Buss, D. M. (2001). "Human Nature and Culture: An Evolutionary Psychological Perspective." *Journal of Personality* 69(6):955–78.
Buss, D. (Ed.). (2005). *The Handbook of Evolutionary Psychology*. Hoboken: John Wiley & Sons, Inc.
Buttree, J. M. (1930). *The Rhythm of the Redman: In Song, Dance and Decoration*. New York: A. S. Barnes.
Byers, John A. (1998). *American Pronghorn: Social Adaptations and the Ghosts of Predators Past*. Chicago: The University of Chicago Press.
Campbell, N. A. (1987). *Biology*. Menlo Park: The Benjamin Cummings Publishing Company, Inc.

Carroll, S. (2016). *The Big Picture: On the Origins of Life, Meaning, and the Universe Itself*. New York: Dutton.

Cashdan, E. (2001). "Ethnic Diversity and Its Environmental Determinants: Effects of Climate, Pathogens, and Habitat Diversity." *American Anthropologist* 103(4):968–91.

Cassidy, J. and L. J. Berlin. (1994). "The Insecure/Ambivalent Pattern of Attachment: Theory and Research." *Child Development* 65:971–91.

Cassidy, J. and P. R. Shaver (Eds.). (1999). *Handbook of Attachment: Theory, Research, and Clinical Applications*. New York: Guilford Press.

Cavalli-Sforza, L. L. (2000). *Genes, Peoples, and Languages*. New York: Farrar, Strauss & Giroux.

Cavalli-Sforza, L. L., P. Menozzi, and A. Piazza. (1994). *The History and Geography of Human Genes*. Princeton: Princeton University Press.

Chisholm, J. S. (1996). "The Evolutionary Ecology of Attachment Organization." *Human Nature* 7(1):1–38.

Cho, F., and R. K. Squier. (2008). "Reductionism: Be Afraid, Be Very Afraid." *Journal of the American Academy of Religion* 76(2):412–17.

Churchland, P. (2005). "A Neurophilosophical Slant on Consciousness Research." *Progress in Brain Research* 149:285–93.

Clark, D. P. (2010). *Germs, Genes & Civilization: How Epidemics Shaped Who We Are Today*. Upper Saddle River: FT Press.

Clark, J. A. and D. M. T. Fessler. (2014). "Recontextualizing the Behavioral Immune System Within Psychoneuroimmunology." *Evolutionary Behavioral Sciences* 8(4):235–43.

Clay, R., J. A. Terrizzi Jr., and N. J. Shook. (2012). "Individual Differences in the Behavioral Immune System and the Emergence of Cultural Systems." *Social Psychology* 43(4):174–84.

Cohen, E. (2007). "Witchcraft and Sorcery." In H. Whitehouse and J. Laidlaw (Eds.), *Religion, Anthropology, and Cognitive Science* (pp. 135–60). Durham: Carolina Academic Press.

Cohen, F., D. Sullivan, S. Solomon, J. Greenberg, and D. M. Ogilvie. (2011). "Finding Everland: Flight Fantasies and the Desire to Transcend Mortality." *Journal of Experimental Social Psychology* 47:88–102.

Cohen, S. and T. B. Herbert. (1996). "Psychological Factors and Physical Disease from the Perspective of Human Psychoneuroimmunology." *Annual Review of Psychology* 47:113–42.

Consedine, N. S. and C. Magai. (2003). "Attachment and Emotion Experience in Later Life: The View from Emotions Theory." *Attachment & Human Development* 5(2):165–87.

Cox, C. R., J. L. Goldenberg, T. Pyszczynski, and D. Weise. (2007). "Disgust, Creatureliness and the Accessibility of Death-Related Thoughts." *European Journal of Social Psychology* 37:494–507.

Crawford, D. H. (2007). *Deadly Companions: How Microbes Shaped Our History*. Oxford: Oxford University Press.

Crespi, B. and K. Summers. (2014). "Inclusive Fitness Theory for the Evolution of Religion." *Animal Behaviour* 92:313–23.

Cronk, L. (1991). "Human Behavioral Ecology." *Annual Review of Anthropology* 20:25–53.

Curtis, V. (2001). "Hygiene: How Myths, Monsters, and Mothers-in-Law can Promote Behaviour Change." *Journal of Infection* 43:75–9.

Curtis, V., R. Aunger, and T. Rabie. (2004). "Evidence that Disgust Evolved to Protect from Risk of Disease." *Proceedings of the Royal Society B (Suppl.)* 271(Suppl. 4): S131–33.

Curtis, V. and A. Biran. (2001). "Dirt, Disgust, and Disease: Is Hygiene in Our Genes?" *Perspectives in Biology and Medicine* 44(1):17–31.

Curtis, V., M. de Barra, and R. Aunger. (2011). "Disgust as an Adaptive System for Disease Avoidance Behaviour." *Philosophical Transactions of the Royal Society B* 366:389–401.

Curtis, V. and M. de Barra. (2018). "The Structure and Function of Pathogen Disgust." *Philosophical Transactions of the Royal Society B* 373:1–17.

Curtis, V. A. (2007a). "Dirt, Disgust and Disease: A Natural History of Hygiene." *Journal of Epidemiology and Community Health* 61:660–4.

Curtis, V. A. (2007b). "A Natural History of Hygiene." *Canadian Journal of Infectious Diseases and Medical Microbiology* 18(1):11–14.

Damasio, A. (2018). *The Strange Order of Things: Life, Feeling, and the Making of Cultures*. New York: Pantheon Books.

Darwin, C. R. (1859). *On the Origin of Species by Means of Natural Selection, or the Preservation of Favoured Races in the Struggle for Life*. London: John Murray.

Davies, M. F. and H. E. Kirby. (1985). "Multidimensionality of the Relationship Between Perceived Control and Belief in the Paranormal: Spheres of Control and Types of Paranormal Phenomena." *Personality and Individual Differences* 6(5):661–3.

Dawkins, R. (1976). *The Selfish Gene*. New York: Oxford University Press.

Dawkins, R. (1982). *The Extended Phenotype*. New York: Oxford University Press.

de Jong, P. J. and M. L. Peters. (2009). "Sex and the Sexual Dysfunctions: The Role of Disgust and Contamination Sensitivity." In B. O. Olatunji and D. McKay (Eds.), *Disgust and Its Disorders: Theory, Assessment, and Treatment Implications* (pp. 253–70). Washington, DC: American Psychological Association.

Dennett, D. C. (1989). *The Intentional Stance*. Cambridge: Massachusetts Institute of Technology.

Dennett, D. C. (1991). *Consciousness Explained*. Boston: Little, Brown and Co.

Dennett, D. C. (1995). *Darwin's Dangerous Idea: Evolution and the Meanings of Life*. New York: Touchstone.

Dennett, D. C. (2006). *Breaking the Spell: Religion as a Natural Phenomenon*. New York: Viking.

Deodhar, N. S. (2003). "Epidemiological Perspective of Domestic and Personal Hygiene in India." *International Journal of Environmental Health Research* 13(Suppl. 1):S47–S56.

Dethlefson, L., M. McFall-Ngai, and D. A. Relman. (2007). "An Ecological and Evolutionary Perspective on Human-Microbe Mutualism and Disease." *Nature* 449(7163):811–18.

Dhabhar, F. S. (2002). "Stress-Induced Augmentation of Immune Function – The Role of Stress Hormones, Leukocyte Trafficking, and Cytokines." *Brain, Behavior, and Immunity* 16:785–98.

Dhabhar, F. S. (2008). "Enhancing versus Suppressive Effects of Stress on Immune Function: Implications for Immunoprotection versus Immunopathology." *Allergy, Asthma, and Clinical Immunology* 4(1):2–11.

Dhabhar, F. S. (2009). "A Hassle a Day May Keep the Pathogens Away: The Fight-or-Flight Stress Response and the Augmentation of Immune Function." *Integrative and Comparative Biology* 49(3):215–36.

Dhabhar, F. S. (2014). "Effects of Stress on Immune Function: The Good, the Bad, and the Beautiful." *Immunologic Research* 58:193–210.

Dhabhar, F. S. (2018). "The Short-Term Stress Response – Mother Nature's Mechanism for Enhancing Protection and Performance under Conditions of Threat, Challenge, and Opportunity." *Frontiers in Neuroendocrinology* 49:175–92.

Dhabhar, F. S. and B. S. McEwan. (1996). "Stress-induced Enhancement of Antigen-Specific Cell-Mediated Immunity." *The Journal of Immunology* 156:2608–15.

Dhabhar, F. S. and K. Viswanathan. (2005). "Short-Term Stress Experienced at Time of Immunization Induces a Long-Lasting Increase in Immunologic Memory." *American Journal of Physiology: Regulatory, Integrative and Comparative Physiology* 289: R738–44.

Dhabhar, F. S., W. B. Malarkey, E. Neri, and B. S. McEwan. (2012). "Stress-Induced Redistribution of Immune Cells – From Barracks to Boulevards to Battlefields: A Tale of Three Hormones." *Psychoneuroendocrinology* 37:1345–68.

Diamond, J. (1997). *Guns, Germs, and Steel: The Fates of Human Societies*. New York: W.W. Norton.

Diamond, J. (2004). *Collapse: How Societies Choose to Fail or Succeed*. New York: Penguin Books.

Diamond, L. M. (2015). "Stress and Attachment." In J. A. Simpson and W. S. Rholes (Eds.), *Attachment Theory and Research: New Directions and Emerging Themes* (pp. 97–123). New York: The Guilford Press.

Dobzhansky, T. (1973). "Nothing In Biology Makes Sense Except in the Light of Evolution." *American Biology Teacher* 35(3):125–9.

Doniger, W. (trans.). (1991). *The Laws of Manu*. New York: Penguin.

Doniger, W. and S. Kakar (Eds.). (2002). *Kamasutra of Vatsyayana*. Oxford: Oxford University Press.

Doron, Guy, Richard Moulding, Maja Nedeljkovic, Michael Kyrios, Mario Mikulincer, and Dar Sar-El. (2012). "Adult Attachment Insecurities are Associated with Obsessive Compulsive Disorder." *Psychology and Psychotherapy: Theory, Research and Practice* 85:163–78.

Douglas, M. (2010 [1966]). *Purity and Danger: An Analysis of Concepts of Pollution and Taboo.* New York: Frederick A. Praeger.

DuBose, T. (2014). "Homo Religiosus." In D. A. Leeming (Ed.), *Encyclopedia of Psychology and Religion.* Boston: Springer. https://doi.org/10.1007/978-0-387-71802-6_308

Dubuisson, D. (2003 [1998]). *The Western Construction of Religion: Myths, Knowledge, and Ideology,* trans. W. Sayers. Baltimore: The Johns Hopkins University Press.

Duncan, L. A., M. Schaller, and J. H. Park. (2009). "Perceived vulnerability to disease: Development and validation of a 15-item self-report instrument." *Personality and Individual Differences* 47:541–6.

Durkheim, E. (1962 [1895]). *The Rules of the Sociological Method.* Glencoe: Free Press.

Dwyer, G. (2003). *The Divine and the Demonic: Supernatural affliction and its treatment in North India.* London: RoutledgeCurzon.

Edmondson, D., C. L. Park, S. R. Chaudoir, and J. H. Wortmann. (2008). "Death Without God: Religious Struggle, Death Concerns, and Depression in the Terminally Ill." *Psychological Science* 19(8):654–758.

Edwards, K. M., V. E. Burns, D. Carroll, M. Drayson, and C. Ring. (2007). "The Acute Stress-Induced Immunoenhancement Hypothesis." *Exercise and Sport Sciences Reviews* 35(3):150–5.

Egnor, M. T. (1984). "The Changed Mother or What the Smallpox Goddess Did When There Was No More Smallpox." *Contributions to Asian Studies* 18:24–45.

Eibl-Eibesfeldt, I. and C. Sutterlin. (1990). "Fear, Defence and Aggression in Animals and Man: Some Ethological Perspectives." In P. F. Brain, S. Parmigiani, R. J. Blanchard, and D. Mainardi (Eds.), *Fear and Defence* (pp. 381–408). Chur: Harwood Academic Publishers.

Eilam, D., R. Izhar, and J. Mort. (2011). "Threat Detection: Behavioral Practices in Animals and Humans." *Neuroscience and Biobehavioral Reviews* 35:999–1006.

Ein-Dor, T., M. Mikulincer, G. Doron, and P. R. Shaver. (2010). "The Attachment Paradox: How Can So Many of Us (the Insecure Ones) Have No Adaptive Advantages?" *Perspectives on Psychological Science* 5(2):123–41.

Ekman, P. (1992). "An Argument for Basic Emotions." *Cognition and Emotion* 6 (3/4):169–200.

Eliade, M. (1958). *Patterns in Comparative Religion,* trans. R. Sheed. New York: Sheed & Ward.

Eliade, M. (1964). *Shamanism: Archaic Techniques of Ecstasy,* trans. W. R. Trask. Princeton: Princeton University Press.

Ellis, B. J. and M. Del Giudice. (2019). "Adaptation to Stress: An Evolutionary Perspective." *Annual Review of Psychology* 70:111–39.

Ellis, B. J., J. J. Jackson, and W. T. Boyce. (2006). "The Stress Response Systems: Universality and Adaptive Individual Differences." *Developmental Review* 26:175–212.

Ellis, T. B. (2008). "On Spirituality: Natural and Non-natural." *Religion Compass* 2(6):270–90.

Ellis, T. B. (2009). "Natural Gazes, Non-natural Agents: The Biology of Religion's Ocular Behaviors." In J. R. Feierman (Ed.), *The Biology of Religious Behavior: The Evolutionary Origins of Faith and Religion* (pp. 36–51). Westport: Praeger Press.

Ellis, T. B. (2011). "Disgusting Bodies, Disgusting Religion." *Journal of the American Academy of Religion* 79(4):879–927.

Ellis, T. B. (2015). "Evoked Puja: The Behavioral Ecology of an Equatorial Ritual." *Journal of the American Academy of Religion* 83(4):1108–56.

Ellis, T. B. (2016). "Of Gods and Devils: Differential Cognition and the Adaptive Illusions of Control." *Method and Theory in the Study of Religion* 28:479–511.

England, J. (2013). "Statistical Physics of Self-Replication." *The Journal of Chemical Physics* 139(12):121923, 1-8.

Eppig, C., C. L. Fincher, and R. Thornhill. (2010). "Parasite Prevalence and the Worldwide Distribution of Cognitive Ability." *Proceedings of the Royal Society B* 277:3801–8.

Evans, E. M. (2001). "Cognitive and Contextual Factors in the Emergence of Diverse Belief Systems: Creation versus Evolution." *Cognitive Psychology* 42:217–66.

Eveland, W. C., W. J. Oliver, and J. V. Neel. (1971). "Characteristics of *Escherichia coli* Serotypes in the Yanomama, a Primitive Indian Tribe of South America." *Infection and Immunity* 4(6):753–6.

Fabrega, Jr., H. (1997). *Evolution of Sickness and Healing*. Berkeley: University of California Press.

Fabrega, Jr., H. (2004). "Consciousness and Emotions are Minimized." *Behavioral and Brain Sciences* 27(6):736–7.

Fabrega, Jr., H. and D. B. Silver. (1973). *Illness and Shamanistic Curing in Zinacantan: An Ethnomedical Analysis*. Stanford: Stanford University Press.

Fales, E. (2013). "Is a Science of the Supernatural Possible?" In M. Pigliucci and M. Boudry (Eds.), *Philosophy of Pseudoscience: Reconsidering the Demarcation Problem* (pp. 247–62). Chicago: University of Chicago Press.

Faulkner, J., M. Schaller, J. H. Park, and L. A. Duncan. (2004). "Evolved Disease-Avoidance Mechanisms and Contemporary Xenophobic Attitudes." *Group Processes & Intergroup Relations* 7(4):333–53.

Feierman, J. R. (Ed.). (2009a). *The Biology of Religious Behavior: The Evolutionary Origins of Faith and Religion*. Westport: Praeger.

Feierman, J. R. (2009b). "The Evolutionary History of Behavior." In J. R. Feierman (Ed.), *The Biology of Religious Behavior: The Evolutionary Origins of Faith and Religion* (pp. 71–86). Westport: Praeger.

Fenichel, O. (1945). *The Psychoanalytic Theory of Neurosis*. New York: W. W. Norton & Company.

Fessler, D. M. T. and K. J. Haley. (2006). "Guarding the Perimeter: The Outside-Inside Dichotomy in Disgust and Bodily Experience." *Cognition and Emotion* 20(1):3–19.

Fessler, D. M. T. and C. D. Navarette. (2003a). "Domain-Specific Variation in Disgust Sensitivity across the Menstrual Cycle." *Evolution and Human Behavior* 24:406–17.

Fessler, D. M. T. and C. D. Navarrete. (2003b). "Meat Is Good to Taboo: Dietary Proscriptions as a Product of the Interaction of Psychological Mechanisms and Social Processes." *Journal of Cognition and Culture* 3(1):1–40.

Fincher, C. L. and R. Thornhill. (2008a). "A Parasite-Driven Wedge: Infectious Disease May Explain Language and Other Biodiversity." *Oikos* 117:1289–97.

Fincher, C. L. and R. Thornhill. (2008b). "Assortative Sociality, Limited Dispersal, Infectious Disease and the Genesis of the Global Pattern of Religion Diversity." *Proceedings of the Royal Society B* 275:2587–94.

Fincher, C. L. and R. Thornhill. (2012). "Parasite-Stress Promotes In-Group Assortative Sociality: The Cases of Strong Family Ties and Heightened Religiosity." *Behavioral and Brain Sciences* 35:61–119.

Fincher, C. L., R. Thornhill, D. R. Murray, and M. Schaller. (2008). "Pathogen Prevalence Predicts Human Cross-Cultural Variability in Individualism/Collectivism." *Proceedings of the Royal Society of London B* 275:1279–85.

Finlay-Jones, R. (1983). "Disgust with Life in General." *Australian and New Zealand Journal of Psychiatry* 17:149–52.

Fitzgerald, T. (2000). *The Ideology of Religious Studies*. New York: Oxford University Press.

Flanagan, O. (2002). *The Problem of the Soul: Two Visions of Mind and How to Reconcile Them*. New York: Basic Books.

Flanagan, O. (2007). *The Really Hard Problem: Meaning in a Material World*. Cambridge: The MIT Press.

Flanagan, O. (2013). *The Bodhisattva's Brain: Buddhism Naturalized*. Cambridge: The MIT Press.

Flanagan, O. and D. Barack. (2010). "Neuroexistentialism." *EurAmerica* 40(3):573–90.

Forrest, B. (2000). "Methodological Naturalism and Philosophical Naturalism: Clarifying the Connection." *Philo* 3(2):7–23.

Frankenhuis, W. E. (2010). "Did Insecure Attachment Styles Evolve for the Benefit of the Group?" *Frontiers in Psychology* 1(172):1–3.

Freeland, W. J. (1976). "Pathogens and the Evolution of Primate Sociality." *Biotropica* 8(1):12–24.

Freud, S. (1927). *The Future of an Illusion*, trans. J. Strachey. New York: W. W. Norton & Company.

Fuller, R. C. (2008). *Spirituality in the Flesh: Bodily Sources of Religious Experiences*. New York: Oxford University Press.

Gadamer, H-G. (2004 [1960]). *Truth and Method*. New York: Continuum.

Gangestad, S. W. and D. M. Buss. (1993). "Pathogen Prevalence and Human Mate Preferences." *Ethology and Sociobiology* 14:89–96.

Gangestad, S. W., M. G. Haselton, and D. M. Buss. (2006). "Evolutionary Foundations of Cultural Variation: Evoked Culture and Mate Preferences." *Psychological Inquiry* 17(2):75–95.

Gangestad, S. W. and N. M. Grebe. (2014). "Pathogen Avoidance Within an Integrated Immune System: Multiple Components with Distinct Costs and Benefits." *Evolutionary Behavioral Sciences* 8(4):226–34.

Geary, D. C. (2005). "Evolution of Paternal Investment." In D. Buss (Ed.), *The Handbook of Evolutionary Psychology* (pp. 483–505). Hoboken: John Wiley & Sons, Inc.

Geertz, C. (1973). *The Interpretation of Culture.* New York: Basic Books.

Gelfand, M. J., D. P. S. Bhawuk, L. H. Nishi, and D. J. Bechtold. (2004). "Individualism and Collectivism." In R. J. House, P. J. Hanges, M. Javidan, P. W. Dorfman, and V. Gupta (Eds.), *Culture, Leadership, and Organizations: The GLOBE Study of 62 Societies* (pp. 437–512). Thousand Oaks: SAGE Publications.

Gibson, T. P. (1986). *Sacrifice and Sharing in the Philippine Highlands: Religion and Society among the Buid of Mindoro.* London: Routledge.

Giesbrecht, T., H. Merckelbach, M. Kater, and A. F. Sluis. (2007). "Why Dissociation and Schizotypy Overlap: The Joint Influence of Fantasy Proneness, Cognitive Failures, and Childhood Trauma." *The Journal of Nervous and Mental Disease* 195(10):812–18.

Gilbert, P. (2006). "Evolution and Depression: Issues and Implications." *Psychological Medicine* 36:287–97.

Girard, R. (1977). *Violence and the Sacred*, trans. P. Gregory. Baltimore: The Johns Hopkins University Press.

Glaser, R. (2005). "Stress-Associated Immune Dysregulation and Its Importance for Human Health: A Personal History of Psychoneuroimmunology." *Brain, Behavior, and Immunity* 19:3–11.

Glaser, R. and J. K. Kiecolt-Glaser. (2005). "Stress-Induced Immune Dysfunction: Implications for Health." *Nature Reviews Immunology* 5(3):243–51.

Glucklich, A. (2001). *Sacred Pain: Hurting the Body for the Sake of the Soul.* New York: Oxford University Press.

Goetz, A. T., T. K. Shackelford, V. G. Starratt, and W. F. McKibbin. (2008). "Intimate Partner Violence." In J. D. Duntley and T. K. Shackelford (Eds.), *Evolutionary Forensic Psychology* (pp. 67–78). New York: Oxford University Press.

Goldenberg, J. L. (2005). "The Body Stripped Down: An Existential Account of the Threat Posed by the Physical Body." *Current Directions in Psychological Science* 14(4):224–8.

Goldenberg, J. L., T. Pyszczynski, S. K. McCoy, and J. Greenberg. (1999). "Death, Sex, Love, and Neuroticism: Why Is Sex Such a Problem?" *Journal of Personality and Social Psychology* 77(6):1173–87.

Goldenberg, J. L., T. Pyszczynski, J. Greenberg, and S. Solomon. (2000). "Fleeing the Body: A Terror Management Perspective on the Problem of Human Corporeality." *Personality and Social Psychology Review* 4(3):200–18.

Goldenberg, J. L., T. Pyszczynski, J. Greenberg, S. Solomon, B. Kluck, and R. Cornwell. (2001). "I Am *Not* and Animal: Mortality Salience, Disgust, and the Denial of Human Creatureliness." *Journal of Experimental Psychology: General.* 130(3):427–35.

Goldenberg, J. L., C. R. Cox, T. Pyszczynski, J. Greenberg, and S. Solomon. (2002). "Understanding Human Ambivalence about Sex: The Effects of Stripping Sex of Meaning." *The Journal of Sex Research* 39(4):310–20.

Goodwin, J., S. Hill, and R. Attias. (1990). "Historical and Folk Techniques of Exorcism: Applications to the Treatment of Dissociative Disorders." *Dissociation* 3(2):94–101.

Gray, K. and D. M. Wegner. (2010). "Blaming God for Our Pain: Human Suffering and the Divine Mind." *Personality and Social Psychology Review* 14(1):7–16.

Graziano, M. S. (2010). *God Soul Mind Brain: A Neuroscientist's Reflections on the Spirit World*. Teaticket: Leapfrog Press.

Gredeback, G. and A. Melinder. (2011). "Teleological Reasoning in 4-Month-Old Infants: Pupil Dilations and Contextual Constraints." *PLoS ONE* 6(10):1–5.

Greene, J. (2013). *Moral Tribes: Emotion, Reason, and the Gap Between Us and Them*. New York: Penguin.

Guernier, V., M. Hochberg, and J-F Guegan. (2004). "Ecology Drives the Worldwide Distribution of Human Diseases." *PLoS Biology* 2(6):740–6.

Guinn, J. (2018). *The Road to Jonestown: Jim Jones and Peoples Temple*. New York: Simon & Schuster.

Guthrie, S. (1993). *Faces in the Clouds: A New Theory of Religion*. New York: Oxford University Press.

Haack, S. (2003). *Defending Science – Within Reason: Between Science and Cynicism*. Amherst: Prometheus Books.

Haidt, J. (2012). *The Righteous Mind: Why Good People are Divided by Politics and Religion*. New York: Vintage Books.

Haidt, J., C. McCauley, and P. Rozin. (1994). "Individual Differences in Sensitivity to Disgust: A Scale Sampling Seven Domains of Disgust Elicitors." *Personality and Individual Differences* 16(5):701–13.

Halbfass, W. (1990). *Tradition and Reflection: Explorations in Indian Thought*. Albany: SUNY Press.

Hamer, D. H. (2005). *The God Gene: How Faith is Hardwired into Our Genes*. New York: Anchor.

Hames, R. (2001). "Human Behavioral Ecology." In N. J. Smelser and P. B. Bates (Eds.), *International Encyclopedia of the Social & Behavioral Sciences* (pp. 6946–51). Amsterdam: Elsevier Science Ltd.

Harari, Y. N. (2015). *Sapiens: A Brief History of Humankind*. London: Vintage.

Harmon, W. (2011). "Possession as Protection and Affliction: The Goddess Mariyamman's Fierce Grace." In F. M. Ferrari (Ed.), *Health and Religious Rituals in South Asia* (pp. 185–98). London: Routledge.

Harpending, H. C., P. Draper, and R. Pennington. (1990). "Cultural Evolution, Parental Care, and Mortality." In A. C. Swedlund and G. J. Armelagos (Eds.), *Disease in Transition: Anthropological and Epidemiological Perspectives*. New York: Bergin and Garvey.

Harris, S., S. A. Sheth, and M. S. Cohen. (2008). "Functional Neuroimaging of Belief, Disbelief, and Uncertainty." *Annals of Neurology* 63:141–7.

Hart, B. L. (1990). "Behavioral Adaptations to Pathogens and Parasites: Five Strategies." *Neuroscience & Biobehavioral Reviews* 14:273–94.

Hart, B. L. (2011). "Behavioural Defences in Animals Against Pathogens and Parasites: Parallels with the Pillars of Medicine in Humans." *Philosophical Transactions of the Royal Society B* 366:3406–17.

Hart, J., Phillip R. Shaver, and J. L. Goldenberg. (2005). "Attachment, Self-Esteem, Worldviews, and Terror Management: Evidence for a Tripartite Security System." *Journal of Personality and Social Psychology* 88(6):999–1013.

Haught, John. (2006). *Is Nature Enough? Meaning and Truth in the Age of Science.* Cambridge: Cambridge University Press.

Haught, John. (2008). *God and the New Atheism: A Critical Response to Dawkins, Harris and Hitchens.* Louisville: Westminster John Knox Press.

Hayden, Brian. (2003). *Shamans, Sorcerers, and Saints: A Prehistory of Religion.* Washington: Smithsonian Books.

Hejmadi, A., P. Rozin, and M. Siegal. (2004). "Once in Contact, Always in Contact: Contagious Essence and Conceptions of Purification in American and Hindu Indian Children." *Developmental Psychology* 40(4):467–76.

Herz, R. (2012). *That's Disgusting: Unraveling the Mysteries of Repulsion.* New York: W. W. Norton & Company.

Hewlett, B. S., M. E. Lamb, B. Leyendecker, and A. Scholmerich. (2000). "Parental Investment Strategies among Aka Foragers, Ngandu Farmers, and Euro-American Urban-Industrialists." In L. Cronk, N. Chagnon, and W. Irons (Eds.), *Adaptation and Human Behavior: An Anthropological Perspective* (pp. 155–78). London: Routledge.

Hill, K. (1993). "Life History Theory and Evolutionary Anthropology." *Evolutionary Anthropology* 2(3):78–88.

Hinde, R. A. (1999). *Why Gods Persist: A Scientific Approach to Religion.* London: Routledge.

Hitchens, C. (2012). *The Missionary Position: Mother Teresa in Theory and Practice.* London: Atlantic Books.

Hochberg, M. E., B. Sinervo, and S. P. Brown. (2003). "Socially Mediated Speciation." *Evolution* 57(1):154–8.

Hodson, G. and K. Costello. (2007). "Interpersonal Disgust, Ideological Orientations, and Dehumanization as Predictors of Intergroup Attitudes." *Psychological Science* 18(8):691–8.

Hofstede, G. (2001). *Culture's Consequences: Comparing Values, Behaviors, Institutions, and Organizations Across Nations.* 2nd ed. Thousand Oaks: Sage Publications.

Hofstede, G. and R. R. McCrae. (2004). "Personality and Culture Revisited: Linking Traits and Dimensions of Culture." *Cross-Cultural Research* 38(1):52–88.

Hogg, M. A. (2004). "Uncertainty and Extremism: Identification with High Entitativity Groups under Conditions of Uncertainty." In V. Yzerbyt, C. M. Judd, and O. Corneille (Eds.), *The Psychology of Group Perception: Perceived Variability, Entitativity, and Essentialism* (pp. 401–18). New York: Psychology Press.

Hogg, M. A., D. K. Sherman, J. Dierselhuis, A. T. Maitner, and G. Moffitt. (2007). "Uncertainty, Entitativity, and Group Identification." *Journal of Experimental Social Psychology* 43:135–42.

Horton, R. (1993). *Patterns of Thought in Africa and the West: Essays on Magic, Religion and Science*. New York: Cambridge University Press.

Huxley, J. S. (2009 [1942]). *Evolution: The Modern Synthesis*. Cambridge: The MIT Press.

Hruschka, D. J. and J. Hackman. (2014). "When are Cross-Group Differences a Product of a Human Behavioral Immune System?" *Evolutionary Behavioral Sciences* 8(4):265–73.

Inden, R. (1990). *Imagining India*. Bloomington: Indiana University Press.

Inhorn, M. C., and P. J. Brown. (1997). *The Anthropology of Infectious Disease: International Health Perspectives*. Amsterdam: Gordon and Breach Publishers.

Irons, W. (2001). "Religion as a Hard-to-Fake Sign of Commitment." In R. Nesse (Ed.), *Evolution and the Capacity for Communication* (pp. 292–309). New York: Russell Sage.

Irons, W. and L. Cronk. (2000). "Two Decades of a New Paradigm." In L. Cronk, N. Chagnon, and W. Irons (Eds.), *Adaptation and Human Behavior: An Anthropological Perspective* (pp. 3–26). London: Routledge.

Jain, A. (2014). *Selling Yoga: From Counterculture to Pop Culture*. New York: Oxford University Press.

James, W. (1961 [1902]). *The Varieties of Religious Experience*. New York: Macmillan.

Jha, S. N. (1995). "Cari-Candra Bhed: Use of the Four Moons." In R. K. Ray (Ed.), *Mind, Body and Society: Life and Mentality in Colonial Bengal* (pp. 65–108). Calcutta: Oxford University Press.

Jones, J. (1991). *Contemporary Psychoanalysis & Religion: Transference and Transcendence*. New Haven: Yale University Press.

Jong, J. and J. Halberstadt. (2016). *Death Anxiety and Religious Belief: An Existential Psychology of Religion*. London: Bloomsbury.

Jonsdottir, I. H., P. Hoffmann, and P. Thoren. (1997). "Physical Exercise, Endogenous Opioids and Immune Function." *Acta Physiologica Scandinavica* 640:47–50.

Kagan, S. (2012). *Death*. New Haven: Yale University Press.

Kahneman, D. (2011). *Thinking, Fast and Slow*. New York: Farrar, Strauss & Giroux.

Kakar, Sudhir. (1979). *Indian Childhood: Cultural Ideals and Social Reality*. Delhi: Oxford University Press.

Kakar, Sudhir. (1981). *The Inner World: A Psycho-Analytic Study of Childhood and Society in India*. Oxford: Oxford University Press.

Kaplan, H., K. Hill, J. Lancaster, and A. M. Hurtado. (2000). "A Theory of Human Life History Evolution: Diet, Intelligence, and Longevity." *Evolutionary Anthropology: Issues, News, and Reviews* 9(4):156–85.

Kaufman, G. D. (1981). *The Theological Imagination: Constructing the Concept of God*. Cambridge: MIT Press.

Kavaliers, M. and E. Choleris. (2018). "The Role of Social Cognition in Parasite and Pathogen Avoidance." *Philosophical Transactions of the Royal Society B* 373(1751):20170206.

Kay, A. C., D. Gaucher, I. McGregor, and K. Nash. (2010). "Religious Belief as Compensatory Control." *Personality and Social Psychology Review* 14(1):37–48.

Kay, A. C., S. Shepherd, C. W. Blatz, S. N. Chua, and A. D. Galinsky. (2010). "For God (or) Country: The Hydraulic Relation Between Government Instability and Belief in Religious Sources of Control." *Journal of Personality and Social Psychology* 99(5):725–39.

Keinan, G. (2002). "The Effects of Stress and Desire for Control on Superstitious Behavior " *Personality and Social Psychology Bulletin* 28(1):102–8.

Keleman, D. (2004). "Are Children 'Intuitive Theists'?: Reasoning About Purpose and Design in Nature." *Psychological Science* 15(5):295–301.

Kelly, D. (2011). *Yuck!: The Nature and Moral Significance of Disgust*. Cambridge: The MIT Press.

Kenrick, D. T, S. Nieuweboer, and A. P. Buunk. (2010). "Universal Mechanisms and Cultural Diversity: Replacing the Blank Slate With a Coloring Book." In M. Schaller, A. Norenzayan, S. J. Heine, T. Yamagishi, and T. Kameda (Eds.), *Evolution, Culture, and the Human Mind* (pp. 257–72). New York: Psychology Press.

Kinsley, D. R. (1997). *Tantric Visions of the Divine Feminine: The Ten Mahåavidyåas*. Berkeley: University of California Press.

Kirkpatrick, L. A. (1998). "God as a Substitute Attachment Figure: A Longitudinal Study of Adult Attachment Style and Religious Change in College Students." *Personality and Social Psychology Bulletin* 24(9):961–73.

Kirkpatrick, L. A. (2005). *Attachment, Evolution, and the Psychology of Religion*. New York: Guilford Press.

Kirkpatrick, L. A. (2006). "Religion is Not an Adaptation." In P. McNamara (Ed.), *Where God and Science Meet*, vol. 1 (pp. 173–93). Westport: Praeger.

Kirkpatrick, L. A. and B. J. Ellis. (2004). "An Evolutionary-Psychological Approach to Self-esteem: Multiple Domains and Multiple Functions." In M. B. Brewer and M. Hewstone (Eds.), *Self and Social Identity* (pp. 52–77). Hoboken: Blackwell Publishing.

Kitcher, P. (2015). *Life After Faith: The Case for Secular Humanism*. New Haven: Yale University Press.

Klenerman, P. (2017). *The Immune System: A Very Short Introduction*. New York: Oxford University Press.

Koenig, H. G. (2008). *Medicine, Religion, and Health: Where Science and Spirituality Meet*. West Conshohocken: Templeton Foundation Press.

Koenig, H. G., D. E. King, and V. B. Carson. (2001). *Handbook of Religion and Health*. New York: Oxford University Press.

Koffel, E. and D. Watson. (2009). "Unusual Sleep Experiences, Dissociation, and Schizotypy: Evidence for a Common Domain." *Clinical Psychology Review* 29(6):548–59.

Koleva, S. P., D. Selterman, R. Iyer, and P. H. Ditto. (2014). "The Moral Compass of Insecurity: Anxious and Avoidant Attachment Predict Moral Judgment." *Social Psychological and Personality Science* 5(2):185–94.

Konvalinka, I., D. Xygalatas, J. Bulbulia, U. Schjodt, E. M. Jegindo, S. Wallot, G. Van Orden, and A. Roepstorff. "Synchronized Arousal between Performed and Related Spectators in a Fire-Walking Ritual." *PNAS* 108(20):8514–19.

Kripal, J. J. (1995). *Kali's Child: The Mystical and the Erotic in the Life and Teachings of Ramakrishna*. Chicago: The University of Chicago Press.

Kumar, V. (2017). "Foul Behavior." *Philosopher's Imprint* 17(15):1–17.

Kurtz, S. N. (1992). *All the Mothers are One: Hindu India and the Cultural Reshaping of Psychoanalysis*. New York: Columbia University Press.

Lafferty, K. D. (2005). "Look What the Cat Dragged In: Do Parasites Contribute to Human Cultural Diversity?" *Behavioral Processes* 68(3):279–82.

Laland, K. N. and G. R. Brown. (2002). *Sense & Nonsense: Evolutionary Perspectives on Human Behavior*. New York: Oxford University Press.

Lambert, W. W. (1992). "Cultural Background to Aggression: Correlates and Consequences of Benevolent and Malevolent Gods and Spirits." In A. Fraczek and H. Zumkley (Eds.), *Socialization and Aggression* (pp. 217–30). Berlin: Springer-Verlag.

Lambert, W. W., L. Minturn Triandis, and M. Wolf. (1959). "Some Correlates of Beliefs in the Malevolence and Benevolence of Supernatural Beings: A Cross-Societal Study." *Journal of Abnormal and Social Psychology* 58:162–9.

Lane, N. (2015). *The Vital Question: Why Is Life the Way It Is?* London: Profile Books.

Langer, E. J. (1975). "The Illusion of Control." *Journal of Personality and Social Psychology* 32(2):311–28.

Langner, T. S. (2002). *Choices for Living: Coping with Fear of Dying*. New York: Kluwer Academic/Plenum Publishers.

Laurin, K., A. C. Kay, and D. A. Moscovitch. (2008). "On the Belief in God: Towards an Understanding of the Emotional Substrates of Compensatory Control." *Journal of Experimental Social Psychology* 44:1559–62.

Lee, A. J., R. C. Brooks, K. J. Potter, and B. P. Zietsch. (2015). "Pathogen Disgust Sensitivity and Resource Scarcity are Associated with Mate Preference for Different Waist-to-Hip Ratios, Shoulder-to-Hip Ratios, and Body Mass Index." *Evolution and Human Behavior* 36:480–8.

Leeming, D. A. and M. A. Leeming. (1994). *Encyclopedia of Creation Myths*. Santa Barbara: ABC-CLIO.

Legare, C. H. and A. L. Souza. (2014). "Searching for Control: Priming Randomness Increases the Evaluation of Ritual Efficacy." *Cognitive Science* 38:152–61.

Letendre, K., C. L. Fincher, and R. Thornhill. (2010). "Does Infectious Disease Cause Global Variation in the Frequency of Intrastate Armed Conflict and Civil War?" *Biological Reviews* 85:669–83.

LeVine, R. A. (1977). "Child Rearing as Cultural Adaptation." In P. H. Leiderman, S. R. Tulkin and A. Rosenfeld (Eds.), *Culture and Infancy: Variations in the Human Experience* (pp. 15–27). New York: Academic Press.

LeVine, R. A. (2007). "Ethnographic Studies of Childhood: A Historical Overview." *American Anthropologist* 109(2):247–60.

LeVine, R. A., S. LeVine, P. H. Leiderman, T. B. Brazelton, S. Dixon, A. Richman, and C. H. Keefer. (1994). *Child Care and Culture: Lessons from Africa*. Cambridge: Cambridge University Press.

Lewis, I. M. (1971). *Ecstatic Religion: An Anthropological Study of Spirit Possession and Shamanism*. New York: Penguin Books.

Lewis, K. (1998). "Pathogen Resistance as the Origin of Kin Altruism." *Journal of Theoretical Biology* 193(2):359–63.

Lieberman, D. and D. Patrick. (2014). "Are the Behavioral Immune System and Pathogen Disgust Identical?" *Evolutionary Behavioral Sciences* 8(4):244–50.

Lienard, P. and P. Boyer. (2006). "Whence Collective Rituals? A Cultural Selection Model of Ritualized Behavior." *American Anthropologist* 108(4):814–27.

Loehle, C. (1995). "Social Barriers to Pathogen Transmission in Wild Animal Populations." *Ecology* 76(2):326–35.

Lourenco, M., L. P. Azevedo, and J. L. Gouveia. (2011). "Depression and Sexual Desire: An Exploratory Study in Psychiatric Patients." *Journal of Sex & Marital Therapy* 37:32–44.

Low, B. S. (1990). "Marriage Systems and Pathogen Stress in Human Societies." *American Zoologist* 30:325–39.

Lowie, R. H. (1966 [1917]). *Culture and Ethnology*. New York: Basic Books.

Lumsden, C. J. and E. O. Wilson. (1981). "Genes, Mind, and Ideology." *The Sciences* 21(9):6–8.

Lutgendorf, S. K, P. P. Vitaliano, T. Tripp-Reimer, J. H. Harvey, and D. M. Lubaroff. (1999). "Sense of Coherence Moderates the Relationship Between Life Stress and Natural Killer Cell Activity in Healthy Older Adults." *Psychology and Aging* 14(4):552–63.

MacBeth, A., M. Schwannauer, and A. Gumley. (2008). "The Association Between Attachment Style, Social Mentalities, and Paranoid Ideation: An Analogue Study." *Psychology and Psychotherapy: Theory, Research and Practice* 81:79–93.

Mackie, J. L. (1982). *The Miracle of Theism: Arguments for and against the Existence of God*. Oxford: Clarendon Press.

Magai, C., N. Distel, and R. Liker. (1995). "Emotion Socialization, Attachment, and Patterns of Adult Emotional Traits." *Cognition and Emotion* 9(5):461–81.

Magai, C., J. Hunziker, W. Mesias, and L. C. Culver. (2000). "Adult Attachment Styles and Emotional Biases." *International Journal of Behavioral Development* 24(3):301–9.

Mahoney, A. (2015). "The Evolutionary Psychology of Theology." In D. J. Slone and J. A. Van Slyke (Eds.), *The Attraction of Religion: A New Evolutionary Psychology of Religion* (pp. 189–210). London: Bloomsbury.

Main, M., N. Kaplan, and J. Cassidy. (1985). "Security in Infancy, Childhood, and Adulthood: A Move to the Level of Representation." In I. Bretherton and E. Waters (Eds.), *Growing Points of Attachment Theory and Research. Monographs of the Society for Research in Child Development* 50(1–2, Serial no. 209):66–104.

Maimonides. (1995). *The Guide of the Perplexed*, trans. C. Rabin. Indianapolis: Hackett Publishing Company.

Malhotra, K. C. (1990). "Changing Patterns of Disease in India with Special Reference to Childhood Mortality." In A. C. Swedlund and G. J. Armelagos (Eds.), *Disease in Populations in Transition: Anthropological and Epidemiological Perspectives* (pp. 313–31). New York: Bergin and Garvey.

Margulis, L. (1997). *Microcosmos: Four Billion Years of Microbial Evolution*. Berkeley: University of California Press.

Markel, H. and A. M. Stern. (2002). "The Foreignness of Germs: The Persistent Association of Immigrants and Disease in American Society." *The Milbank Quarterly* 80(4):757–88.

Martin, L. H. and D. Wiebe. (2016). "Religious Studies as a Scientific Discipline: The Persistence of a Delusion." In L. H. Martin and D. Wiebe (Eds.), *Conversations and Controversies in the Scientific Study of Religion: Collaborative and Co-Authored Essays* (pp. 221–32). Leiden: Brill.

Masson, J. M. (1976). "The Psychology of the Ascetic." *Journal of Asian Studies* 35(4):611–25.

Mattausch, J. (2012). "With Whom May British Gujaratis Identify, to Whom May They be Compared?" In S. Mawani and A. Mukadam (Eds.), *Gujarati Communities Across the Globe: Memory, Identity and Continuity* (pp. 27–42). Stoke-on-Trent: Trentham Books.

Matzinger, P. (2002). "The Danger Model: A Renewed Sense of Self." *Science* 296:301–5.

Maunder, R. G. and J. J. Hunter. (2001). "Attachment and Psychosomatic Medicine: Developmental Contributions to Stress and Disease." *Psychosomatic Medicine* 63:556–67.

Maunder, R. G., W. J. Lancee, R. P. Nolan, J. J. Hunter, and D. W. Tannenbaum. (2006). "The Relationship of Attachment Insecurity to Subjective Stress and Autonomic Function During Standardized Acute Stress in Healthy Adults." *Journal of Psychosomatic Research* 60:283–90.

May, R. M. and R. M. Anderson. (1979). "Population Biology of Infectious Diseases: Part II." *Nature* 280:455–61.

Mayr, E. (2001). *What Evolution Is*. New York: Basic Books.

McCabe, C. M., S. M. Reader, and C. L. Nunn. (2015). "Infectious Disease, Behavioural Flexibility and the Evolution of Culture." *Proceedings of the Royal Society B* 282:1–9.

McCauley, R. N. and G. Graham. (2020). *Hearing Voices and Other Matters of the Mind: What Mental Abnormalities Can Teach Us About Religions*. New York: Oxford University Press.

McClenon, J. (1997). "Shamanic Healing, Human Evolution, and the Origin of Religion." *Journal for the Scientific Study of Religion* 36(3):345–54.

McClenon, J. (2002). *Wondrous Healing: Shamanism, Human Evolution, and the Origin of Religion*. Dekalb: Northern Illinois University Press.

McClenon, J. (2006). "The Ritual Healing Theory." In P. McNamara (Ed.), *Where God and Science Meet*, vol. 1 (pp. 135–58). Westport: Praeger.

McCorkle, W. W. (2010). *Ritualizing the Disposal of the Deceased: From Corpse to Concept*. New York: Peter Lang.

McCrae, R. R. and Juri Allik (Eds.). (2002). *The Five-Factor Model of Personality*. New York: Springer.

McCrae, R. R. and A. Terracciano. (2005). "Personality Profiles of Cultures: Aggregate Personality Traits." *Journal of Personality and Social Psychology* 89:3407–25.

McCutcheon, R. T. (2001). *Critics Not Caretakers: Redescribing the Public Study of Religion*. Albany: State University of New York Press.

McDade, T. W. (2003). "Life History Theory and the Immune System: Steps Toward a Human Ecological Immunology." *Physical Anthropology* 46:100–25.

McDaniel, J. (1989). *The Madness of the Saints: Ecstatic Religion in Bengal*. Chicago: The University of Chicago Press.

McFalls, J. A. (1979). *Psychopathology and Subfecundity*. New York: Academic Press.

McGregor, H., J. Lieberman, J. Greenberg, S. Solomon, J. Arndt, and L. Simon. (1998). "Terror Management and Aggression: Evidence that Mortality Salience Promotes Aggression Toward Worldview-Threatening Individuals." *Journal of Personality and Social Psychology* 74:590–605.

McGuire, M. and A. Troisi. (1998). *Darwinian Psychiatry*. New York: Oxford University Press.

McGuire, M. T. and L. Tiger. (2009). "The Brain and Religious Adaptations." In J. F. Feierman (Ed.), *The Biology of Religious Behavior: The Evolutionary Origins of Faith and Religion* (pp. 125–40). Santa Barbara: Praeger.

McIntyre, L. (2019). *The Scientific Attitude: Defending Science from Denial, Fraud, and Pseudoscience*. Cambridge: The MIT Press.

McNamara, P. (2009). *The Neuroscience of Religious Experience*. Cambridge: Cambridge University Press.

McNamara, P., J. Andresen, J. Clark, M. Zborowski, and C. A. Duffy. (2001). "Impact of Attachment Styles on Dream Recall and Dream Content: A Test of the Attachment Hypothesis of REM Sleep." *Journal of Sleep Research* 10:117–27.

McNeill, W. H. (1976). *Plagues and Peoples*. New York: Anchor Books.

Metzner, R. (1998). "Hallucinogenic Drugs and Plants in Psychotherapy and Shamanism." *Journal of Psychoactive Drugs* 30(4):333–41.

Mian, R., G. Shelton-Rayner, B. Harkin, and P. Williams. (2003). "Observing a Fictitious Stressful Event: Haematological Changes, Including Circulating Leukocyte Activation." *Stress* 6(1):41–7.

Mian, R., G. McLaren, and D. W. Macdonald. (2005). "Of Stress, Mice and Men: A Radical Approach to Old Problems." In K. V. Oxington (Ed.), *Stress and Health: New Research* (pp. 61–79). New York: Nove Science Publishers, Inc.

Mikulincer, M., V. Florian, and R. Tolmacz. (1990). "Attachment Styles and Fear of Personal Death: A Case Study of Affect Regulation." *Journal of Personality and Social Psychology* 58(2):273–80.

Miller, B. S. (trans.) (1995). *Yoga: Discipline of Freedom (The Yoga Sutra Attributed to Patanjali)*. New York: Bantam Books.

Miller, E. N., M. Fadl, H. S. Mohamad, A. Elzein, S. E. Jamieson, . . . and J. M. Blackwell. (2007). "Y Chromosome Lineage- and Village-Specific Genes on Chromosomes 1p22 and 6q27 Control Visceral Leishmaniasis in Sudan." *PLoS Genetics* 3:679–88.

Miller, S. L. and J. K. Maner. (2011). "Sick Body, Vigilant Mind: The Biological Immune System Activates the Behavioral Immune System." *Psychological Science* 22(12):1467–71.

Milner Jr., M. (1994). *Status and Sacredness: A General Theory of Status Relations and An Analysis of Indian Culture*. New York: Oxford University Press.

Mithen, S. (1996). *The Prehistory of the Mind: A Search for the Origins of Art, Religion and Science*. London: Thames and Hudson.

Modiano, D., V. Petrarca, B. S. Sirima, I. Nebie, D. Diallo, F. Esposito, and M. Coluzzi. (1996). "Different Response to Plasmodium falciparum Malaria in West African Sympatric Ethnic Groups." *PNAS* 93(23):13206–11.

Monod, J. (1971). *Chance and Necessity: On the Natural Philosophy of Modern Biology*. New York: Penguin.

Mordeniz, C and A. Verit. (2009). "Is Circumcision a Modified Ritual of Castration?" *Urologia Internationalis* 82(4):399–403.

Morelli, G. A. and F. Rothbaum. (2007). "Situating the Child in Context: Attachment Relationships and Self-Regulation in Different Cultures." In S. Kitayama and D. Cohen (Eds.), *Handbook of Cultural Psychology* (pp. 500–27). New York: The Guilford Press.

Munz, P. (1985). *Our Knowledge of the Growth of Knowledge: Popper or Wittgenstein?* London: Routledge.

Murdock, G. P. (1932). "The Science of Culture." *American Anthropologist* 4:200–15.

Murray, D. R. and M. Schaller. (2010). "Historical Prevalence of Infectious Diseases Within 230 Geopolitical Regions: A Tool for Investigating Origins of Culture." *Journal of Cross-Cultural Psychology* 41(1):99–108.

Murray, D. R., R. Trudeau, and M. Schaller. (2011). "On the Origins of Cultural Differences in Conformity: Four Tests of the Pathogen Prevalence Hypothesis." *Personality and Social Psychology Bulletin* 37(3):318–29.

Murray, D. R., D. Fessler, and N. Kerry. (2016). "The Kiss of Death: Three Tests of the Relationship between Disease Threat and Ritualized Physical Contact within Traditional Cultures." *Evolution and Human Behavior* 38(1):63–70.

Nations, M. K. (1986). "Epidemiological Research on Infectious Disease: Quantitative Rigor or Rigormortis? Insights from Ethnomedicine." In C. R. Janes, R. Stall, and S. M. Gifford (Eds.), *Anthropology and Epidemiology: Interdisciplinary Approaches to the Study of Health and Disease* (pp. 97–124). Dordrecht: D. Reidel Publishing Company.

Navarrete, C. D. and D. M. T. Fessler. (2006). "Disease Avoidance and Ethnocentrism: The Effects of Disease Vulnerability and Disgust Sensitivity on Intergroup Attitudes." *Evolution and Human Behavior* 27(4):270–82.

Nesse, R. M. and E. A. Young. (2000). "Evolutionary Origins and Functions of the Stress Response." In *Encyclopedia of Stress*, vol. 2 (pp. 79–84). Amsterdam: Academic Press.

Nesse, R. M. and G. C. Williams. (1996). *Why We Get Sick: The New Science of Darwinian Medicine*. New York: Vintage.

Nettle, D. (2006). "The Evolution of Personality Variation in Humans and Other Animals." *American Psychologist* 61(6):622–31.

Nettle, D. (2009). "Beyond Nature Versus Culture: Cultural Variation as an Evolved Characteristic." *Journal of the Royal Anthropological Institute* 15:223–40.

Nettle, D., M. A. Gibson, D. W. Lawson, and R. Sear. (2013). "Human Behavioral Ecology: Current Research and Future Prospects." *Behavioral Ecology* 24(5):1031–40.

Neuberg, S. L. (2014). "Contention, Consensus, and the Behavioral Immune System: From the Forum Forward." *Evolutionary Behavioral Sciences* 8(4):284–8.

Neuberg, S. L., D. T. Kenrick, and M. Schaller. (2011). "Human Threat Management Systems: Self-Protection and Disease Avoidance." *Neuroscience and Biobehavioral Reviews* 35:1042–51.

Newton, T. and D. N. McIntosh. (2013). "Unique Contributions of Religion to Meaning." In J. A. Hicks and C. Routledge (Eds.), *The Experience of Meaning in Life: Classical Perspectives, Emerging Themes, and Controversies* (pp. 257–69). New York: Springer Science + Business Media.

Nilsson, M. P. (1954). *Religion as Man's Protest Against the Meaninglessness of Events*. Bokforlag: CWK Gleerup.

Nisbett, R. E. (2003). *The Geography of Thought: How Asians and Westerners Think Differently . . . and Why*. New York: Free Press.

Noftle, E. E. and P. R. Shaver. (2006). "Attachment Dimensions and the Big Five Personality Traits: Associations and Comparative Ability to Predict Relationship Quality." *Journal of Research in Personality* 40(2):179–208.

Norenzayan, A. (2013). *Big Gods: How Religion Transformed Cooperation and Conflict*. Princeton: Princeton University Press.

Oaten, M., R. J. Stevenson, and T. I. Case. (2009). "Disgust as a Disease-Avoidance Mechanism." *Psychological Bulletin* 135(2):303–21.

Offit, P. A. (2011). *Deadly Choices: How the Anti-Vaccination Movement Threatens Us All*. New York: Basic Books.

Ogilvie, D. M. (2003). *Fantasies of Flight*. New York: Oxford University Press.

Ohman, A. and S. Mineka. (2001). "Fears, Phobias, and Preparedness: Toward an Evolved Module of Fear and Fear Learning." *Psychological Review* 108 (3):483–522.

Olatunji, B. O. and D. McKay (Eds.). (2009). *Disgust and Its Disorders: Theory, Assessment, and Treatment Implications*. Washington, DC: American Psychological Association.

Openshaw, J. (2002). *Seeking Bauls of Bengal*. Cambridge: Cambridge University Press.

Otto, R. (1923 [1917]). *The Idea of the Holy*, trans. J. W. Harvey. New York: Oxford University Press.

Oviedo, L. (2016). "Response to Donald Wiebe, 'Religions as Hazard-Precaution Systems,' and Luther Martin, 'The Ecology of Threat Detection and Precautionary Response': Try to Explain Religion (Again)." In L. Martin and D. Wiebe (Eds.), *Conversations and Controversies in the Scientific Study of Religion: Collaborative and Co-authored Essays* (pp. 106–10). Leiden: Brill.

Palmer, C. T., and R. O. Begley (2015). "Costly Signaling Theory, Sexual Selection, and the Influence of Ancestors on Religious Behavior." In D. J. Slone and J. A. Van Slyke (Eds.), *The Attraction of Religion: A New Evolutionary Psychology of Religion* (pp. 93–109). London: Bloomsbury.

Panchin, A. Y., A. I. Tuzhikov, and Y. V. Panchin. (2014). "Midichlorians – The Biomeme Hypothesis: Is There a Microbial Component to Religious Rituals?" *Biology Direct* 9(14):1–14.

Parry, J. (1989). "The End of the Body." In M. Feher, R. Naddaff and N. Tazi (Eds.), *Fragments for a History of the Human Body* (pp. 491–517). New York: UrZone.

Paul, G. (2009). "The Chronic Dependence of Popular Religiosity upon Dysfunctional Psychosociological Conditions." *Evolutionary Psychology* 7(3):398–441.

Pazhoohi, F. and K. Luna. (2018). "Ecology of Musical Preference: The Relationship Between Pathogen Prevalence and the Number and Intensity of Metal Bands." *Evolutionary Psychological Science* 4:294–300.

Pellerin, J. and M. B. Edmond. (2013). "Infections Associated with Religious Rituals." *International Journal of Infectious Disease* 17(11):e945–8.

Penn, D. J. and W. K. Potts. (1999). "The Evolution of Mating Preferences and Major Histocompatibility Complex Genes." *The American Naturalist* 153(2):145–64.

Pennock, R. T. (1999). *Tower of Babel: The Evidence Against the New Creationism*. Cambridge: The MIT Press.

Peoples, H. C., P. Duda, and F. W. Marlowe. (2016). "Hunter-Gatherers and the Origins of Religion." *Human Nature* 27:261–82.

Perlman, R. L. (2013). *Evolution & Medicine*. New York: Oxford.

Petersen, M. B. (2017). "Healthy Out-Group Members are Represented Psychologically as Infected In-Group members: Corrigendum." *Psychological Science* 30(2):1792–4.

Philipse, H. (2014). *God in the Age of Science?: A Critique of Religious Reason*. New York: Oxford University Press.

Piertney, S. B. and M. K. Oliver. (2006). "The Evolutionary Ecology of the Major Histocompatibility Complex." *Heredity* 96(1):7–21.

Pinker, S. (2002). *The Blank Slate: The Modern Denial of Human Nature*. New York: Viking.

Pinker, S. (1999). *How the Mind Works*. New York: W. W. Norton & Company.

Pinker, S. (2018). *Enlightenment Now: The Case for Reason, Science, Humanism, and Progress*. New York: Viking.

Pinker, S. (2021). *Rationality: What It Is, Why It Seems Scarce, Why It Matters*. New York: Viking.

Pitchappan, R. M. (2002). "Castes, Migration, Immunogenetics and Infectious Diseases in South India." *Community Genetics* 5:157–61.

Pitchappan, R. M., K. V. John, and M. Jayalakshmi. (2008). "HLA Genomic Diversity of India and its implications in HIV Pandemic." *International Journal of Human Genetics* 8(1):143–53.

Pluckrose, H. and J. Lindsay. (2020). *Cynical Theories: How Activist Scholarship Made Everything about Race, Gender, and Identity – An Why That Harms Everybody*. Durham: Pitchstone Publishing.

Polimeni, J. and J. P. Reiss. (2002). "How Shamanism and Group Selection May Reveal the Origins of Schizophrenia." *Medical Hypotheses* 58(3):244–8.

Powell, R. and S. Clarke. (2012). "Religion as an Evolutionary Byproduct: A Critique of the Standard Model." *Journal of the British Society for the Philosophy of Science* 63:457–86.

Preston, B. T., I. Capellini, P. McNamara, R. A. Barton, and C. L. Nunn (2009). "Parasite Resistance and the Adaptive Significance of Sleep." *BMC Evolutionary Biology* 9(7):1–9.

Preston, J. L. and R. S. Ritter. (2012). "Cleanliness and Godliness: Mutual Association Between Two Forms of Personal Purity." *Journal of Experimental Social Psychology* 48(1):1365–8.

Preus, J. S. (1987). *Explaining Religion: Criticism and Theory from Bodin to Freud*. New Haven: Yale University Press.

Proudfoot, W. (1985). *Religious Experience*. Berkeley: University of California Press.

Prugnolle, F., A. Manica, M. Charpentier, J. F. Guegan, V. Guernier, and F. Balloux. (2005). "Pathogen-Driven Selection and Worldwide HLA Class I Diversity." *Current Biology* 15(11):1022–7.

Pyszczynski, T., J. Greenberg, and S. Solomon. (2003). *In the Wake of 9/11: The Psychology of Terror*. Washington, DC: American Psychological Association.

Pyszczynski, T., J. Greenberg, S. Solomon, J. Arndt, and J. Schimel. (2004). "Why Do People Need Self-Esteem? A Theoretical and Empirical Review." *Psychological Bulletin* 130(3):435–68.

Ramacharaka, Y. (1904). *Hatha Yoga of the Yogi Philosophy of Physical Well-Being*. London: L. N. Fowler.

Rammohan, A., K. Rao, and D. K. Subbakrishna. (2002). "Religious Coping and Psychological Wellbeing in Carers of Relatives with Schizophrenia." *Acta Psychiatrica Scandinavica* 105:356–62.

Rappaport, Roy A. (1999). *Ritual and Religion in the Making of Humanity*. Cambridge: Cambridge University Press.

Ray, D. W. (2009). *The God Virus: How Religion Infects Our Lives and Culture*. Ashland: Ipc Press.

Revonsuo, A. (2000). "The Reinterpretation of Dreams: An Evolutionary Hypothesis of the Function of Dreaming." *Behavioral Brain Science* 23(6):877–901.

Reynaert, C., P. Janne, A. Bosly, P. Staquet, N. Zdanowicz, M. Vause, B. Chatelain, and D. Lejeune. (1995). "From Health Locus of Control to Immune Control: Internal Locus of Control has a Buffering Effect on Natural Killer Cell Activity Decrease in Major Depression." *Acta Psychiatrica Scandinavica* 92(4):294–300.

Reynolds, V. and R. Tanner. (1995 [1983]). *The Social Ecology of Religion*. New York: Oxford University Press.

Richerson, P. J. and R. Boyd. (2006). *Not By Genes Alone: How Culture Transformed Human Evolution*. Chicago: The University of Chicago Press.

Ridley, M. (1993). *The Red Queen: Sex and the Evolution of Human Nature*. New York: Macmillan Publishing Company.

Ridley, M. (1996). *The Origins of Virtue: Human Instincts and the Evolution of Cooperation*. New York: Penguin.

Ridley, M. (2015). *The Evolution of Everything: How New Ideas Emerge*. New York: HarperCollins.

Ritter, R. S. and J. L. Preston. (2011). "Gross Gods and Icky Atheism: Disgust Responses to Rejected Religious Beliefs." *Journal of Experimental Social Psychology* 47:1225–30.

Rizzuto, A-M. (1979). *The Birth of the Living God: A Psychoanalytic Study*. Chicago: University of Chicago Press.

Robbins-Schug, G., K. Elaine, B. C. Blevins, K. Gray, and V. Mushrif-Tripathy. (2013). "Infection, Disease, and Biosocial Processes at the End of the Indus Civilization." *PLoS ONE* 8(12):1–20.

Robertson, S. A., J. R. Prins, D. J. Sharkey, and L. M. Moldenhauer. (2013). "Seminal Fluid and the Generation of Regulatory T Cells for Embryo Implantation." *American Journal of Reproductive Immunology* 69:315–30.

Robertson, S. A. and D. J. Sharkey. (2016). "Seminal Fluid and Fertility in Women." *Fertility and Sterility* 106(3):511–19.

Rochat, P. (2001). *The Infant's World*. Cambridge: Harvard University Press.

Rock, K. L., A. Hearn, C.-J. Chen, and Y. Shi. (2005). "Natural Endogenous Adjuvants." *Seminars in Immunopathology* 26:231–46.

Rohner, R. P. (1975). *They Love Me, They Love Me Not: A Worldwide Study of the Effects of Parental Acceptance and Rejection*. New Haven: HRAF Press.

Roland, A. (1988). *In Search of Self in India and Japan: Toward a Cross-Cultural Psychology*. Princeton: Princeton University Press.

Rosenberg, A. (2011). *The Atheist's Guide to Reality: Enjoying Life without Illusions*. New York: W. W. Norton & Company.

Rosenberg, A. (2017). "Why Social Science is Biological Science." *Journal for General Philosophy of Science* 48:341–69.

Rosenberg, A. (2018). *How History Gets Things Wrong: The Neuroscience of Our Addiction to Stories*. Cambridge: The MIT Press.

Rothbaum, F., G. Morelli, and N. Rusk. (2011). "Attachment, Learning, and Coping: The Interplay of Cultural Similarities and Differences." In M. J. Gelfand, C-y. Chiu, Y-y.

Hong (Eds.), *Advances in Culture and Psychology* (pp. 153–215). New York: Oxford University Press.

Rozin, P. and A. E. Fallon. (1987). "A Perspective on Disgust." *Psychological Review* 94(1):23–41.

Rozin, P., J. Haidt, and C. R. McCauley. (2000). "Disgust." In M. Lewis and J. M. Haviland-Jones (Eds.), *Handbook of Emotions* (pp. 757–76). New York: The Guilford Press.

Rue, L. D. (2005). *Religion is Not about God: How Spiritual Traditions Nurture Our Biological Nature and What To Expect When They Fail*. New Brunswick: Rutgers University Press.

Rutjens, B. T., R. M. Sutton, and R. van der Lee. (2018). "Not All Skepticism Is Equal: Exploring the Ideological Antecedents of Science Acceptance and Rejection." *Personality and Social Psychology Bulletin* 44(3):384–405.

Saad, G. (2020). *The Parasitic Mind: How Infectious Ideas Are Killing Common Sense*. Washington, DC: Regnery Publishing.

Sagan, C. (1997). *The Demon-Haunted World: Science as a Candle in the Dark*. New York: Ballantine Books.

Salsman, J. M., T. L. Brown, E. H. Brechting, and C. R. Carlson. (2005). "The Link Between Religion and Spirituality and Psychological Adjustment: The Mediating Role of Optimism and Social Support." *Personality and Social Psychology Bulletin* 31(4):522–35.

Sanderson, S. K. (2018). *Religious Evolution and the Axial Age: From Shamans to Priests to Prophets*. London: Bloomsbury.

Sapolsky, R. M. (2004). *Why Zebras Don't Get Ulcers*. New York: St. Martin's Griffin.

Sapolsky, R. M. (2005). "The Influence of Social Hierarchy on Primate Health." *Science* 308:648–52.

Sapolsky, R. M. (2017). *Behave: The Biology of Humans at Our Best and Worst*. New York: Penguin Press.

Sarabian, C., V. Curtis, and R. McMullan. (2018). "Evolution of Pathogen and Parasite Avoidance Behaviours." *Philosophical Transactions of the Royal Society B* 373:20170256.

Sarbacker, S. R. (2005). *Samadhi: The Numinous and Cessative in Indo-Tibetan Yoga*. Albany: State University of New York Press.

Saroglou, V. and L. Anciaux. (2004). "Liking Sick Humor: Coping Styles and Religion as Predictors." *Humor: International Journal of Humor Research* 17(3):257–77.

Schaller, M. (2006). "Parasites, Behavioral Defenses, and the Social Psychological Mechanisms Through Which Cultures Are Evoked." *Psychological Inquiry* 17(2):96–137.

Schaller, M. (2014). "When and How Disgust Is and Is Not Implicated in the Behavioral Immune System." *Evolutionary Behavioral Sciences* 8(4):251–6.

Schaller, M. and L. A. Duncan. (2007). "The Behavioral Immune System: Its Evolution and Social Psychological Implications." In J. P. Forgas, M. G. Haselton, and W. von Hippel (Eds.), *Evolution and the Social Mind: Evolutionary Psychology and Social Cognition* (pp. 293–307). New York: Psychology Press.

Schaller, M. and D. R. Murray. (2008). "Pathogens, Personality, and Culture: Disease Prevalence Predicts Worldwide Variability in Sociosexuality, Extraversion, and Openness to Experience." *Journal of Personality and Social Psychology* 95(1):212–21.

Schaller, M. and D. R. Murray. (2010). "Infectious Disease and the Evolution of Cross-Cultural Differences." In M. Schaller, A. Norenzayan, S. J. Heine, T. Yamagishi and T. Kameda (Eds.), *Evolution, Culture, and the Human Mind* (pp. 243–56). New York: Psychology Press.

Schaller, M. and D. R. Murray. (2011). "Infectious Disease and the Creation of Culture." In M. J. Gelfand, C.-Y. Chiu, and Y.-Y. Hong (Eds.), *Advances in Culture and Psychology* (pp. 99–151). New York: Oxford University Press.

Schaller, M. and J. H. Park. (2011). "The Behavioral Immune System (and Why It Matters)." *Current Directions in Psychological Science* 20(2):99–103.

Schaller, M., G. E. Miller, W. M. Gervais, S. Yager, and E. Chen. (2010). "Mere Visual Perception of Other People's Disease Symptoms Facilitates a More Aggressive Immune Response." *Psychological Science* 21(5):649–52.

Schaller, M., J. H. Park, and J. Faulkner. (2003). "Prehistoric Dangers and Contemporary Prejudices." *European Review of Social Psychology* 14:105–37.

Schjenken, J. E. and S. A. Roberston. (2014). "Seminal Fluid and Immune Adaptation for Pregnancy – Comparative Biology in Mammalian Species." *Reproduction in Domestic Animals* 49(Suppl. 3):27–36.

Schmidt, M. H. (2014). "The Energy Allocation Function of Sleep: A Unifying Theory of Sleep, Torpor, and Continuous Wakefulness." *Neuroscience & Biobehavioral Reviews* 47:122–53.

Schmitt, D. P. (2005). "Fundamentals of Human Mating Strategies." In D. Buss (Ed.), *The Handbook of Evolutionary Psychology* (pp. 258–91). Hoboken: John Wiley & Sons, Inc.

Schmitt, D. P., G. Diniz, L. Alcalay . . . and D. Herrera. (2004). "Patterns and Universals of Adult Romantic Attachment Across 62 Cultural Regions." *Journal of Cross-Cultural Psychology* 35(4):367–402.

Schmitt, D. P. and R. C. Fuller. (2015). "On the Varieties of Sexual Experience: Cross-Cultural Links Between Religiosity and Human Mating Strategies." *Psychology of Religion and Spirituality* 7(4):314–26.

Schulenburg, H., J. Kurtz, Y. Moret, and Michael T. Siva-Jothy. (2009). "Introduction. Ecological immunology." *Philosophical Transactions of the Royal Society B* 364:3–14.

Schumaker, J. F. (1995). *The Corruption of Reality: A Unified Theory of Religion, Hypnosis, and Psychopathology*. Amherst: Prometheus.

Searle, J. (2005). *Mind: A Brief Introduction*. New York: Oxford University Press.

Segal, R. A. (1983). "In Defense of Reduction." *Journal of the American Academy of Religion* 51(1):97–124.

Segerstrom, S. C. and G. E. Miller. (2004). "Psychological Stress and the Human Immune System: A Meta-Analytic Study of 30 Years of Inquiry." *Psychological Bulletin* 130(4):601–30.

Sela, Y., T. K. Shackelford, and J. R. Liddle. (2015). "When Religion Makes It Worse: Religiously Motivated Violence as a Sexual Selection Weapon." In D. J. Slone and J. A. Van Slyke (Eds.), *The Attraction of Religion: A New Evolutionary Psychology of Religion* (pp. 111–31). London: Bloomsbury.

Seligman, M. E. P. (1975). *Helplessness: On Depression, Development, and Death.* San Francisco: Freeman.

Shanks, N. and I. Karsai. (2005). "Self-Organization and the Origin of Complexity." In M. Young and T. Edis (Eds.), *Why Intelligent Design Fails: A Scientific Critique of the New Creationism* (pp. 85–106). New Brunswick: Rutgers University Press.

Shaver, P. R. and K. A. Brennan. (1992). "Attachment Styles and the 'Big Five' Personality Traits: Their Connections with Each Other and With Romantic Relationship Outcomes." *Personality and Social Psychology Bulletin* 18(5):536–45.

Shaver, P. R. and M. Mikulincer. (2002). "Attachment-Related Psychodynamics." *Attachment and Human Development* 4:133–61.

Shaver, P. R., M. Mikulincer, I. Alonso-Arbiol, and S. Lavy. (2010). "Assessment of Adult Attachment Across Cultures: Conceptual and Methodological Considerations." In P. Erdman and K-M. Ng (Eds.), *Attachment: Expanding the Cultural Connections* (pp. 89–108). New York: Routledge.

Sheffler, S. (2016). *Death & the Afterlife.* New York: Oxford University Press.

Sherman, P. W. and J. Billing. (1999). "Darwinian Gastronomy: Why We Use Spices." *BioScience* 49(6):453–63.

Shultz, S., C. Opie, and Q. D. Atkinson. (2011). "Stepwise Evolution of Stable Sociality in Primates." *Nature* 479:219–24.

Siegel-Itzkovich, J. (2006). "Stringent Religious Purification Proved Lethal." *Jerusalem Post* Nov. 14.

Silver, L. (2006). *Challenging Nature: The Clash Between Biotechnology and Spirituality.* New York: Harper Perennial.

Singer, M. (2015). *Anthropology of Infectious Disease.* London: Routledge.

Singh, N. D., D. R. Criscoe, S. Skofield, K. P. Kohl, E. S. Keebaugh, and T. A. Schlenke. (2015). "Fruit Flies Diversify Their Offspring in Response to Parasite Infection." *Evolution* 349(6294):747–50.

Singleton, M. (2010). *Yoga Body: The Origins of Modern Posture Practice.* New York: Oxford University Press.

Slingerland, E. (2008). *What Science Offers the Humanities: Integrating Body & Culture.* New York: Cambridge University Press.

Slingerland, E. and J. Bulbulia. (2011). "Introductory Essay: Evolutionary Science and the Study of Religion." *Religion* 41(3):307–28.

Slone, D. J. (2008). "The Attraction of Religion: A Sexual Selectionist Account." In J. Bulbulia, R. Sosis, E. Harris, R. Genet, and K. Wyman (Eds.), *The Evolution of Religion: Studies, Theories, & Critiques* (pp. 181–8). Santa Margarita: Collins Foundation Press.

Slone, D. J. and J. A. Van Slyke. (2015). "Introduction: Connecting Religion, Sex, and Evolution." In D. J. Slone and J. A. van Slyke (Eds.), *The Attraction of Religion: A New Evolutionary Psychology of Religion* (pp. 1–9). London: Bloomsbury.

Small, M. F. (1998). *Our Babies, Ourselves: How Biology and Culture Shape the Way We Parent.* New York: Anchor Books.

Smith, J. Z. (2004). *Relating Religion: Essays in the Study of Religion.* Chicago: University of Chicago Press.

Smith, T. (2019). *The Methods of Science and Religion: Epistemologies in Conflict.* Washington: Lexington Books.

Smith, T. B., M. E. McCullough, and J. Poll. (2003). "Religiousness and Depression: Evidence for a Main Effect and the Moderating Influence of Stressful Life Events." *Psychological Bulletin* 129(4):614–36.

Smolin, L. (1999). *The Life of the Cosmos.* New York: Oxford University Press.

Solomon, S., J. Greenberg, and T. Pyszczynski. (2015). *The Worm at the Core: On the Role of Death in Life.* New York: Random House.

Solomon, S., J. Greenberg, T. Pyszczynski, F. Cohen, and D. M. Ogilvie. (2010). "Teach These Souls to Fly: Supernatural as Human Adaptation." In M. Schaller, A. Norenzayan, S. J. Heine, T. Yamagishi, and T. Kameda (Eds.), *Evolution, Culture, and the Human Mind* (pp. 99–118). New York: Psychology Press.

Sommer, S. (2005). "The Importance of Immune Gene Variability (MHC) in Evolutionary Ecology and Conservation." *Frontiers in Zoology* 2(16). https://doi.org/10.1186/1742-9994-2-16

Sosis, R., and C. Alcorta. (2003). "Signaling, Solidarity, and the Sacred: The Evolution of Religious Behavior." *Evolutionary Anthropology* 12:264–74.

Sosis, R. and J. Bulbulia. (2011). "The Behavioral Ecology of Religion: The Benefits and Costs of One Evolutionary Approach." *Religion* 41(3):341–62.

Sovatsky, S. (2014). *Advanced Spiritual Intimacy: The Yoga of Deep Tantric Sensuality.* Rochester: Destiny Books.

Sperber, D. (1990). "The Epidemiology of Beliefs." In G. Gaskell & C. Fraser (Eds.), *The Social Psychological Study of Widespread Beliefs* (pp. 25–44). Oxford: Clarendon Press.

Sperber, D. (1996). *Explaining Culture: A Naturalistic Approach.* Cambridge: Blackwell.

Sperber, D. (2004). "Agency, Religion, and Magic." *Behavioral and Brain Sciences* 27(6):750–1.

Spilka, B., R. W. Hood Jr., B. Hunsberger, and R. Gorsuch. (2003). *The Psychology of Religion: An Empirical Approach.* New York: Guilford Press.

Spiro, M. (1994). *Culture and Human Nature.* New Brunswick: Transaction Publishers.

Stark, R. and R. Finke. (2000). *Acts of Faith: Explaining the Human Side of Religion.* Berkeley: University of California Press.

Steen, F. F. and S. A. Owens. (2001). "Evolution's Pedagogy: An Adaptationist Model of Pretense and Entertainment." *Journal of Cognition and Culture* 1(4):289–321.

Steptoe, A., G. Willemsen, N. Owen, L. Flower, and V. Mohamed-Ali. (2001). "Acute Mental Stress Elicits Delayed Increases in Circulating Inflammatory Cytokine Levels." *Clinical Science* 101:185–92.

Sterelny, Kim. (2018). "Religion Re-explained." *Religion, Brain & Behavior* 8(4):406–25.

Stevenson, R. J., D. Hodgson, M. J. Oaten, J. Barouei, and T. I. Case. (2011). "The Effect of Disgust on Oral Immune Function." *Psychophysiology* 48:900–7.

Stewart-Williams, S. (2010). *Darwin, God and the Meaning of Life: How Evolutionary Theory Undermines Everything You Thought You Knew*. Cambridge: Cambridge University Press.

Stewart-Williams, S. (2018). *The Ape that Understood the Universe: How Mind and Culture Evolve*. Cambridge: Cambridge University Press.

Strassman, B. I., N. Kurapati, B. F. Hug, and E. E. Burke. (2012). "Religion as a Means to Assure Paternity." *Proceedings of the National Academy of Sciences* 109(25):9781–5.

Sweek, J. (2002). "Biology of Religion." *Method & Theory in the Study of Religion* 14:196–218.

Swinburne, R. (1977). *The Coherence of Theism*. New York: Oxford University Press.

Tadd, M. (2012). "The Power of Parasites and Worms." In B. Gardenour and M. Tadd (Eds.), *Parasites, Worms, and the Human Body* (pp. i–xv). New York: Peter Lang.

Taves, A. (2009). *Religious Experience Reconsidered: A Building-Block Approach to the Study of Religion and Other Special Things*. Princeton: Princeton University Press.

Taylor, M. (1984). *Erring: A Postmodern A/theology*. Chicago: University of Chicago Press.

Terrizzi Jr., J. A., N. J. Shook, and W. L. Ventis. (2012). "Religious Conservatism: An Evolutionarily Evoked Disease-Avoidance Strategy." *Religion, Brain & Behavior* 2(2):105–20.

Terrizzi Jr., J. A., N. J. Shook, and M. A. McDaniel. (2013). "The Behavioral Immune System and Social Conservatism: A Meta-Analysis." *Evolution and Human Behavior* 34:99–108.

Tewari, S., S. Khan, N. Hopkins, N. Srinivasan, and S. Reicher. (2012). "Participation in Mass Gatherings Can Benefit Well-Being: Longitudinal and Control Data from a North Indian Hindu Pilgrimage Event." *PLoS One* 7(10):e47291.

Thompson, N. S. and P. G. Derr. (2000). "Intentionality is the Mark of the Vital." In F. Tonneau and N. S. Thompson (Eds.), *Perspectives in Ethology, Vol. 13, Evolution, Culture, and Behavior* (pp. 213–29). Boston: Kluwer Academic Publishers.

Thornhill, R. and C. L. Fincher. (2014a). "The Parasite-Stress Theory of Sociality, the Behavioral Immune System, and Human Social and Cognitive Uniqueness." *Evolutionary Behavioral Sciences* 8(4):257–64.

Thornhill, R. and C. L. Fincher. (2014b). *The Parasite-Stress Theory of Values and Sociality: Infectious Disease, History and Human Values Worldwide*. New York: Springer.

Thornhill, R., C. L. Fincher, and D. Aran. (2009). "Parasites, Democratization, and the Liberalization of Values Across Contemporary Countries." *Biological Reviews* 84:113–31.

Tinbergen, N. (1963). "On Aims and Methods of Ethology." *Zeitschrift fur Tierpsychologie* 20:410–33.

Tooby, J. (1982). "Pathogens, Polymorphism, and the Evolution of Sex." *Journal of Theoretical Biology.* 97:557–76.

Tooby, J. and L. Cosmides. (1990). "The Past Explains the Present: Emotional Adaptations and the Structure of Ancestral Environments." *Ethology and Sociobiology* 11:375–424.

Tooby, J. and L. Cosmides. (1992). "The Psychological Foundations of Culture." In J. H. Barkow, L. Cosmides and J. Tooby (Eds.), *The Adapted Mind* (pp. 19–136). New York: Oxford University Press.

Tooby, J., L. Cosmides, and H. C. Barrett. (2003). "The Second Law of Thermodynamics Is the Frist Law of Psychology: Evolutionary Developmental Psychology and the Theory of Tandem, Coordinated Inheritances." *Psychological Bulletin* 129(6):858–65.

Triandis, H. C. (1995). *Individualism & Collectivism.* Boulder: Westview Press.

Triandis, H. C. (2001). "Individualism-Collectivism and Personality." *Journal of Personality* 69(6):907–24.

Trivers, R. (1971). "The Evolution of Reciprocal Altruism." *Quarterly Review of Biology* 46:35–57.

Trivers, R. (2011). *The Folly of Fools: The Logic of Deceit and Self-Deception in Human Life.* New York: Basic Books.

Turner, J. H., A. Maryanski, A. K. Petersen, and A. Geertz. (2018). *The Emergence and Evolution of Religion: By Means of Natural Selection.* New York: Routledge.

Tybur, J. M. and D. O'Brien. (2014). "The Behavioral Immune System: Taking Stock and Charting New Directions." *Evolutionary Behavioral Sciences* 8(4):223–5.

Tybur, J. M. and D. Lieberman. (2016). "Human Pathogen Avoidance Adaptations." *Current Opinion in Psychology* 7:6–11.

Tybur, J. M., Y. Inbar, L. Aaroe. (2016). "Parasite Stress and Pathogen Avoidance Relate to Distinct Dimensions of Political Ideology Across 30 Nations." *PNAS* 113(44):12408–13.

Tybur, J. M., C. Cinar, A. K. Karinen, and P. Perone. (2018). "Why Do People Vary in Disgust?" *Philosophical Transactions of the Royal Society B* 373:20170204.

Vail III, K. E., Z. K. Rothschild, D. R. Weise, S. Solomon, T. Pyszczynski, and J. Greenberg. (2010). "A Terror Management Analysis of the Psychological Functions of Religion." *Personality and Social Psychology Review* 14(1):84–94.

Valli, K., A. Revonsuo, O. Palkas, K. H. Ismail, K. J. Ali, and R. L. Punamaki. (2005). "The Threat Simulation Theory of the Evolutionary Function of Dreaming: Evidence from Dreams of Traumatized Children." *Consciousness and Cognition* 14(1):188–218.

Valli, K. and A. Revonsuo. (2006). "Recurrent Dreams: Recurring Threat Simulations?" *Consciousness and Cognition* 15(2):464–9.

Varki, A. (2009). "Human Uniqueness and the Denial of Death." *Nature* 460(7256):684.

Van Blerkom, L. M. (2003). "Role of Viruses in Human Evolution." *Yearbook of Physical Anthropology* 46:14–46.

Van Leeuwen, F., J. H. Park, B. L. Koenig, and J. Graham. (2012). "Regional Variation in Pathogen Prevalence Predicts Endorsement of Group-Focused Moral Concerns." *Evolution and Human Behavior* 33:429–37.

Van Slyke, J. A. (2015). "Why Don't Abstinence Education Programs Work? (And Other Puzzles): Exploring Causal Variables in Sexual Selectionist Theories of Religion." In D. J. Slone and J. A. Van Slyke (Eds.), *The Attraction of Religion: A New Evolutionary Psychology of Religion* (pp. 11–27). London: Bloomsbury.

Villarreal, L. P. (2008). "From Bacteria to Belief: Immunity and Security." In R. D. Sagarin and T. Taylor (Eds.), *Natural Security: A Darwinian Approach to a Dangerous World* (pp. 42–68). Berkeley: University of California Press.

Viswanathan, K., C. Daugherty, and F. S. Dhabhar. (2005). "Stress as an Endogenous Adjuvant: Augmentation of the Immunization Phase of Cell-Mediated Immunity." *International Immunology* 17(8):1059–69.

Voland, E. (2005). *Grandmotherhood: The Evolutionary Significance of the Second Half of Female Life*. New Brunswick: Rutgers University Press.

Volk, A. A. and J. A. Atkinson. (2013). "Infant and Child Death in the Human Environment of Evolutionary Adaptation." *Evolution and Human Behavior* 34(3):182–92.

Volk, T. and J. Atkinson. (2008). "Is Child Death the Crucible of Human Evolution?" *Journal of Social, Evolutionary, and Cultural Psychology* December:103–16.

Waller, N. G., B. A. Kojetin Jr., T. J. Bouchard, D. T. Lykken, and A. Tellegen. (1990). "Genetic and Environmental Influences on Religious Interests, Attitudes, and Values: A Study of Twins Reared Apart and Together." *Psychological Science* 1(2):138–42.

Warren, R. (2013). *The Purpose Driven Life: What on Earth Am I Here For?* Grand Rapids: Zondervan.

Watt, C., S. Watson, and L. Wilson. (2007). "Cognitive and Psychological Mediators of Anxiety: Evidence from a Study of Paranormal Belief and Perceived Childhood Control." *Personality and Individual Differences* 42(2):335–434.

Weaver, L. J. and A. C. Hibbs. (2012). "Serpents and Sanitation: A Biocultural Survey of Snake Worship, Cultural Adaptation, and Parasitic Disease in Ancient and Modern India." In B. Gardenour and M. Tadd (Eds.), *Parasites, Worms, and the Human Body* (pp. 1–16). New York: Peter Lang.

Weber, C. and C. Federico. (2007). "Interpersonal Attachment and Patterns of Ideological Belief." *Political Psychology* 28(4):389–416.

Wedekind, C. and S. Furi. (1997). "Body Odour Preferences in Men and Women: Do They Aim for Specific MHC Combinations or Simply Heterozygosity?" *Proceedings of the Royal Society B* 264(1387):1471–9.

Wedekind, C. and D. Penn. (2000). "MHC Genes, Body Odours, and Odour Preferences." *Nephrology Dialysis Transplantation* 15(9):1269–71.

Wedemeyer, C. K. (2007). "Beef, Dog, and Other Mythologies: Connotative Semiotics in Mahayoga Tantra Ritual and Scripture." *Journal of the American Academy of Religion* 75(2):383–417.

Weingarten, C. P. and J. S. Chisholm. (2009). "Attachment and Cooperation in Religious Groups: An Example of a Mechanism for Cultural Group Selection." *Current Anthropology* 50(6):759–85.

West, S. A., A. Gardner, D. M. Shuker, T. Reynolds, M. Burton-Chellow, E. M. Sykes, M. A. Guinnee, and A. S. Griffin. (2006). "Cooperation and the Scale of Competition in Humans." *Current Biology* 16(11):1103–6.

West-Eberhard, M. J. (2003). *Developmental Plasticity and Evolution.* New York: Oxford University Press.

White, D. G. (1996). *The Alchemical Body: Siddha Traditions in Medieval India.* Chicago: University of Chicago Press.

White, D. G. (2003). *Kiss of the Yogini: "Tantric Sex" in Its South Asian Contexts.* Chicago: University of Chicago Press.

White, D. G. (2009). *Sinister Yogis.* Chicago: University of Chicago Press.

Whitehouse, H. (2000). *Arguments and Icons: Divergent Modes of Religiosity.* New York: Oxford University Press.

Whitson, J. A. and A. D. Galinsky. (2008). "Lacking Control Increases Illusory Pattern Perception." *Science* 322:115–17.

Wiebe, D. (2016). "Pseudo-Speciation of the Human Race: Religions as Hazard-Precaution Systems." In L. Martin and D. Wiebe (Eds.), *Conversations and Controversies in the Scientific Study of Religion: Collaborative and Co-Authored Essays* (pp. 46–67). Leiden: Brill.

Wiley, E. O. (1988). "Entropy and Evolution." In B. H. Weber, D. J. Depew, and J. D. Smith (Eds.), *Entropy, Information, and Evolution: New Perspectives on Physical and Biological Evolution* (pp. 173–88). Cambridge: The MIT Press.

Willard, A. K. and A. Norenzayan. (2017). "'Spiritual but Not Religious': Cognition, Schizotypy, and Conversion in Alternative Beliefs." *Cognition* 165:137–46.

Williams, K. and M. F. Reynolds. (2006). "Sexual Dysfunction in Major Depression." *CNS Spectrums* 11 (8[Suppl. 9]):19–23.

Wilson, D. S. (2002). *Darwin's Cathedral: Evolution, Religion, and the Nature of Society.* Chicago: University of Chicago Press.

Wilson, D. S., Y. Hartberg, I. MacDonald, J. A. Lanman, and H. Whitehouse. (2017). "The Nature of Religious Diversity: A Cultural Ecosystem Approach." *Religion, Brain & Behavior* 7:134–53.

Wilson, J. S. and P. R. Costanzo. (1996). "A Preliminary Study of Attachment, Attention, and Schizotypy in Early Adulthood." *Journal of Social and Clinical Psychology* 15(2):231–60.

Wilson, E. O. (1975). *Sociobiology: The New Synthesis.* Cambridge: Belknap Press.

Wilson, E. O. (1978). *On Human Nature.* Cambridge: Harvard University Press.

Wilson, E. O. (1999). *Consilience: The Unity of Knowledge.* New York: Vintage Books.

Wilson, T. D. (2002). *Strangers to Ourselves: Discovering the Adaptive Unconscious*. Cambridge: The Belknap Press of Harvard University Press.

Winkelman, M. (2010). *Shamanism: A Biopsychosocial Paradigm of Consciousness and Healing*. Santa Barbara: Praeger.

Winkelman, M. (2011). "Shamanism and the Evolutionary Origins of Spirituality and Healing." *NeuroQuantology* 9(1):54–71.

Winterhalder, B. and E. A. Smith. (2000). "Analyzing Adaptive Strategies: Human Behavioral Ecology at Twenty-Five." *Evolutionary Anthropology* 9(2):51–72.

Wolfe, N. D., C. P. Dunavan, and J. Diamond. (2007). "Origins of Major Human Infectious Disease." *Nature* 447:279–83.

Wright, R. (1994). *The Moral Animal*. New York: Vintage.

Wright, S. A. (1995). *Armageddon in Waco: Critical Perspectives on the Branch Davidian Conflict*. Chicago: University of Chicago Press.

Wu, C.-h. (2009). "The Relationship Between Attachment Style and Self-Concept Clarity: The Mediation Effect of Self-Esteem." *Personality and Individual Differences* 47(1):42–6.

Yalom, I. (2009). *Staring at the Sun: Overcoming the Terror of Death*. San Francisco: Jossey-Bass.

Young, M. and T. Edis (Eds.). (2005). *Why Intelligent Design Fails: A Scientific Critique of the New Creationism*. New Brunswick: Rutgers University Press.

Zadra, A., M. Pilon, and D. Donderi. (2006). "Variety and Intensity of Emotions in Nightmares and Bad Dreams." *Journal of Nervous & Mental Disease* 194(4):249–54.

Zahavi, A. and A. Zahavi. (1997). *The Handicap Principle: A missing piece of Darwin's puzzle*. New York: Oxford University Press.

Zeller, B. E. (2014). *Heaven's Gate: America's UFO Religion*. New York: NYU Press.

Zerial, T., A. Pandya, K. Thangaraj, E. Y. Ling, J. Kearley, S. Bertoneri, S. Paracchini, L. Singh, and C. Tyler-Smith. (2007). "Y-Chromosomal Insights into the Genetic Impact of the Caste System in India." *Human Genetics* 121(1):137–44.

Zhang, T. Y., R. Bagot, C. Parent, C. Nesbitt, T. W. Brady, C. Caldji, E. Fish, H. Anisman, M. Szyf, and M. J. Meany. (2006). "Maternal Programming of Defensive Responses Through Sustained Effects on Gene Expression." *Biological Psychology* 73(1):72–89.

Zhong, C.-B. and K. Liljenquist. (2006). "Washing Away Your Sins: Threatened Morality and Physical Cleansing." *Science* 313:1451–2.

Zias, J., S. Harter-Lailheugue, and J. Tabor. (2006). "Toilets at Qumran, the Essenes, and the Scrolls: New Anthropological Data and Old Theories." *Revue de Qumran* 22(4):631–40.

Zuckerman, M., J. Silberman, and J. A. Hall. (2013). "The Relation Between Intelligence and Religiosity: A Meta-Analysis and Some Proposed Explanations." *Personality and Social Psychology Review* 17(4):325–54.

Zuckerman, M., C. Li, and E. Diener. (2018). "Religion as an Exchange System: The Interchangeability of God and Government in a Provider Role." *Personality and Social Psychology Bulletin* 44(8):1–13.

Index

ablutions 155
acceptance and rejection 78–9
acetylcholine 85
acute stress 7, 10, 11, 86, 87, 113, 135–42, 177
adapted/special immune system 9, 116–18, 138, 139
adaptive behaviors 3, 27
adjuvants 139, 140
adrenal cortex 85
adrenaline. *See* epinephrine
adrenal medulla 85
adrenocorticotropic hormone (ACTH) 85
affiliative behaviors 99
agential behavior 18, 19, 21, 49
agriculture 91, 92
Alcorta, C. 37, 120, 123
allelic variation 114, 181 n.1
allomothering 186 n.16
Alloy, L. B. 103–5
Amazon 69
amoral behavior 18
anatomical modernity 114
Anciaux, L. 62, 79, 160
animal-nature disgust 11, 12, 83, 97, 98, 144, 159–63, 167–9, 173, 178
animals 99, 100, 137, 159
animate world 23, 24
animism 32, 79, 119
annihilation 93, 187 n.6
antagonism 85
anthropomorphism 3, 33, 100, 128
antibodies 118
antipathogen defense function 58
anti-vaccination 12, 153, 154, 178
anxiety 9, 75, 80, 82, 93, 96, 97, 176. *See also specific entries*
apotropaic rituals 100, 101
artifactual transmission 148
assortative sociality 58
Atkinson, J. A. 52, 134
Atran, S. 33, 99

attachment anxieties 9, 113
attachment system 72, 73, 75
attachment theory 72, 73, 128
Aunger, R. 21, 27, 146–8
autism spectrum disorders (ASD) 182 n.12
autoimmune disorders 10, 13, 88, 142, 143, 158, 172, 178
autoimmunity 10–11, 13, 88, 142, 143, 177, 187 n.2
autonomic nervous system 85, 121
Azande 135

bacteriology 60
Baldwin, James Mark 193 n.5
Baldwin Effect 147
Balon, R. 88
Barrett, H. C. 19
bartaman panthis 169
basophils 117
Baumard, N. 41, 72
Bausell, R. B. 123
B cells 117, 118, 136
Becker, E. 82, 95
Begley, R. O. 39, 45, 46
behavioral gambit 29, 146
behavioral immune system (BIS) 4, 6, 7, 9, 50, 51, 55, 56, 58, 80–2, 107, 111, 118, 129, 137, 141, 143, 150, 158, 175, 176
behavioral paralysis 93, 176
behavioral plasticity 6, 22, 27
behavioral transmission 148
Bell, D. 22, 40
Bering, J. 26
Berlin, L. J. 75
Bible 42
Big Five personality profile 76
Big Gods 38, 92, 152
biological species concept 24
biological success 39, 45
Biology of Religion, The (Reynolds and Tanner) 3

biomeme hypothesis 150
biophobia 16
Biran, A. 60, 171
Blackmore, S. 147, 162
Bloch, M. 112, 145, 146
blood sacrifices 112, 113, 121, 133–6, 140–2, 177, 192 n.15
Blume, M. 46
bosons 20
Boudry, M. 146, 148, 149
Bowlby, J. 186 n.18
Boyd, R. 83, 150
Boyer, P. 30, 131, 182 n.9
Branch Davidians 161
Bretherton, I. 79
Brown, G. R. 27–9
Brown, P. J. 155
Buid 124, 134
Bulbulia, J. 16, 19, 22, 27, 28, 31, 33, 36, 37, 40, 104, 112, 119, 132–5, 140, 143, 150
Burkert, W. 3, 33

Calvinism 102, 103
Campbell, N. A. 19
Cassidy, J. 75
Catalhoyuk 92
catecholamine hormones 85, 86
Cavalli-Sforza, L. L. 67, 68
celibacy 161–2
cellular response 117, 118
cessative yoga 166
Chagga Tribe 160
Chevallier, C. 41, 72
childhood trauma 126–8
childrearing 7, 51, 69–80, 185 nn.14, 15
 authoritarian 78, 79
 pedagogical 71, 72, 78
 pediatric 7, 71, 72, 74, 76, 78–80, 126–8, 131, 141, 164, 192 n.14
Chisholm, J. S. 38, 74
Choleris, E. 75
Christian beliefs 161
Christian Scientists 154, 158, 165
chronic medical risk 72
chronic stress 7, 8, 10, 11, 82, 86–9, 93, 95, 104, 105, 109, 113, 141, 176
circumcision 42, 162–3, 193 n.6
Clark, D. P. 50

Clements, C. M. 103–5
climatically-based energy hypothesis 64
cognition 22, 25, 54, 144
cognitive adaptations 17, 27
cognitive immunity 9, 84, 106, 109
cognitive infections 83, 150, 161
cognitive niche 22, 40, 49, 145, 147
cognitive plumes 40
cognitive sciences 5, 17, 22, 23, 27, 34, 90, 99
coital inability 88, 89, 122
collective action 5, 37, 49
collectivism 6, 7, 51, 53, 56–8, 66, 70, 71, 76, 81, 164, 176, 184 n.4
collectivist cultures 56, 57
Coltrane, John 149
comfort hypothesis 7, 10
communions 99
complementary and alternative medicine (CAM) 192 n.13
complement system 118
congenital brain defects 84
consciousness, altered states of 10, 113, 120–2, 124, 126, 129
conspecific agents 49
cooperation 5, 17, 22, 30, 31, 34–47, 49, 56, 175, 179. *See also specific entries*
Cortes, Hernan 65
corticosteroids 85
corticotropin-releasing hormone (CRH) 85, 86
cortisol 85–7
Cosmides, L. 19, 29
costly-signaling theory (CST) 5, 17, 36, 38, 39, 45, 65, 111, 112, 135
costly signals 5, 36, 38–40, 44, 49, 111, 175
Cox, C. R. 97
Crawford, D. H. 118, 179
Creation of the Sacred: Tracks of Biology in Early Religions (Burkert) 3
credibility-enhancing display (CRED) 38–9, 155, 161
Crespi, B. 46
cross-culture 19, 51, 70, 184 n.4
cui bono 148
culture 28, 53, 59, 79, 80, 145, 146, 150, 188 n.9

anthropology 19
  evoked 28, 51, 172
  evolution 11, 46, 63, 144
  selection 41
  wisdom 70
  worldviews 94, 95, 176
curative violence 112, 120, 133–42
Curtis, V. 21, 27, 43, 44, 50, 56, 60, 61, 63, 77, 137, 171
cytokines 117

Damasio, A. 20, 95
Darwin, Charles 15, 16, 192 n.4
Darwinian algorithm 27, 145
Dawkins, Richard 145, 149
death 82–4, 90, 93, 96, 98, 106
death anxiety 82, 93, 96, 98, 105, 107, 162
de Barra, M. 43, 44, 137
degree of agency 21
demons and devils 33, 99–105
Dennett, D. 21, 25, 30, 100, 115, 116, 148
depression 7, 8, 10, 80, 82, 88–90, 104, 105, 129, 176, 187 n.3
Descartes, Rene 26, 27
descendant-leaving (DL) hypothesis 17, 45, 148
design stance 99–101, 104
détente dualism/dualists 12, 144, 159, 166, 178
devadasis 167
developmental psychology 80
Dhabhar, F. 136, 137, 139
Diamond, L. M. 80, 186 n.18
disaffiliative behaviors 99
disagreement 106, 158
discreet functions 22–3
disease avoidance 54, 63, 66
disease ecologies 6, 7, 51, 58, 64, 67–9, 71, 72, 76, 78, 80, 81, 141, 176
disembodied minds 32, 49, 183
disgust 6, 9, 11, 35, 43, 44, 50, 54, 55, 61–3, 77, 83, 84, 97, 137, 170, 176
disgusting other 105–9
dissociation 10, 125, 127–9, 132
Dobzhansky, Theodor 16
Dogon 42
domain generality 27

domain specificity 27
Douglas, Mary 19, 58–60, 62, 65, 170, 184 n.5
DRD4 gene 191 n.9
dualism 11–12, 26–7, 119, 128, 144. See also specific entries
Durkheim, Emile 19
Dwyer, G. 128

ecological contingencies 28
ecological stress 72
economic cooperation 11, 42, 81, 96, 97, 109, 111, 112, 120, 162–3
economic success 17, 39, 175
ecstatic behaviors 113, 121, 124
Eddy, Mary Baker 154
Edington, A. 18
Edmond, M. B. 156
educated guesses 25
Edwards, K. M. 139
Eibl-Eibesfeldt, I. 26
ekak 168
Eliade, M. 124, 125
Ellis, B. J. 86
embodied condition 97, 170
embryonic stem (ES) cells 157
emotions 55, 63, 71–2, 84
endogamy 66, 68
endogenous opioids 128, 132
England, J. 20
entropy 20
environmental insult 84
environment of evolutionary adaptedness (EEA) 29–31, 34, 35, 41, 52, 57, 72, 74, 75, 86, 90, 98, 104, 122
eosinophils 117
epinephrine 85
erectile dysfunction 89
erythrocytes 117
esoteric consanguinity 46
Essene community 156
ethnocentrism 6, 7, 51, 53, 57, 65, 69, 176, 178
Eveland, W. C. 69
evolution 5, 7, 15–17, 19–21, 37, 46, 63, 181 n.3
evolutionarily stable strategy (ESS) 120
evolutionary biology 27, 30, 49, 183 n.13

evolutionary psychology 5, 17, 22, 23, 27, 50, 90
evolutionary theory 18, 52
existential anxieties 9, 176
existential stress 84, 90, 91, 93, 108, 111, 124, 141
existential terror 82, 90, 91, 93, 95, 97
exorcism 99–105, 188 n.10
exploratory behaviors 73
external control, perception of 102, 103
extra-tribal other 51

Fabrega, H., Jr. 50, 53, 134, 179
Faces in the Clouds: A New Theory of Religion (Guthrie) 3
faith-based charities 152
Fallon, A. E. 163
fantasies 94, 95, 98, 125, 126, 141
fear 54, 55, 137
fermions 20
Fessler, D. M. T. 43, 63
fictive kin 46, 162
fight-or-flight response 85, 121, 130, 137
Fincher, C. 47, 57, 64, 65, 68, 69, 77, 115
First Amendment, Constitution of the United States 153, 157
folk biology 24, 100, 182 n.8
folk cosmologies 59
folk economics 25, 182 n.10
folk pharmacology 10
folk physics 23–4, 26
folk psychology 24, 25
folk science 24, 54
fraternal polyandry 43, 44
Freeland, W. J. 66
free riders 5, 9, 37, 53, 56, 111, 120, 175
Fuller, R. C. 42

Galinsky, A. D. 102, 104
Galli 162
game theory 34
Gangestad, S. W. 28
Geertz, Clifford 19
generational inheritance 15
genes 11, 15–16, 28–30, 144, 148, 149, 151, 181 n.1, 192–3 n.4
genetic mutation 191 n.9
genetic resistance 69

genetic signatures 67, 68
genital mutilation 36, 42
germ theory 54, 60, 61
Gibson, T. P. 124, 134
Gilbert, P. 90
Glucklich, A. 2, 121, 126, 127, 163
glucocorticoids 57, 85, 87–8, 187 n.2
Gobekli Tepe 91–2, 162
God gene 191 n.9
God(s) 3, 19, 32, 33, 78, 79, 99–105, 158
Goldenberg, J. L. 97, 98, 106, 159
Golden Rule 45, 46, 148
Goodwin, J. 101
Graham, G. 112, 133, 134
granulocytes. *See* myeloid leukocytes
Gray, K. 151
Guthrie, S. 3, 33

Haack, Susan 181 n.1
habituation/dishabituation paradigm 23
habituation hypothesis 136
Haidt, J. 55
Halberstadt, J. 96
hard-core tantra 168–70, 172
hardship rituals 37, 42, 65–6
hard-to-fake signs 5, 36, 38–40, 49, 65, 66, 111–13, 135, 167, 175
Harmon, W. 133, 134
Harpending, H. C. 72
Harris, S. 107
Hart, B. L. 53, 64, 66, 132, 140
hatha yoga 165–8
Hatha Yoga (Ramacharaka) 165
Hatha Yoga Pradipika, The (HYP, Svatmarama) 165, 193 n.7
Hayden, B. 2, 30, 98, 119, 160
Hazard-Precaution System 131
Heaven's Gate 161
heightened vigilance 86
herbal remedies 132, 177
Herz, R. 55, 84, 97, 138
Hewlett, B. S. 185 n.15
Hibbs, A. C. 60
Hindu caste system 67–8
Hochberg, M. E. 67
Hofhuis, S. 146, 148, 149
Hofstede, G. 51, 77, 78, 79
Hogg, M. A. 78
holy springs/water 156

Homo religiosus 96
Homo sapiens 96
Horton, R. 33, 99
human animals 3–8, 11, 17, 22, 25–30, 47, 49, 50, 54–5, 60, 82, 90, 92, 93, 97, 98, 100, 101, 105, 114, 118, 144, 145, 159, 175, 190 n.4
human behavioral ecology (HBE) 5, 17, 27–9
human genome 114, 115
Human Leukocyte Antigen (HLA) complex 67, 68, 115, 116, 169, 172, 190 n.3
human mind/brain and behavior 5, 11, 19, 22–31, 96, 137, 144, 147
humoral response 117–18
hunter-gatherers (HGs) 37, 38, 91–3, 113, 114, 125, 177, 190–1 n.6
hygiene 6, 50, 60–3, 68, 109
hyperactive agency detection device (HADD) 5, 17, 26, 50, 54, 114
hyperactive pathogen detection device (HPDD) 50, 54, 114
hyper-reactivity 86
hypnosis 10, 121–3, 125, 132, 133
hypothalamic-pituitary-adrenal axis (HPA) 86
hypothalamus 85

idealism 191 n.8
Idea of the Holy, The (Otto) 1
illusion of external control (IoEC) 103
illusion of internal control (IoIC) 103
illusion of qualified, internal control (IoQC) 83, 104, 176
illusions of control 8, 10, 11, 83, 84, 98, 103–5, 109, 111, 141
illusory pattern perception 104
immortality 8, 11, 94, 95, 105–7, 176
immune systems 64, 138, 139, 171, 172, 190 n.4. *See also specific entries*
immunocompetence 6, 64–9, 80, 104, 109, 175, 178
immunoenhancement 7, 10, 11, 104, 113, 125, 128, 132, 135–7, 139, 141
immunoglobulins (Ig) 67, 68, 118
immunological memory 9, 117

immunosuppression 4, 7, 8, 10, 43, 82, 87, 88, 109, 129, 176
implicit germ theory 54
inanimate objects 23, 24
incest elicit sexual disgust 43
inclusive fitness 2, 5, 28, 30, 31, 37, 41, 45, 88, 97, 137, 143, 147, 149, 159, 161, 175, 179
India 67, 68
indigenous psychotherapy 132
individualism 51, 53, 70, 184 n.4
infant and child survival 52, 70, 80, 184 n.3
infant cognition 23
infectious disease 1–2, 4, 6, 7, 12, 13, 17, 47, 49–51, 55, 57, 60, 67, 76, 77, 78, 114, 116, 118, 133, 134, 141, 155, 156, 179, 184 n.3, 189–90 n.2
  diversity 63, 64
  selection pressure 52–6
in-group collectivism 68
Inhorn, M. C. 155
innate/natural immune system 9, 116, 138, 139
innocent ignorance 106
insecure-anxious attachments 7, 9, 51, 74–81, 86, 90, 98, 126–33, 141, 164, 176, 177
insecure-avoidant/dismissing attachments 74
insecure-avoidant/fearful attachments 74, 79
institutionalized patterns 70
insular social geographies 67
integrated immune system 4, 6, 7, 9, 50, 81, 109, 111, 112, 143, 170, 175, 176
intentional stance 25, 99–102, 104
intergroup vigilance theory 63
interleukin (IL) 1 117, 118
internal control, perception of 102, 103
internal working model (IWM) 73–5, 90, 127
interpersonal death anxiety 187–8 n.6
intersexual competition 40
intrapersonal death anxiety 187 n.6
intrasexual competition 39
intuitive microbiology 54

Irons, W. 31
irrational behavior 36
irrational signals 36
Iyer, K. V. 165

James, W. 18
Jehovah's Witnesses 154, 157
Jha, S. N. 168–9, 171
Jones, Jim 161
Jong, J. 96

Kama Sutra (Vatsyayana) 98, 160
Kant, Immanuel 15, 16
Kaulajnananirnaya 168
Kavaliers, M. 75
Kay, A. C. 98, 152
Keinan, G. 103
kin altruism 30, 45, 116
King, B. 7
Kirkpatrick, L. A. 17, 18, 23, 78, 126
Klenerman, P. 115
Koenig, H. G. 103, 154
Koleva, S. P. 98
Koresh, David 161
Kripal, J. J. 169
Kumar, V. 35

Lafferty, K. D. 51
Laland, K. N. 27–9
Lambert, W. W. 134
Lane, N. 20
Langer, E. J. 102, 103
Laws of Manu 42, 172
learned opponent 106–8
Legare, C. H. 98
leishmaniasis 69
leukocytes 117, 130, 136, 137
LeVine, R. 70, 72, 185 n.15
Lieberman, D. 54
Lienard, P. 131
life, definition 20
Liljenquist, K. 61
literal immortality 95, 96, 176
local ecological pressures 51
locally immunized groups 69
locus coeruleus-norepinephrine (LC-NE) systems 86
Loehle, C. 88
Lord Alfred Tennyson 21

Love Supreme, A (Coltrane) 149
Luguru 160
lymphocytes 87, 88, 117
lymphoid leukocyte 117

Macbeth effect 62
McCauley, R. N. 112, 133, 134, 140
McClenon, J. 114, 121, 123, 127, 131
McCrae, R. R. 51, 78
McFalls, J. A. 89
McGuire, M. 83
McIntosh, D. N. 95
McNamara, P. 112, 131–4, 136, 140
McNeil, W. H. 67
macrophage 118
Mahoney, A. 36
maithuna 169
major histocompatibility complex (MHC). *See* Human Leukocyte Antigen (HLA) complex
maladaptive behavior 10, 159
manipulations 10, 99
marital unions 42–4
Mariyamman 133, 134
Masson, J. M. 163, 164
mass suicide 161
Mattausch, J. 67
Maunder, R. G. 86
Mayr, E. 66
mechanical manipulations 100, 101
memes 11–13, 144–53, 155, 157–9, 161, 162, 164, 165, 173
memetic infections 11, 12, 150–9, 177
memetic lineages 147, 148, 158, 159, 163–73
memetics 11, 144–50
Mendel, Gregor 15–16, 192 n.4
menstrual huts 42
menstrual pollution 42
mental contamination 83
mental healing 10
mental health 4, 81, 82, 84
mental instability 123–5, 128
mesolimbic dopamine system 57
Metzitzah b'peh 157
Mian, R. 137, 138
microbiology 54
microbiome 190 n.4
Mikulincer, M. 90

militant dualism   12, 144, 145, 159–63, 167, 170–2, 178
Miller, E. N.   69
Miller, G. E.   118
Milner, M., Jr.   99, 100
modal personalities   28, 51
modern medicine   47, 51, 121
Modiano, D.   69
monocytes   117, 136
monogamy   42–4
moral behavior   18
moral elevation   39
moral impurity   62, 107
moral righteousness   61, 62
morbidity   2, 52, 88, 111, 139, 141, 154
Mordeniz, C.   162
Morris, M. W.   100
Morrison, Jim   13
mortality   2, 13, 82, 88, 93, 107, 108, 111, 139, 153, 154
motivation, theory of   18
Murdock, G. P.   19
Murray, D.   28, 64, 67, 70
myeloid leukocytes   117

natural agents   32, 33, 100
natural killer (NK) cells   117, 125
natural selection   2, 4, 5, 7, 8, 15, 18, 20, 24, 43, 50, 52, 54, 55, 80, 82, 89, 116, 129, 137, 143, 175, 181 n.3
Navarette, C. D.   43, 63
neophobia   57
Nesse, R. M.   41, 44, 115
Nettle, D.   27, 77
Neuberg, S. L.   139
neuroendocrine stress response   139, 140
neuroticism   76, 77, 80, 97, 98, 129, 176
neurotransmitter   85
neutrophils   117
Newton, T.   95
New York State   153–4
Nisbett, R. E.   56
Noftle, E. E.   90
non-agential behavior   18
non-fraternal polyandry   43, 44
nonkin conspecifics   30–1
non-natural agents   31–3, 99–104, 124, 133
non-sororal polygyny   43, 44

non-zero-sumness   35
nonzoonotic infections   68, 184 n.3
Norenzayan, A.   38, 92, 127, 161
norepinephrine   85
numinous yoga   166, 167
numinous yogis   166

Oaten, M.   54
Obamacare   153
Offit, P. A.   154
On the Origin of Species by Means of Natural Selection, or the Preservation of Favoured Races in the Struggle for Life (Darwin)   15
Openshaw, J.   169
open systems   20, 21, 93
Otto, Rudolf   1, 179, 181 n.1
Owens, S. A.   131

Paleolithic disease   114
Palmer, C. T.   39, 45, 46
Panchin, A. Y.   150, 156
parakiya   168
paranormal beliefs   103
parasympathetic nervous system   121
parental manipulation   45–6
parenting   70–2, 79
Park, J. H.   138
Parry, J.   163
paternity   41, 42, 44
pathogenicity   59, 60, 171
pathogens   53, 54, 58, 61, 63–5, 69, 109, 137, 140, 171, 172
Paul, G.   152, 153
Pellerin, J.   156
Penn, D. J.   115
Pentecostals   154–5
People's Temple   161
perceptions and misperceptions   86
Perlman, R. L.   66
personality profiles   6, 7, 51, 69, 76, 79, 176
personality traits   28, 51, 77
Petersen, M. B.   184 n.7
phagocytic cells   117
phenotypic effect   147
phenotypic gambit   29
phenotypic traits   39, 40, 114

physical cleanliness   50, 61, 62, 79
physicalism   191 n.8
physical pressure   52
physical stressor   85, 86
physiological homeostasis   83, 84
physiological immune system   4, 9, 10, 43, 44, 67, 68, 81, 82, 87, 88, 109, 111–18, 129, 136–9, 143, 175–7
physiological pressure   52
Pinker, S.   20
Pitchappan, R. M.   68
pituitary gland   85
placebo effect   10, 121, 123, 125, 132, 133
Plato   27
Pleistocene   29, 30, 37, 80, 91, 114
pluripotency   157
Polimeni, J.   129
political instability   153
pollution   6, 7, 11, 50, 58–64, 68, 70, 79, 80, 109, 154, 155, 160, 172, 176
polymatry   186 n.16
polymorphism   115, 181 n.1
polymorphs. *See* myeloid leukocytes
postzygotic isolating mechanisms   66, 185 n.9
Potts, W. K.   115
precarity   8, 59
predation anxiety   33
prereproductive pressure   52
Preston, B. T.   129, 130
Preston, J. L.   61, 107
prezygotic isolating mechanism   66, 68, 69, 185 n.9
primary emotions   90, 170
progeny   6, 30, 31, 33, 36, 39, 41, 45, 46, 116, 143
promiscuous riders   5, 6, 11, 40, 41, 53, 56, 111, 175
pronoun drop   56
prophylactic behaviors   50, 55, 62, 69, 83, 109, 111, 176
prophylactic collective   80
propositional isolation   66, 68, 69
proximity-seeking behaviors   72, 73
pseudospeciation   63
psychological adaptations   22, 27, 49
psychological homeostasis   108–9

psychological immune system   4, 7, 9, 81–4, 91, 105, 107–9, 111, 118, 120, 127, 141, 143, 158, 175, 176
psychological manipulations   10
psychological pressures   52, 90
psychological stress   87, 89
psychological threat   84
psychological well-being   82
psychoneuroimmunology   8
psychosocial stressor   85, 86
psychosomatic disorders   113
public health   50, 56, 96, 97, 153, 157, 179
purity   6, 7, 11, 50, 58–64, 68, 70, 79, 80, 109, 154, 155, 160, 172, 176
Purity and Danger (Douglas)   58
Pyszczynski, T.   90

raja yoga   166, 168
Ramakrishna   168
Ramayana   42
Rank, Otto   96, 107
rational agent   25
rational behavior   25
rational choice theory   25, 34, 182 n.11
reciprocal altruism   34
reciprocity   35, 77, 120
Reiss, J. P.   129
religion   1–2, 31–6, 55, 56, 58, 78, 81, 95, 98, 104, 118, 188 n.9. *See also individual entries*
   beliefs and practices   11, 42, 66, 83, 84, 96, 103, 104, 143, 150, 152, 159, 160
   biology of   3–4, 16, 17, 19, 36, 111, 175
   conventions   50
   definition   101
   development   53
   diversity   63, 64, 68
   fundamentalist   193 n.1
   pilgrimage   156–8
   practices   84, 103, 133
   traditions   11, 13, 46, 61, 62, 65, 69, 81, 103, 118, 193 nn.6, 11
   tribes   6, 60, 66, 80, 106, 111, 176
   vital lies   7–8, 10, 11, 82–4, 91–8, 105, 109, 111, 141

religiosity   55, 64, 77, 84, 103–4, 112, 142, 153
reproductive cooperation   11, 42, 81, 96, 97, 109, 111, 112, 163
reproductive fitness   20, 52, 90, 115
reproductive isolation   66
reproductive success   5, 7, 8, 11, 17, 44, 70, 82, 111, 123, 132, 162, 175
reverse causation hypothesis   51, 69, 76
reverse domination   37–8
Revonsuo, A.   80, 130, 138
Reynaert, C. P.   90, 104
Reynolds, V.   3, 135, 152, 154, 155
Richerson, P. J.   83, 150
Ridley, M.   31, 34
right-wing authoritarianism (RWA)   57–8
Ritter, R. S.   61, 107
ritual healing   10, 112, 113, 121, 122, 126, 128, 129, 133–5, 140
ritualized behaviors   36, 64, 83, 84, 98, 131, 140
Robertson, S. A.   44
Rochat, P.   25
romantic love   98
Rosenberg, A.   5, 31, 36, 41, 147
Rothbaum, F.   186 n.18
Rozin, P.   163

sacrificial behaviors   39
sadhaks   172
St. Paul   159
Samkhya   166
Sanderson, S. K.   44, 84
Sapolsky, R. M.   44, 56, 57, 62, 76, 78, 84, 87–91, 93, 101, 103, 107, 114, 136, 138
Sarbacker, S.   166
Saroglou, V.   62, 79, 160
Satya Yuga   160
Schaller, M.   28, 64, 67, 138
schistosomiasis   155, 156
schizophrenia   32
schizotypy   127–9, 132, 141
Schmidt, K.   92
Schmitt, D. P.   42
second law of thermodynamics   5, 13, 17–22, 46, 64, 94, 178, 179
secure attachments   74, 186 n.18

Segerstrom, S. C.   118
Sela, Y.   42
self-castration   162
self-esteem   93–5
self-model   73
self-protection system   63
semen   43, 44, 167
semi-allogenic conceptus   43, 44
sexual intercourse   12, 40, 42, 43, 66, 68, 88, 97–8, 105, 122, 160, 162, 167, 169–72, 186 n.16
sexuality   98, 162
sexual ornaments   40
sexual promiscuity   183 n.18
sexual reproduction   115, 116, 122, 161, 162
sexual selection theory   17, 39
sexual weapon   39
shamanic syndrome   127
shamanism   9, 79, 111–13, 118–33, 142, 163, 177, 190 n.5
shamans   9–10, 79, 113, 119–28, 132, 140–2, 160, 163, 164, 166, 167, 177, 190 n.5
shared arousal hypothesis   141
Sharkey, D. J.   44
Shaver, P. R.   90
Silver, L.   134, 158
Singer, M.   52, 114
Singh, N. D.   116
Singleton, M.   164, 165, 167
Skoptzy   162
Slingerland, E.   16, 18, 27
Slone, D. J.   36
Slone, J.   2, 40, 44
Small, M. F.   70, 72
Smith, T.   129
social/cooperative behavior   22
social dominance orientation (SDO)   58
Social Ecology of Religion, The (Reynolds and Tanner)   3
sociality   22, 51
social learning   150
social manipulation   99, 100
Sociobiology: The New Synthesis (Wilson)   2
socioeconomic intercourse   99–101
Solar Temple   161

Solomon, S.   82, 92, 93, 96, 106, 108, 145, 155, 160
sororal polygyny   43, 44
Sosis, R.   28, 37, 120, 123
soul mates   98
souls   11, 144, 159, 178
sound body and mind   50, 55, 80, 84, 109
south Asia   67, 68, 172, 192 n.14
South India   68, 133
Souza, A. L.   98
speciation   15
species diversity   63, 64
sperm   44
Standard Social Science Model (SSSM)   17–20
Steen, F. F.   130, 131
stem cell technology   157–8
Steptoe, A.   138
steroids   85, 86
Stewart-Williams, S.   24, 45, 96, 149, 151
Strassman, B. I.   42
stress   84–91, 113, 133, 135–7
stressors   84, 85, 138
subfecundity   4, 7, 8, 10, 82, 88, 89, 105, 109, 111, 139, 141
subsistence technology   91
Sudan   69
suicidal dualism   12–13, 145, 160–1, 178
Summers, K.   46
supernatural agents   32, 79
Sutterlin, C.   26
Swami Nikhilananda   168
Swinburne, R.   32
Swiss Army Knife   23, 27
symbolic constructions   105–6
symbolic immortality   95, 176
sympathetic-adrenal-medullary axis (SAM)   85
sympathetic nervous system   85, 89, 121

Tabor, J.   156
Tadd, M.   61
Tamils   133, 137
Tanner, R.   3, 135, 152, 154, 155
tantra   12, 145, 146, 151, 163–73, 178
tantric sex   164, 169, 171
T cells   117, 136
T cytotoxic cells   117

teleo-functional reasoning   26
Terrizzi, J. A., Jr.   69
terror management theory (TMT)   8, 82, 93–6, 102, 105, 108, 176, 187 n.6
Texas Chain Saw Massacre, The (1974)   138
thanatocentric theories   188 n.8
T helper cells   117, 118
theological knowledge   36
theory of mind (ToM)   5, 17, 25–7, 49, 99, 114, 128, 146
theriomorphic model   33
Thevenot, Jean de   168
Thornhill, R.   47, 57, 64, 65, 68, 77, 115
threat and challenge   85, 86
threat management systems   63
threat simulation theory   130, 131, 138
Tiger, L.   83
tightness   57
tit-for-tat   34, 35, 37, 77, 120
Tooby, J.   18, 19, 29
transpersonal death anxiety   187 n.6
tribalism   6, 7, 51, 56, 58, 63–9, 66, 69, 78, 80, 81, 109, 111, 175, 176, 178
Trivers, R.   81
trust   31, 35–47
Turner, J. H.   32, 108, 120
Tybur, J. M.   22, 54, 58, 69

uncertainty   78, 82, 99
  avoidance   77, 79, 80, 82
  unexpected   93
United States   153
usable energy   20–1, 46, 47, 64

Vail III, K. E.   95, 96
Valli, K.   80, 138
Van Slyke, J. A.   44
Varki, A.   90, 91, 93
Verit, A.   162
vertebrate immune system   115
Villarreal, L. P.   84
violation-of-expectation gazing   23
Viswanathan, K.   86, 139
Volk, A. A.   52

Wana   134
Watt, C.   103
Weaver, L. J.   60

Wegner, D. M.   151
Weingarten, C. P.   38, 74
West-Eberhard, M. J.   28
White, D. G.   97, 164, 165
Whitson, J. A.   102, 104
Wiebe, D.   178
Wiley, E. O.   18
Willard, A. K.   127
willful ignorance   106
Williams, G. C.   31, 41, 44, 115
Wilson, D. S.   57, 63, 66, 83, 151
Wilson, E. O.   2–3, 5, 32, 35, 175
Wilson, T. D.   82
Winkelman, M.   84, 96, 119, 120–2, 125, 127, 128, 163, 165
Wolfe, N. D.   113
worship   99–105
Wright, R.   35

xenophobia   6, 7, 51, 53, 57, 63, 65, 69, 78, 176, 178

Yalom, I.   96
yoga   12, 145, 146, 151, 163–73, 178. *See also specific entries*
Yoga Sutras (Patanjali)   166
yogini   169, 171
yogis   165–7
Young, M. J.   100
yugal   168
yugal-parakiya sadhana   168, 169

Zerial, T.   68
Zhong, C.-b.   61
Zias, J.   156
Zinacantecos   134
Zuckerman, M.   103, 104

www.ingramcontent.com/pod-product-compliance
Lightning Source LLC
Chambersburg PA
CBHW062144300426
44115CB00012BA/2030